Psychology
in
Progress

General editor: Peter Herriot

Brain
and
Mind

Psychology in Progress

Already available

Philosophical Problems in Psychology
edited by Neil Bolton

The Pathology and Psychology of Cognition
edited by Andrew Burton

Thinking in Perspective
Critical essays in the study of thought processes
edited by Andrew Burton and John Radford

The School Years
Current issues in the socialization of young people
edited by John C. Coleman

Issues in Person Perception
edited by Mark Cook

Applications of Conditioning Theory
edited by Graham Davey

Personality
Theory, measurement and research
edited by Fay Fransella

Aspects of Memory
edited by Michael M. Gruneberg and Peter Morris

Issues in Childhood Social Development
edited by Harry McGurk

Developing Thinking
Approaches to children's cognitive development
edited by Sara Meadows

Brain, Behaviour and Evolution
edited by David A. Oakley and H. C. Plotkin

Aspects of Psychopharmacology
edited by D. J. Sanger and D. E. Blackman

Small Groups and Personal Change
edited by Peter B. Smith

Brain
and
Mind

edited by

DAVID A. OAKLEY

METHUEN
London and New York

First published in 1985 by
Methuen & Co. Ltd
11 New Fetter Lane, London EC4P 4EE
Published in the USA by
Methuen & Co.
in association with Methuen, Inc.
733 Third Avenue, New York, NY 10017

Typeset by Scarborough Typesetting Services
and printed in Great Britain by
Richard Clay, The Chaucer Press,
Bungay, Suffolk

British Library Cataloguing in Publication Data

Brain and mind. − (Psychology in progress)
1. Psychology, Physiological.
2. Mind and body.   3. Brain
I. Oakley, David A.   II. Series
612'.82   QP376

ISBN 0−416−31620−4
ISBN 0−416−31630−1 Pbk

Library of Congress Cataloging in Publication Data
Main entry under title:

Brain and mind.
(Psychology in progress)
Includes bibliographies and indexes.
1. Consciousness − Physiological aspects.
2. Brain.   Mind and body.
I. Oakley, David A.   II. Series.
[DNLM: 1. Brain − physiology.
2. Consciousness.
BF 311 B8143]
QP411.B75   1985   612'.82   84−29604

ISBN 0−416−31620−4
ISBN 0−416−31630−1 (pbk)

Contents

Notes on the contributors   vii
Editor's introduction   x
Human brain anatomy   xiv

1 On the evolution of mind   1
  Harry J. Jerison

2 Representations of the physical and social world   32
  Keith Oatley

3 Is consciousness the gateway to the hippocampal
  cognitive map? A speculative essay on the neural basis of
  mind   59
  John O'Keefe

4 Cognition and imagery in animals   99
  David A. Oakley

5 Animal awareness, consciousness and self-image   132
  David A. Oakley

6 Neuropsychology of consciousness: a review of
  human clinical evidence   152
  Freda Newcombe

7 Brain, mind and language   197
      Joseph E. LeDoux

8 The plurality of consciousness   217
      David A. Oakley and Lesley C. Eames

   Name index   252
   Subject index   261

Notes on the contributors

Lesley Eames is a child psychologist in the Bristol area. Her doctoral research was centred around the role played by the neocortex in association learning and cognitive processes in animals. Her present interest in neurodevelopmental problems of learning and behaviour in children stems from this earlier work with animals. She is also interested in the use of hypnosis as a therapeutic tool with children and in the use of microcomputers in remedial teaching.

Harry J. Jerison is a Professor in the Department of Psychiatry and Biobehavioral Sciences at the Medical School of the University of California at Los Angeles (UCLA). His scientific interests have been in the evolution of the vertebrate brain and its significance for the evolution of intelligence. For many years he has also done research on human and animal vigilance, or sustained attention.

Joseph LeDoux is an Assistant Professor in the Neurology Department at Cornell University and is working on the neuroanatomical and neurochemical substrates of emotional processing. He graduated from Louisiana State University in 1971 and then carried out the research for his Ph.D. thesis on cognitive and emotional mechanisms in split-brain patients at the State University of New York at Stony Brook. He is the co-author of *The Integrated Mind* (Plenum Press, 1978) with Michael Gazzaniga.

Freda Newcombe is a Member of the External Staff of the Medical Research Council and is affiliated to the University Department of Clinical Neurology in Oxford. She is President-elect of the International Neuropsychology Society and the INS editor of *The Journal of Clinical and Experimental Psychology*. Her main interests are in the functional architecture of acquired and developmental cognitive disorders, notably reading, pattern perception, and spatial orientation, their neural correlates, and their evolution with time and remedial intervention.

David A. Oakley lectures in psychology at University College London. He spent a number of years as a scientific member of the MRC Unit on Neural Mechanisms of Behaviour before joining the academic staff of the Department of Social Science and Humanities at the City University. He has published theoretical and research papers on the role of the neocortex in learning and memory and has contributed chapters to *Animal Models of Human Behaviour* (Wiley, 1983) and *Memory in Animals and Humans* (Van Nostrand Reinhold, 1983). He is also the co-editor, with Henry Plotkin, of *Brain, Behaviour and Evolution* (Methuen, 1979). He is currently working on the role of neocortex in cognitive processes and behavioural flexibility in animals, on extrapolations from the animal-based research to human clinical situations and on dissociations of consciousness, particularly those encountered in hypnosis.

Keith Oatley is a Lecturer in Experimental Psychology at the University of Sussex. His current work is on cognitive theories of emotion, and the relation between life events and depression. He is the author of *Perceptions and Representations* (Methuen, 1978) and *Selves in Relation* (Methuen, 1984).

John O'Keefe is Reader in Psychobiology in the Anatomy Department, University College London and the Chairman of the Brain Research Association. He studied engineering at New York University and psychology at the City College of New York. From there he went to the Psychology Department at McGill University and received his Ph.D. degree in 1967.

Editor's introduction

An earlier volume in this series considered the impact which evolutionary theory is having on psychology, particularly in providing a new perspective from which to view its subject matter (*Brain, Behaviour and Evolution*, 1979, edited by David A. Oakley and H. C. Plotkin). Individual authors discussed the evolution and genetics of behaviour, the evolution of the central nervous system and its neurotransmitters as well as pointing out the importance of an evolutionary perspective when attempting to draw meaningful conclusions from studies of brain/behaviour relationships involving different animal species. Other topics included the evolution and function of sleep, the relationship between brain size and intelligence, the extent to which adaptive behaviours such as learning could be identified with a particular region of the central nervous system, the significance of both symmetry and asymmetry in the nervous system for psychological functions and the implications of split-brain studies for views of consciousness. In all these cases the need to consider human beings and their individual behavioural and psychological attributes as only part, albeit an important part, of a much broader evolutionary picture helped to clear away many of the preconceptions which we as humans bring to any evaluation of the functional significance of particular mental and physical characteristics.

In the course of writing my own chapter for *Brain, Behaviour and Evolution* it became evident, after I had presented the relevant experimental evidence, that I could not provide an adequate account of the relationship between neocortex and adaptive behaviour without departing from the simpler forms of learning with which I was most familiar in animal studies. In particular it appeared necessary to adopt a view, which was being increasingly stressed by a number of theorists, that the most significant advance in information processing in animal brains was the emergence of an ability to form central representations, or models, of the world and to use these as a means of controlling behaviour. This essentially cognitive approach to animal behaviour clearly diminishes the gulf between models of information processing in animal brains in general and in human brains in particular.

Once the brain is attributed an autonomous model-making role it is a short step to see the contents of this internal world as equivalent to the contents of mind. If both human and animal brains house minds, new questions arise with regard to the problem of consciousness, both in defining it and deciding its distribution within the brain and within the animal kingdom. The present volume tackles these problems, again from a predominantly evolutionary perspective, and attempts to provide a view (or views) of mental life which encompasses both human and non-human animals. In the first chapter Jerison considers the evolution of mind (or minds) in animal species in terms both of the development of the ability to create internal worlds and the pressure which these capacities place upon brain size. Oatley (chapter 2) then provides a formal presentation of representational theory using examples from circadian rhythms and visual perception. He follows this with his own view of the role in social interaction of representations of more abstract concepts and the influence which these have on the contents of mind. In chapter 3 O'Keefe presents evidence for the involvement of a particular brain structure, the hippocampus, in forming cognitive maps or models of the environment. He uses behavioural and electrophysiological evidence, derived predominantly from animal studies, as a basis for developing a Cartesian view of mind which can accommodate both the physiological evidence and data derived from introspection regarding the nature of consciousness in humans.

Oakley (chapter 4) reviews evidence from animal studies to determine the range of objects or situations which might form the subject matter of representations and also the likely sources of such information in exploration, play, self-observation, or watching others. He goes on in chapter 5 to discuss the implications of this evidence for views of awareness, consciousness and self-image in animals, and to provide a simple model in terms of both their anatomical substrates and the modes of information processing which underly them. The question of human consciousness is tackled in chapter 6 by Newcombe, from the perspective of the practical and theoretical problems raised by changes in either the level or the contents of consciousness which result from damage to different parts of the brain. After reviewing the neuropsychological evidence she goes on to draw a number of parallels between the divisions and dissociations in consciousness produced by brain injury and those which can be observed in the everyday working of normal brains. One of the most powerful representational systems is based on language, and it is this system which above all others colours the content of human consciousness. The relationship of language to consciousness in humans is discussed in the context of split-brain studies by LeDoux in chapter 7, with particular reference to the case of a patient with an unusually good linguistic representation in his right hemisphere. In the final chapter (chapter 8) Oakley and Eames present a more detailed model of human consciousness based on that developed in chapter 5. The aim is to provide a framework within which to organize the behavioural, experiential and neurological data already presented; to provide working definitions of awareness, consciousness and self-awareness; and to extend the discussion to include functional dissociations in consciousness, as seen in hypnosis, hysterical conversion symptoms and multiple personality.

The reader will discover that though the authors in this volume adopt for the most part the view that mind can be profitably considered as an evolved biological system which processes information in the form of representations, they are by no means unanimous in their definition of its most perplexing attribute, consciousness. Lesley Eames and I have presented what we feel is a useful working definition in the final chapter. It would have been both presumptuous and counterproductive however had I attempted, as editor, to impose a uniform definition on the contributing authors. Many of the apparent conflicts of opinion which emerge from a comparison of the diverse views of these writers stem from differences in definition of terms rather than any fundamental disagreement about the nature of the phenomena under discussion. Newcombe, for instance, takes it as self-evident that 'consciousness' is not dependent on language, whilst

LeDoux asserts that 'consciousness' is directly related to our capacity for natural language, though neither would disagree, I suspect, that there is an aspect of mental life in humans which is uniquely associated with language. This is not the place to attempt to resolve such differences, and the reader is referred to the final chapter for further discussion.

Progress in theories of consciousness will be slow until a conceptual framework which at least diminishes the semantic confusions is adopted. This book offers representational theory as a way of describing the informational transactions which underlie mind in animals and humans alike, and points the way to operationally based definitions of awareness, consciousness and self-awareness. This approach provides a common frame of reference for evolutionary biologists, comparative psychologists, neuropsychologists, clinical and cognitive psychologists and psychodynamically oriented therapists in discussing brain, mind and consciousness.

I am grateful to the series editor, Peter Herriot, for his initial support of this project, to Mary, Sam, Ben and Dan for their patience during its progress, to the contributors for their hard work and to the students on C444 for their good humour in the face of ever more complex models of mind.

DAVID A. OAKLEY

Human brain anatomy

In several of the chapters in this book reference is made to parts of the central nervous system. In order to prevent duplication of figures, and to assist readers who are less familiar with human neuroanatomy, the following five figures show the majority of structures referred to in the text. For more detailed information see N. R. Carlson, *Physiology of Behavior* (Boston: Allyn & Bacon, 1981) or M. B. Carpenter, *Core Text of Neuroanatomy* (Baltimore: Williams & Wilkins, 1972).

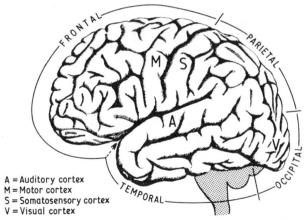

A = Auditory cortex
M = Motor cortex
S = Somatosensory cortex
V = Visual cortex

Fig. A   The left hemisphere of a human brain showing its convoluted covering of cortex and its subdivision into four areas or lobes. Part of the brainstem, spinal cord and cerebellum are shown as a dotted silhouette (see **Fig. B**).

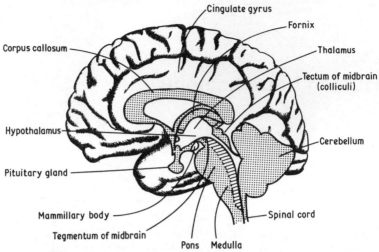

Cingulate gyrus

Fornix

Corpus callosum

Thalamus

Tectum of midbrain (colliculi)

Hypothalamus

Cerebellum

Pituitary gland

Mammillary body

Spinal cord

Tegmentum of midbrain

Pons   Medulla

Fig. B   The right hemisphere of a human brain viewed from the midline and showing that cortex continues as a convoluted surface deep into the cleft between the hemispheres. The deepest, less convoluted area of cortex is the cingulate gyrus and is part of the limbic system. In order to separate the two halves of the brain to produce this view of the right hemisphere it would be necessary to cut through the corpus callosum, the diencephalon, the midbrain (mesencephalon), the hindbrain (metencephalon and myelencephalon), the cerebellum and the spinal cord. Cut surfaces are shown as densely dotted areas. The thalamus and hypothalamus are diencephalic structures located in the walls of the third ventricle. The midbrain and hindbrain (pons and medulla) together form the brainstem. The location of the reticular formation within the brainstem is shown as a cross-hatched area.

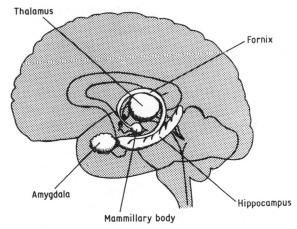

Fig. C Hippocampus and amygdala nucleus within the temporal lobe of the human brain. The prominent C-shaped pathway is the fornix, shown here terminating in the mammillary body of the posterior hypothalamus. The thalamus is shown for purposes of orientation.

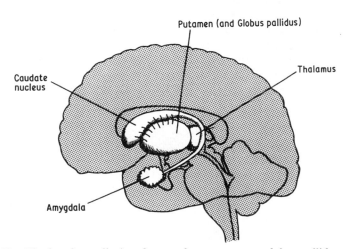

Fig. D The basal ganglia (caudate nucleus, putamen, globus pallidus and amygdala). The caudate nucleus has a long C-shaped 'tail' linking it with the amygdala in the temporal lobe. The globus pallidus is obscured by the putamen in this view (see Fig. E).

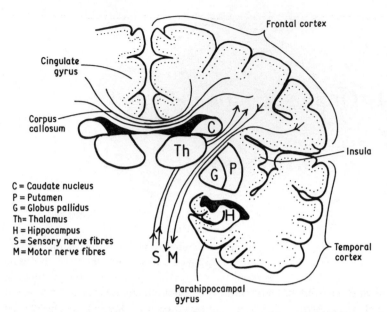

Fig. E A coronal (frontal) section of the human brain to show the internal structure of the cerebral hemispheres. A complete hemisphere is shown to the right but, for clarity, only the upper middle region of the other hemisphere is shown to the left. Lateral ventricles are solid black. The amygdala lies in front of the hippocampus in the same location and so cannot be included in this drawing. Sensory nerve fibres (S) and motor nerve fibres (M) run together as the internal capsule between the caudate and putamen in this figure. The depth of the cortex covering the hemisphere is indicated by the dotted line. The remainder of the hemisphere is filled with nerve fibres (white matter).

1 On the evolution of mind

Harry J. Jerison

Most of us think of mind as a little person in the head, the 'knower' of reality (cf. Attneave, 1960). It is this intuition that will be elaborated for an evolutionary analysis of the place of mind in nature. Our major task, in this chapter, is to develop the intuition into an idea about the activity of an organ of the body, because evolutionary biology is about organic evolution, and the evolutionary biology of mind must be about the organic basis of mind.

The organ of mind is the brain, of course. The task, then, is to identify aspects of the brain that are correlated with its work as the organ of mind, and to describe the *organic* evolution of this brain/mind system. Most of the chapter is on this substantive problem.

Darwinism has traditionally been a doctrine about phyletic history, about the origin and change of species. As a doctrine it has been rooted in the similarities and differences among species and in the reconstruction of phyletic histories, of family trees and the bundles of related species (clades) that are the branches in a family tree. Yet in the evolution of behavior there is evidence of correlated advances in mental capacity across broad spectra of species. Progressive, or anagenetic, evolution is sometimes evident to comparable degrees in the evolution of behavioral capacity, or mind, in distantly related species (Gould, 1976; Rensch, 1959). Misunderstandings of the relation between cladistic and anagenetic approaches to the evolution of behavior should be cleared up, or at least discussed, in a chapter like this.

Following the outline just presented, this chapter has four main themes. First we review the nature of mind from a perspective that lends itself to evolutionary analysis. That perspective emphasizes a role for perceptual-motor and cognitive integration. The second theme is the hierarchical organization of very large nervous systems in effecting the integration. Third, in the light of that perspective on the nature of mind, we review the evolution of mind as the history of encephalization – the history of the enlargement of the brain beyond the grade expected from trends towards the evolution of larger bodies. Finally, we compare anagenetic with cladistic evolution in order to put the evolution of mind into an appropriate evolutionary perspective.

On mind

These are our premises: the phenomenon of mind is manifested as the 'real' world constructed by the brain; the quotation marks about 'real' are to distinguish this created world from the external world that we know exists, but which is translated into experienced reality by sensori-motor systems and by the brain. The construction of 'reality', discussed more fully below, is the most demanding work that the brain does, and it is primarily for this work that very large amounts of brain tissue are required. ('Very large', for present purposes, is of the order of 10^7 or more nerve cells, a gram or so of human cerebral cortex, or 0.1 gram of cerebral cortex in a rat, in which neurons are packed much more densely than in the human brain; see Jerison, 1973.)

These premises about mind as a construction of the brain are fundamental hypotheses about the work of the brain and about brain/behavior relations in higher vertebrates, that is, in birds and mammals. They imply that the perceptual worlds of different species may be different, that their 'realities' may be different because their sensorimotor systems and brains are different. They are the bases for an analysis of mind as an evolutionary character, or trait.

Perceptual worlds

The most accessible part of the 'reality' that is mind is the naively known 'real world', the *Umwelt*, or perceptual world (von Uexküll, 1934).

This perceptual world is related to the reality implied by physical measurement and physical theory, but a century of analysis (Carterette and Friedman, 1974) has made it clear that the physical and psychological are different worlds. Physical reality, the external world revealed by physical measurement (Bridgman, 1959), is a world we all believe exists though we do not know it directly. Experienced reality is based on that physical world, shaped by the way information about the external world is transformed at the sensory surfaces of the body and by the way that information is processed in the central nervous system. Different individuals live in different realities, depending on the nature of the transformations and processing. A color-blind person's reality differs from that of a normal trichromat's, for example. A classic problem in comparative psychology has been to reconstruct the perceptual worlds of other species, in which differences in sensory transformations and presumed differences further along in the central nervous system could imply fantastically different realities in different species (von Uexküll, 1934).

Some of the differences among species that have been established are, indeed, fantastic. Echolocating bats (microchiropterans), for example, apparently use auditory-vocal information to construct worlds that may be equivalent in *spatial* extension to our visual worlds (Griffin, 1976). These species must build their realities from time-encoded bits of information, transformed into a spatial as well as temporal world, a three-dimensional analogue, perhaps, to the picture generated by successive dots that form the image we see on a television screen. We may have a sense of how this works for a bat if we recognize something comparable that we humans do.

The finest temporal resolution of mammalian nervous systems is for the difference in the time of arrival of acoustic signals to the two ears, a difference of about 10 microseconds (Masterton and Diamond, 1973). Although demonstrated experimentally in cats and monkeys, the function is clearly the same in humans, and it functions to translate time differences into information about space rather than about time. It is the basis for the ability to localize sound in space. We humans make this transformation when we recognize the 'where' (rather than 'when') of a sound, when we localize its source in space. This can be a primary source for the construction of space by the congenitally blind. Bats may construct their 'space' in an analogous way, using information processed primarily by their auditory rather than visual nervous system.

The perceptual worlds of different species should be similar to the extent that they are constrained by similar physical features of the environment and are constructed by nervous systems that, at least in vertebrates, work in fundamentally similar ways. The constructed realities will, therefore, retain appropriate isomorphisms with physical reality. The realities of different species should be analogous to translations of the same ideas into different languages.

Perception, experience and consciousness

The naively known perceptual world is only part of what we would describe as mind, and we can play a kind of word game to improve our sense of the nature of mind. If we recognize the depth of the problem of knowledge, we may take 'mind' and 'knowing' as approximately synonymous. A second step can be to pair knowing with being aware (or conscious) of the experiences of the moment. The words 'awareness' and 'immediate experience' are still not quite right, but a measure of our progress in this word game is that we can be more precise about where the words are wrong. Here are a few of the problems:

First, 'awareness' and 'immediate experience' are incomplete descriptions of intuitions about mind. Careful perceptual experiments have shown that many important mental events occur without awareness (e.g. Posner, 1978), and this proves that aspects of mind other than the vague ones described in psychoanalytic practice must be unconscious. That won't surprise many people. Second, the words are misleading. If we are serious about equating awareness with *immediate* experience, there is a problem with the immediacy. Experience of the moment is colored by memories and anticipations. So mind, even if restricted to immediate experience, includes expectations and memories. Developing this understanding with the help of words that make our thoughts more precise, we should also be sensitive to an important semantic problem. 'Awareness' and 'experience' are passive, and miss the manipulation and active exploration and movement that determine at least some of the work of the mind. This active dimension is important enough to be emphasized in 'motor theories' of consciousness (James, 1890; Sperry, 1952; cf. Held, 1965).

Language and mind

The picture of mind remains incomplete. We could add sensory dimensions: kinaesthetic, proprioceptive, gustatory, and even olfactory, beyond the visual and auditory dimensions, motor activity and expectations and memories considered thus far. Another, and major dimension of mind in the human species is linguistic. It deserves special discussion as an example of a species-typical cognitive adaptation as well as of an unusual progressive development in behavioral capacity.

Language is a double medium. When we communicate with it we use a neurobehavioral system that I believe (Jerison, 1973, 1976) evolved as a unique adaptation to contribute to the construction of 'reality'. If I talk to you with words I send you messages that are also elements of my reality. When you hear my words you receive my messages and incorporate them into your reality. In short, when we talk we share realities. Now that is unusual for animal communication. More normal is a dog's signaling another dog, for example, by baring its teeth. The message is a command: 'Retreat, or face the consequences!' There is a lack of ambiguity about the message that is rare in human communication, and to a significant extent its behavioral expression appears to be encoded in the genetic material. We communicate in this way when we blush, flinch, smile, laugh (if these are not staged) and so on. Our natural gestural 'language' is probably the genuine homologue of communicational systems of other species (MacLean, 1970). But when we talk (or write, or 'sign' with the sign languages of the deaf) we share what is on our minds. Of course, when we read we are doing some delayed sharing of the mind of the writer, and when we watch a film, all of us in attendance may live directly in the cleverly created worlds of the director, editor and actors as we experience the pleasures and pains as participant-observers. Language is a medium for sharing consciousness.

In our immediate experience of the external world we live in a created world that includes our selves as individuals. The experience has linguistic dimensions, which give it a special kind of meaning. We like to think of experience as private. Yet when we converse, or read, or watch a film we are no longer completely individual. We share the lives of others, or, more accurately, we live the lives of others, which merge with our own lives. These are not mere metaphors but state what are surely facts of mind: our minds are not limited by the boundaries of our bodies. We share the lives of others through the medium of language as if we shared information from their senses, experienced the sights they saw and the sounds they heard. In effect, we share a set of experiences that are marked by the language 'sense' as surely as they are marked by the conventional senses. Language enables us to share more, because we can also share more subtle experiences, such as feelings, emotions and expectations.

Mind goes beyond immediate experience and the awareness of the external world. We may achieve a better understanding than hinted at by these intuitions about language, and by the evidence on the nature of perceptual, cognitive and motor activities, if we turn now to the analysis that must take place in the brain. This is a hierarchical analysis that transforms the elementary information represented by the neural code into building blocks that are the components of the behaviors, experiences and memories, of the motoric, linguistic, perceptual and cognitive worlds that are at least components of mind.

Hierarchical structures in brain/behavior systems

Perceptual worlds may be thought of as possible worlds created by the brain to make sense of the otherwise overwhelming amount of activity of nervous systems. Our perceptual world allows a coin to be turned and moved to project changing oval and circular images on different parts of the retina, and yet there is a 'constancy' to the coin as an object, despite its changed stimulus configuration peripherally and the inevitably changed central neural events generated by the peripheral image.

This is the work involved in the construction of *Umwelten*. It is costly neural activity in that much neural machinery is used to build these worlds, which maintain their constant structure and also reflect changing events within the structure. The construction should be thought of as occurring at certain levels of the hierarchical organization of the brain's work. At lower levels it is the work of single neurons and then of relatively small networks of neurons. The work at one level may be described with a different vocabulary from the work at another level. Lower level work might be described with the language of cellular neurophysiology, and higher level work with the language of nerve networks and neural systems.

Like all large information processing systems, whether artificial or natural, large brains must function hierarchically (Simon, 1974). The elements of neural information, which are changes of state in individual nerve cells, must be combined or chunked into subroutines within higher order programs, and it is the higher order programs that actually control behavior and experience.

Physiological hierarchies

Important transformations change the information available to and used by living organisms, and the sequence of changes takes place at successive levels of organization. Environmental information is in the form of physical energy: photons, the movement of molecules of air, chemicals that can reach sensory surfaces, the mechanical deformation of the skin, inertial changes in body fluids, and so on. Such information is transformed by sense cells into neural events in peripheral parts of the visual, auditory, olfactory and gustatory (chemical), tactile, and proprioceptive systems. Other information, feedback from body tissues, is relayed by peripheral parts of the kinaesthetic and autonomic nervous systems. At this stage of information processing, very different kinds of physical information are transformed into a neural code of action potentials and waves of polarization and depolarization. The problem solved by the organism is, in a sense, the translation of an environmental code into a neural code.

If we think of activity at a single synapse as the lowest purely physiological level of neural analysis, we can identify the next level as the synaptic activity that combines to activate a whole neuron, exciting or inhibiting its activity. At a higher level there is the temporal pattern of firing of a single nerve cell, which is recorded as trains of impulses that may also be interpreted as excitatory or inhibitory. And at still higher levels one can identify networks of neurons, or cell-assemblies, that operate jointly on some classes of information. This includes the work of receptor fields and 'tuned' detector neurons, which may represent yet other levels of organization of information processing in the nervous system.

Even higher physiological levels of organization of the nervous system are in the activities of the major projection areas of the brain, such as the several visual, somatic, auditory cortical areas and so forth. Then there are more broadly organized brain systems that can be identified as handling classes of information. These classes may be referred to sense modality (e.g. the visual system represented in many interconnected cortical, thalamic, midbrain, retinal and oculomotor subsystems); to polysensory systems in which several modalities are represented in the same region (Jones and Powell, 1970); to language systems (in the human brain); or even to a whole-brain functional level represented by the still poorly understood electroencephalogram, which can identify behavioral levels of arousal and attentiveness. There are many levels of organization.

For a better perspective on the relationship of neurophysiological evidence to the problem of mind, it is helpful to think of the nervous system as one of a class of systems that handles very large amounts of information. How can an information processing system use the thousands of millions of identifiable neural events that take place in a moderately large mammalian brain every minute? Well understood information processing systems that are very large, such as computers, must function hierarchically to accomplish this. At the lowest level there are changes of state in on-off devices. At a higher level the changes of state are assembled into groups and described as logical operations, equivalent to 'and', 'or', 'nor' and so forth. The general statement of the solution to handling a lot of information is that the information is chunked, with clusters of elements nested within chunks and clusters of chunks nested within larger chunks and so on. The analogy is to computer programs in which subroutines are constructed and used as parts of more inclusive subroutines and so on (Simon, 1974).

Vertebrate brains are all large information processing systems. In addition to the functional hierarchies for information processing, there are structural hierarchies (e.g. forebrain v. mid- or hindbrain), which have been important for describing the way brains are organized and work. Beyond the level of the nerve cell, and of assemblies of cells, the higher levels of physiological organization may be distributed through many parts of the structural hierarchy (Mountcastle, 1978). But the distribution is to homologous brain structures in different species. A particular function may be organized at spinal, bulbar, midbrain, diencephalic and the various telencephalic levels; the same distribution of the function would generally be found in all species in which the structures and the function can be identified. For example, networks of neurons in the visual attention-system in tree shrews, lemurs, and, one assumes, humans are spread through the superior colliculi, pulvinar and other thalamic nuclei, temporal cortex, frontal eyefields, midbrain nuclei and peripheral ganglia that ultimately control the various muscles of the eye, determining eye-fixation, convergence and accommodation. At higher levels the networks act in combination and often reflexly as an operating system that points the eyes toward points in space to which one is attending (Diamond, 1979; Merzenich and Kaas, 1980).

It is usually assumed that physiological controls by lower levels of the structural hierarchy are more automatic and stereotyped than those at higher levels of the structural hierarchy. The highest 'physiological' levels of this hierarchical organization can be described only by introducing behavioral concepts such as arousal and attention; they verge on the concept of mind.

The place of mind in the hierarchy

The 'physiological' hierarchy must include a system of controls that enables one to maintain the 'constancy' mentioned earlier, what Klüver (1933) has called the 'constancy of the external environment'. Present methods in neurophysiology are not adequate to study and describe such controls, but no one doubts their presence. The descriptive language has to be psychological. At some level of *physiological* organization of the nervous system there must be systems describable not by words like 'edge-detector', or 'visual cortex', or even 'speech and language' areas but by words denoting functions that can be related to imagery, reality and knowledge. We can return to the computer analogy to appreciate that one of the most difficult problems in computer science is the problem of pattern recognition – how to write programs, for example, that would recognize words spoken by men as opposed to women or by people with different regional accents as being the same or different. The problem is solvable, but it requires very large amounts of computing machinery – in that sense it may be comparable to the way the organism handles such problems, i.e. by investing in very large brains. (We should remind ourselves that 'very large' with respect to neural machinery may imply a brain that can be packed into a cubic centimeter or less of space.)

These very large systems must be organized hierarchically in order to function. The question is about the highest levels in the hierarchy, the levels at which a model of reality, of a possible world, is built (Craik, 1943). Objects in space and time are structures of the highest level of the hierarchy according to the view presented here. They represent the final stage in the transformation of physical events in the external world into a perceived reality that is configured as a real world supported by many other mental activities: memory, predictions, anticipations, feelings and imagination. Experience itself, and the knowledge of the experience, i.e. self-consciousness, are part of the model and contribute to the capacity of the organism to deal with the external world (cf. Humphrey, 1978).

Another way to put this conclusion is that the real world that we know in ordinary experience is a creation of the brain. This familiar insight has been verified many times with many examples: the world that we know depends on our capacity to perceive it. To extend the examples presented at the beginning of the chapter, just as the world of the color-blind differs from that of the visually normal, so does the world of the expert observer differ from that of the ignorant; a neighborhood is experienced differently when one knows it well from when it is new and strange. Craik's (1943) view, as I interpret it and which I am following here, was that higher functional levels of organization of the brain create the reality of immediate experience. Following our intuition and original definition, these higher levels of functional organization of the brain include what we know as mind.

Information processing and brain size

We should now be ready to accept the proposition that mind in man and other animals is a consequence of the enormous processing capacity of the brain and is part of the solution of the problem of putting that capacity to work. This conclusion enables us to undertake an analysis of the evolution of mind by analyzing the evolution of brain size, more specifically, by analyzing the evolution of the brain to sizes greater than those that would be associated merely with the evolution of larger bodies. There is a missing link in the argument, however, which we must now establish, namely to show how information processing capacity is related to brain size.

Neural modules and processing capacity

As a structure, the mammalian neocortex is surprisingly uniform microscropically (Rockel, Hiorns and Powell, 1980). The neuronal structure of the neocortex has been analyzed as consisting of integrative columnar modules (Mountcastle, 1978; Szentágothai, 1978), again remarkably uniform in their structure. The columns extend through the full depth of the cortex, which may vary from 0.5 to 3.0 mm or so, depending on species and region of the cortex, but all contain comparable numbers of nerve cells, something of the order of 2000. The columns are about 250 micrometers in diameter and are the units of information processing. They overlap one another, but their number in a given species is determined by the total cortical surface area.

Because of the high correlation between the extent of the neocortex and the total size of the brain in mammals, the analysis of the relationship between processing capacity and brain size is probably equivalent to that between processing capacity and the extent of the neocortex. But the unit of processing, the column or module, is not restricted to the cortex. As Mountcastle puts it:

> The large entities of the brain we know as areas (or nuclei) of the neocortex, the limbic lobe, basal ganglia, dorsal thalamus, and so forth, are themselves composed of replicated *local neural circuits*, modules which vary in cell number, intrinsic connections, and processing mode from one large entity to another but are basically similar within any given entity.   (Mountcastle, 1978, p. 8)

Eccles (1979) considers these modules to be even more general. In any case, the important point is to recognize that there is more structural uniformity in the brain than had been appreciated, and that the diversity in the information that is processed is probably reflected in specialized connections within the modules. Modules in the visual system will process visual information and those in the auditory system will process auditory information, but the modules in the two systems may be built in similar ways and communicate with one another to significant extents.

Considering for the moment only cortical columns, their columnar structure is the feature that relates processing capacity to gross brain size, because the number of columnar modules in any mammalian species is necessarily proportional to the area of the cerebral surface. For comparisons among species, the area of the cerebral cortex (including surface hidden within convolutions) can be estimated from brain size, with an error of only a few percentage points. The correlation coefficient for the two measures in logarithmic units, determined in 48 different species, is 0.995, a perfect correlation to two significant figures (Jerison, 1983). Since the number of cortical columns is proportional to processing capacity, processing capacity is proportional to brain size. QED.

The argument is valid for processing capacity in mammalian cortex. It seems reasonable to assume that it is also true for all of the brain's processing capacity in mammals, and, by extension, in other vertebrates.

Behavioral demands on neural tissue

One of the problems in analyzing brain evolution with respect to the brain's work in the control of behavior, is that most behavior, even complex behavior, does not seem to require much brain tissue for its control. The behaviors that are correlated with the evolution of extensive neural control systems involve sensory-perceptual activity, and motor activity correlated with sensory-perceptual integration. One reason for identifying human language as a cognitive system is that it encumbers very large amounts of neural tissue, whereas communication systems in most species apparently evolved with relatively little neural apparatus to control them (MacLean, 1970). It is 'creating reality' — the work that we assume is done by sensory-perceptual systems — that seems to be so difficult for the neural computer that it requires a major investment in neural processing capacity.

Sensory-perceptual systems involve much more of the brain in their work than is usually recognized, much more than the mapped areas identified with them. The visual system, for example, is represented in primary visual neocortex, but also in bands of brain tissue around primary cortex (Areas 18 and 19), in visual 'attention systems' in the temporal lobe of primates and homologous areas in other orders, in frontal eye fields (Area 8, etc.) and in various regions of the basal ganglia, cerebellum and other parts of the brain (Merzenich and Kaas, 1980). Well mapped and well mappable, the system is diffuse as well as focalized. There is no reason to assume that other brain systems that are differentiated by human scientific analysis are not equally complex. They may be functionally coherent yet structurally diffuse.

Mountcastle (1978) has analyzed the problem in depth, describing the brain as a 'distributed system' in which the module is the unit of processing. The idea of mind and intelligence is represented organically by the work of such brain systems, organized functionally as hierarchical systems, with their parts widely distributed throughout the brain. Enormous amounts of brain tissue may be encumbered by the activity of sensory-perceptual systems. If we accept the idea that the highest level of the brain's work is the construction of realities, the grade of intelligence or mental capacity assigned to a species would be proportional to the complexity of the reality that it constructs and, therefore, related to the gross size of its brain.

It is legitimate to emphasize overall capacity while recognizing that the organization of that capacity is also important. Specialized organization should reflect specialized requirements of the niche, whereas overall capacity may reflect the complexity of the neurobehavioral system that evolved to meet the requirements. In that sense we may think of more intelligent (involving more processing capacity) and less intelligent (involving less processing capacity) ways of doing approximately the same thing. We are led to a paradoxical conclusion: the economical response of animals to an adaptive requirement with respect to neural control is to minimize the size of the neural control system, and less intelligent rather than more intelligent behaviors should be preferred as solutions of the evolutionary game. 'Less intelligent' behaviors are economical energetically, because neural control systems are metabolically the most expensive organ-systems in the body. The paradox is that despite its energetic cost, the brain in many species has evolved to larger size than required for the control of ordinary bodily functions, and its residual capacity must be thought of as controlling more intelligent behavior. There must, therefore, have been some benefit associated with higher intelligence, despite its energetic cost, though, as we shall see, most species of vertebrates did not 'invest' in intelligence as a solution for adaptive problems.

Encephalization and brain/body allometry

Information processing capacity is related to brain size. But a bigger brain, like a bigger heart or liver, is one of the things that has to evolve when a larger body evolves. There must be a component of brain size allocated, as it were, to the control of body functions, and one would be reluctant to relate the processing performed by that component to higher mental processes, or mind. This issue has been handled biometrically by taking into account the normal relations among organ sizes in species of different size, which is called an allometric relationship. Brain/body allometry can be used to estimate a body-control component in brain size, and the 'residual' (in the statistical sense) component, which can be taken as a measure of encephalization, can be used to estimate the amount of processing capacity related to the evolution of mind.

There remain a number of uncertainties in the statistical analysis of brain/body data to determine empirical allometric functions (see for example Jerison (in press), Martin (1983) and Russell (1979)), but for the discussion of encephalization that follows these technical issues raise no major problems. The 'allometric' analysis is nonparametric. It depends on identifying a body size factor in processing capacity by examining the orientation of polygons drawn about brain/body data, graphed on log-log coordinates (Figure 1.1). Such minimum convex polygons may be used to define a brain/body 'space' as regions in the coordinate system, in which it has been possible for species to evolve with respect to two traits: brain size and body size. The avian polygon, for example, would indicate the limits of the adaptive radiation of

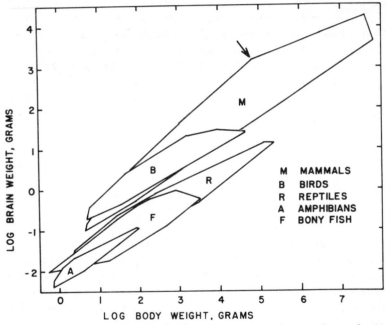

Fig. 1.1 Brain/body relations in living species from five vertebrate classes. The polygons are minimum convex hulls drawn about the data of each class. For example the human datum and the dolphin (*Tursiops truncatus*) datum, together at the arrow, form one vertex of the mammalian polygon, and a large alligator provides the datum for the highest point on the reptilian polygon. (Adapted from H. J. Jerison, 'Animal intelligence as encephalization', *Philosophical Transactions of the Royal Society of London B 308* (1985): 21–35.)

birds with respect to brain and body size, and although more extreme sizes may be possible, the absence of living (or fossil) species at the more extreme sizes would suggest that some limitation of avian morphology and neurobiology may prevent the evolution of these extremes. Encephalization is the vertical displacement of polygons relative to one another for species or groups of species that are to be compared. If the brain/body datum of the fossil bird *Archaeopteryx* was below the polygon for living birds, for example, this would be taken as evidence that it was less encephalized than living birds. Encephalization determined in this way does not depend on the many assumptions hidden in numerical computations of encephalization quotients.

The evolution of encephalization

Fossil evidence of encephalization has been available for more than a century. Darwin (1871) was impressed by it and cited it, and the evidence remains impressive. I have discussed it and reviewed the extensive literature on it elsewhere (Jerison, 1973, 1982a, 1983, in press); this is a summary of the major results and conclusions. Since encephalization represents an increase in processing capacity beyond that required for the control of basic body functions, it is appropriate to treat it as the morphological correlate of mind in man and animals. The history of encephalization is, therefore, fundamental evidence about the evolution of mind.

The vertebrate classes

There is a fossil record of endocranial casts (endocasts) suitable for the analysis of encephalization in all of the classes of vertebrates with the exception of the jawless fishes (agnathans). That record is entirely consistent with data on living species. If we draw polygons about brain/body points of the classes of living species (cartilaginous fish, bony fish, amphibians, reptiles, birds and mammals), the interpretation of the polygons is not affected by adding data on fossil species to the graph. Fossil bony fish with good endocasts (small species that lived about 300 million years ago) were apparently much like living fish of similar size in brain/body relations. Adding dinosaurs to reptilian data makes the reptilian polygon longer, by including some very large species, but the elongation occurs without any change of the orientation of the polygon in brain/body space. Dinosaurs were 'good' reptiles. This is no surprise to evolutionists, who recognize it as an example of 'uniformitarianism'. The evidence on dinosaurs shows that the uniformity of nature with respect to brain/body relations in reptiles was maintained in the geological record. This evidence puts to rest the myth that dinosaurs became extinct because of their small brains. With few exceptions, they were like living reptiles in relative brain size. Their brains were just right for their reptilian bodies. (The exceptions to be described presently were, in fact, more encephalized than living reptiles.

Appropriately combined, the classes of vertebrates fall into two somewhat larger polygons that are similar in size and orientation but are displaced vertically from one another. Bony fish, amphibians and reptiles are together in the lower polygon as 'lower vertebrates', and birds and mammals are in the higher polygon, the 'higher vertebrates'. The cartilaginous fish – sharks, rays and skates – are exceptional in this kind of analysis, because the polygon that encloses their brain/body data overlaps the other two. They are neither primitive nor generalized with respect to encephalization. Finally, living agnathans (lampreys and hagfish), relics of the earliest vertebrates, are significantly below the lower polygon, but they may be degenerate rather than primitive, with a reduction in neural control to a level adequate for life in their present parasitic niches.

An unusual exception in this simple picture of evolutionary history occurred during the adaptive radiation of the dinosaurs. Endocasts of 'ostrich dinosaurs', a group that included species similar in size and shape to living ostriches, indicate that their brains were similar in size to those of living ostriches. In other words, the dinosaurs 'experimented' with encephalization in at least one of their families.

Transitional forms

About 500 million years ago the only vertebrates were jawless fish, but the great adaptive radiation that followed saw the appearance of both bony and cartilaginous fish, and when terrestrial niches became available, amphibians and reptiles evolved. This history, and the history of the later evolution of mammals and birds, between 200 and 150 million years ago, is now well known and reasonably well understood. The great transition was the advance in grade that occurred when mammals and birds evolved.

The earliest known mammalian endocasts, about 150 million years old, indicate a grade of encephalization comparable to that of living opossums and hedgehogs. The transition from a reptilian grade to a mammalian grade must have occurred earlier, and it is possible that some species of reptiles (therapsids) immediately ancestral to mammals were advanced beyond the present grade of reptilian encephalization (see Jerison, in press). No transitional mammals below the lowest grade of present mammalian encephalization are known as fossils.

Birds probably evolved later than mammals, from a very different group of reptiles, closely related to dinosaurs. The earliest of their fossils, *Archaeopteryx*, lived about 150 million years ago and is an excellent example of a transitional form in many respects (Ostrom, 1976). Of the two specimens with known endocasts, one was apparently less encephalized than any living bird, but brain/body data for the second, which was smaller and perhaps a juvenile, lie within the living avian polygon.

Taking the evolution of encephalization as evidence on the evolution of mind, these results demonstrate an interesting conservatism. Animals evolved as little behavioral capacity as possible, consistent with their niches, rather than as much as possible. Adaptive problems were not usually 'solved' by the evolution of flexible behavioral systems that we associate with high mental capacity. This evidence lies in the stability of encephalization in the fossil record of most groups. The stability of the 'lower vertebrates' is outstanding, indicating that the grade of encephalization achieved in these great vertebrate classes has been maintained without significant advances for between 200 and 400 million years, and remains the present level of encephalization for their living representatives. Of the 45,000 or so species of living vertebrates, some 30,000 are lower vertebrates. Evolving enlarged brains has clearly been an unusual adaptation.

Higher vertebrates

Stability of encephalization is also evident in the evolution of birds and mammals. Fossil avian brains are known from only a few specimens, but these show that when birds had become recognizably modern in general body structure (beyond the grade of *Archaeopteryx*), 50 million or more years ago or so, they were also recognizably modern in encephalization. A much more detailed record is available

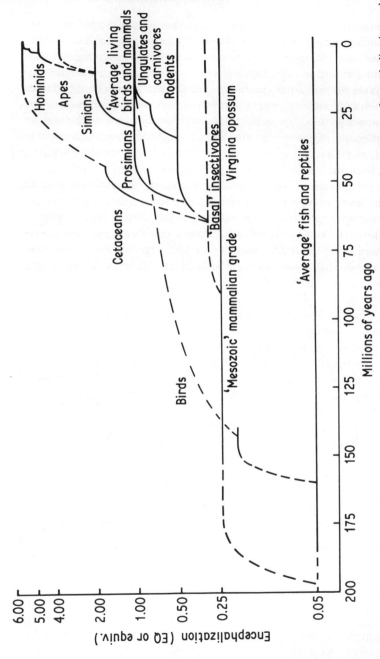

Fig. 1.2 Rates of mammalian brain evolution from the reptilian 'steady state'. The ordinate is a measure of encephalization such as an encephalization quotient relative to the 2/3 power of body size.

for mammalian encephalization, and this record is also consistent with long periods of stability (Figure 1.2).

The most complete records are available for ungulates (hooved mammals) and carnivores. Less complete but extensive records are available for archaic mammalian species, members of orders that are now entirely extinct. There are reasonable records of the cetacean brain, which have not yet been analyzed in sufficient depth, considering their potential importance. The record for primates is now also good, and especially good for the evolution of the hominids during the past four million years.

A polygon drawn to contain the archaic mammals (Figure 1.3) is at the lower margin of the one for living mammals, with the largest archaic species being somewhat less encephalized than any living species of comparable body size. (Low encephalization in large species probably reflects their evolution as a result of selection for body size rather than brain size; see Lande, 1979.) If living marsupials,

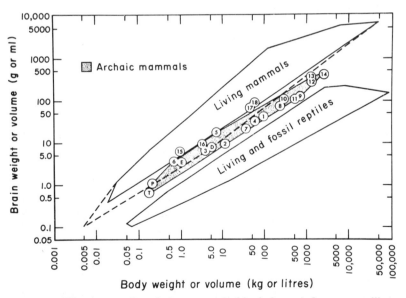

Fig. 1.3 Divergence of archaic mammals (shaded area) from a reptilian grade of encephalization. Note that the dashed line is the border for all living mammalian species, and that the solid polygon for mammals excludes living 'primitive' groups, namely the order Insectivora and the didelphids among the marsupials. (From Jerison, 1973, reprinted by permission.)

monotremes (egg-laying mammals) and insectivores are excluded from the living polygons, on the ground that they are relict groups (survivors of 'primitive' orders), then the polygon for archaic mammalian species is entirely below that of living mammals and intermediate between that of lower and higher vertebrates, suggesting the archaic forms as a kind of transitional mammalian grade. However, the living 'primitive' mammalian orders would be well represented within that archaic polygon. Keeping in mind that the archaic polygon represents 100 million years of evolution, between about 150 million years ago for the earliest known endocasts and between 60 and 40 million years ago for the last of the fossils represented in the group, we can appreciate the meaning of stability of encephalization. Living 'primitive' mammals, such as opossums and hedgehogs, are evidence of the adequacy of that grade of encephalization for at least some present mammalian niches. The opossum (*Didelphis*) is represented by D in Figure 1.3. E in the same figure is the moonrat (*Echinosorex*), a close living relative of the hedgehog. Other points are fossil species.

Major advances in encephalization occurred in early primates and cetaceans, with somewhat later and less dramatic advances in carnivores and the modern ungulate orders. Primates are represented by good endocasts that date from about 55 million years ago and by evidence of the brain case that is about 60 million years old. The earliest primates were lemur-like, larger-brained than their contemporaries among other orders of mammals but only about half as encephalized as living lemurs. The earliest endocast is of the lower Eocene tarsioid, *Tetonius*. This animal's brain was already large compared to other Eocene mammals of comparable body size, but significantly smaller than in its living descendants, the tarsiers.

The advance in encephalization in prosimians may have been fairly continuous over the period of about 30 million years following the earliest evidence of the brain. The prosimians (lemurlike and tarsierlike species) appeared to reach their present grade of encephalization by about 30 million years ago. Stability in this group is evident in its later history; there have been no significant further advances. The earliest of the simian primates in which there is evidence on the brain (*Aegyptopithecus*, of about 30 million years ago) was at a prosimian grade of encephalization, but later simian primates had apparently achieved the present grade of encephalization about 20 million years ago.

Among living mammals, only the cetaceans include species as

encephalized as many higher primates. The bottlenosed dolphin (*Tursiops*) is comparable to humans in relative brain size, and has become an intriguing species for research on higher mental processes in exotic animals (Herman, 1980). Although the fossil record of cetacean encephalization is incomplete it indicates that, like the primates, this order of mammals has been encephalized for many eons. The present grade of encephalization may have been reached as early as the lower Miocene epoch, about 20 million years ago.

The most recent great advance in encephalization occurred in the hominids. The present view (Martin, 1983) is that the earliest hominids appeared about 5 million years ago. These were the australopithecines, with brains that had already become enlarged beyond the grade of monkeys and great apes, according to the oldest data on endocasts of between 3 and 4 million years ago. Within the several species of australopithecines there is no evidence of further encephalization; differences in brain size are appropriate for their body sizes.

The next advance in grade occurred about 2 million years ago with the appearance of *Homo habilis*, with almost a doubling in brain size. About 1.6 million years ago, the earliest pithecanthropine (*Homo erectus*) appeared, with an additional step in brain size, followed by *Homo sapiens* within the past 200,000 years or so, the living human species, with yet another increment in brain size. These advances in grade in the genus *Homo* are not especially easy to interpret. One widely distributed group of fossil *Homo sapiens*, the Neandertals, may have been slightly larger-brained than any living human populations. Differences in body size among the species of *Homo* are not clear enough or great enough to account for the enlargement of the brain. Some of the problem of interpretation is related to the variability of brain size; the coefficient of variation is about 10 per cent in larger mammals, including humans. This means that an average brain size of 1300 grams in living humans implies an expected range for normal brains between 1040 and 1560 grams for 95 per cent of the population. The average pithecanthropine brain was probably only slightly smaller than the lower figure, and some pithecanthropines had brains of 1100 grams or more. These hominid grades apparently overlapped, except for the step from *Australopithecus* to *Homo*.

There are five points to emphasize in summing up this evidence.

1. The allometric brain/body relationship, represented by the orientation of minimum convex polygons drawn about brain/body data (or the angle of the regression lines through the centroids of the

polygons), is comparable for archaic and living mammals, as it is for birds and lower vertebrates. There is, therefore, stability in the expected values of brain size for a given body size, i.e. conservation of brain/body allometry.

2. All mammals, even the oldest, were big-brained compared to the reptiles from which they evolved.

3. Mammals were at a steady state in encephalization for more than 100 million years, between the oldest endocasts of 150 million years ago and those of archaic species of about 40 million years ago.

4. There was a great leap forward in mammalian encephalization between the archaic grade and the modern mammalian grade represented by living orders of mammals, a leap that began about 50 million years ago.

5. Finally, the most recent encephalization apparently occurred in the hominid lineage, and within the genus *Homo* body size was similar enough to permit one to see encephalization as changes in brain size. These occurred as steps from species to species, as should be expected from any evolutionary analysis, but there was probably stability within each species (and within the genus *Australopithecus*) during its survival as a taxon.

The anagenetic evolution of mind

Victorians outraged by the publication of Darwin's *Origin of Species* were troubled by the obvious implication, which Darwin diplomatically neglected to develop, that there was mental continuity between man and other animals. The evidence for continuity that has accumulated during the past century is now so strong that serious arguments against it are no longer presented. The problem has become to establish differences among species rather than similarities, and as mentioned at the beginning of this chapter, serious questions have been raised about the validity of evidence for the progressive evolution of mind and of qualitative differences among species. Except for the evolution of language as a species-typical behavior, it has been argued that the human species and other animal species are more similar than different in behavioral capacity (Macphail, 1982), although the consensus still favors the idea of at least some significant differences among species.

Encephalization, mental evolution, and the Red Queen

Advances in encephalization may be taken as advances in mental capacity and evidence of the evolution of mind. They were dramatically evident in the evolution of the birds and mammals. Several grades of encephalization occur in living species of these vertebrate classes.

Among birds, chickens and pigeons are among the least encephalized; songbirds are 'average' birds, fairly typical of the avian grade, and crows and parrots are the most encephalized. If one is concerned with the avian 'mind' the morphological indicators point to this grading of behavioral capacity.

The most interesting feature of mammalian encephalization is the appearance of comparable advances in species that are phylogenetically distant from one another. It would be difficult to find placental mammals more different in lineage than primates and cetaceans, yet the two most encephalized living mammals, humans and dolphins, evolved in these groups. There are comparable pairings at other grades of encephalization. The great apes and the harbor porpoise (*Phocaena*), are about equally encephalized. Lemurs, canids, felids, horses, and deer are at the 'average' grade of encephalization of living mammals. Most rodents are half as encephalized, and the 'primitive' living mammals such as opossums and hedgehogs are about one-quarter as encephalized as average species. Perhaps paradoxically, in view of the low grade of encephalization of 'primitive' living placentals among the insectivores and of the didelphids among the marsupials, some Australian marsupials are almost, but not quite, at the average mammalian grade. The spiny anteater, an egg-laying mammal that is sometimes thought of as a relict of one of the earliest groups of Mesozoic mammals, is also near that grade, with a brain about three-quarters the size of average mammals of its body size. Advances in encephalization evidently occurred in many groups, and must have evolved independently; the advances are outstanding examples of anagenetic evolution above the species level.

A new evolutionary explanation of such correlated progress has been presented by Van Valen (1973), who developed a model of anagenetic evolution based on the interaction of many species in a set of related niches. Progress is not the result of some inherent urge towards a better life. It occurs, as Van Valen explains it, in a framework in which species maintain their status relative to other species.

Evolution is a zero-sum game (cf. Maynard Smith, 1978), in which an adaptive gain by one species always entails losses by other species; adaptation is better described as a maintained balance than as progress. In this view, species evolve 'progressively' to keep their place relative to other species in the grand scheme of things. Like Alice's Red Queen, they have to run, i.e. evolve, as fast as they can merely to stay in place, hence Van Valen's name for the model: 'the Red Queen hypothesis'.

There must be an enormous diversity of adaptations correlated with encephalization, in view of the diversity of encephalized species. For an evolutionist this diversity implies some fitness for mind *per se* as an adaptation, independently of the particular quality of mind that evolved in different species. But the fitness is specific to a species. Depending on their differences in sensory and perceptual adaptations, different species may differ radically in their mental properties, and as noted earlier, this implies the evolution of minds, in the plural, rather than a uniquely defined mind which can be defined according to the human model. The general aspect of mind that may be trans-specific, as it were, may be the functions that contribute to the complexity of the 'reality' created by the brain, even if the realities differ in different species. It is these realities that were kept in balance if the evolution of encephalization proceeded as suggested by the Red Queen hypothesis.

Cladistics and anagenetics

Macphail's (1982) critique was of the idea that there were qualitative differences in learning and problem solving abilities that were supposed to differentiate the classes of vertebrates, specifically those identified by Bitterman (1975) in comparative studies of laboratory performance of goldfish, box turtles, pigeons and rats as representatives of their respective classes. Bitterman reported evidence of progress (anagenesis) as the phylogenetic scale was 'ascended'. Comparisons such as these are often criticized as not being consistent with 'correct' evolutionary analysis, in that they do not compare behaviors in closely related species that may represent a genuine phyletic progression (Hodos and Campbell, 1969). The preferred strategy of most evolutionary biologists is to analyze the relatedness of species and seek to establish clades based on the similarities of species. But Huxley (1942), Simpson (1953), and especially Rensch (1959) made it clear that the cladistic and anagenetic approaches that were contrasted were, in fact, complementary. Both are important for evolutionary theory and analysis (Gould, 1976; Plotkin, 1983).

The analysis of mind is the problem of comparative psychologists, studying psyche, i.e. mind, as a function that *might* be analyzable in any animal species. Fundamental 'laws' of mind might be discovered as easily in rats or pigeons as in humans. The analogy is with the search for fundamental laws of the nerve membrane, of chemical neurotransmitters, and so forth, and it is most elegantly represented in Bitterman's long and impressive analysis of the place of the 'laws' of learning in the behavioral repertoires of species that represent the major vertebrate classes. Unfortunately, the work does not enter the main stream of evolutionary thinking because of its purely functional approach. Its most constructive critics are also functionalists, such as Mackintosh (1974).

The evolution of mind can be studied both cladistically and anagenetically. Mindful of the criticisms of Hodos and Campbell (1969), the cladistic analysis would emphasize comparisons among related species and limit anagenesis to the microevolutionary sense: progressive evolution that would be sufficient to establish a difference between closely related species. The analysis of the comparative psychology of primates, comparing humans with chimpanzees, etc., is in this tradition. The evidence of encephalization reviewed in the previous section demonstrates, however, that mind, in the sense of increased neural processing capacity, or encephalization, evolved in many species and, presumably, in many ways. It seems to be a behavioral dimension that is orthogonal to species-typical behavioral adaptations, so that one might, in principle, characterize some species-typical adaptations as involving more 'mind', i.e. more behavioral capacity, than other adaptations.

Anagenesis of mind in primates

Mason (1976) has argued persuasively for a qualitative difference between monkeys and great apes in their capacity for 'representation' of the external world ('constructing reality' as the idea is developed in this chapter). He suggests that we and the apes are more similar in this regard than are apes and monkeys. Gallup (1979) presents a comparable argument based on the capacity to develop a concept of self. Only chimpanzees and orangs could learn the significance of their images in a mirror as images of themselves. Gorillas have thus far failed on this task, though one suspects that the failure will turn out to be an artifact of an interaction between some overlooked species-typical adaptation of gorillas and Gallup's procedure. Passingham (1982) has analyzed the issue in some depth and also concludes that there is evidence for progressive evolution of mind or intelligence – behavioral capacity appropriately defined – within the primates, which differentiates species more or less as a measure of encephalization differentiates them. Parker and Gibson (1979) see evidence that chimpanzees are at a higher Piagetian grade of intelligence than other nonhuman primates, and Premack and Woodruff (1978) find that they have a 'theory of mind'. This last point is especially intriguing, and is based on the ability of Premack's chimpanzees to predict the behaviors of their human caretakers according to styles of behavior adopted by the caretakers, and in that sense to have theories about the minds of the caretakers.

The analysis is a classic combination of cladistics and anagenetics on the issue of the evolution of mind. Recent speculations on this issue have been summarized by Parker and Gibson (1979), who present a Piagetian framework to explain comparisons among living hominids and monkeys. They suggest a questionable evolutionary model based on discredited notions of the recapitulation of ontogeny in phylogeny, which Piaget had accepted (see Jerison, 1982b, and commentaries appended to the original report by Parker and Gibson). The criticisms are on peripheral theoretical issues, however, and the Parker and Gibson article is strongly recommended for its review of evidence.

The fossil evidence on the evolution of encephalization in primates, as pointed out earlier, indicates that encephalization lagged behind other adaptations. In the hominids it is clear that the earliest species, the australopithecines, were only slightly more encephalized than their cousins among the pongids, and it was only long after the lineage was established that encephalization approached modern grades. In the hominid fossils, the analysis reduces, more or less, to the evolution of brain size since the known fossils were reasonably comparable in body size. One question is whether the evolution of human brain size was continuous in our lineage or proceeded by 'punctuated equilibria', that is, by periods of very rapid evolution which alternated with periods of stasis (Gould, 1980). The assumption is generally that evolution by natural selection is a kind of tracking of environmental change by species evolving in the changing environment. When change is rapid, evolution has to be rapid, and when the environment is static, evolution can be very slow, following the 'neutralist' expectation for 'genetic drift'. The general analysis of the evolution of encephalization presented earlier was consistent with the punctuationalist position, but a gradualist evolutionary model also fits the data on evolution of brain size in our lineage.

Some conclusions

How should such considerations affect programs of research? Let us apply them to the most popular topic in comparative psychology of the past decade, animal languages (generally in chimpanzees) as an entry into the animal mind. The goal is to understand the mind of another species. This may not be an easy goal, but present research proves that we can get answers fairly directly if we devise clever enough 'languages', i.e. communication systems, with which to communicate with other species. For many years this kind of communication has been an unheralded success of classic comparative methods. Operant methods have been used routinely to 'ask' rats and pigeons whether they can recognize various distinctions in their environments, and they 'answer' by pressing levers signifying 'yes' and 'no'. The yes-no answers have even been used to drive machines that graph the psychophysical functions of the animal subject (Blough, 1958). Using a more sophisticated 'language', Premack and Woodruff (1978) found that chimpanzees understood Piagetian questions about the conservation of mass. These are exactly the sort of questions to uncover aspects of the 'realities' of other species.

We may anticipate even more interesting information about the mind of the dolphin, which is likely to be stranger to a human observer than that of our close relative, the chimpanzee. The questions will have to be phrased appropriately, and cleverly, to enter the unusual world of so exotic a species. Herman and his colleagues (Richards, Wolz and Herman, 1984; Herman, Richards and Wolz, 1984) have begun to report the results of an extensive program, which is presently directed toward determining the behavioral capacities of dolphins with a 'language' comparable to that used by Premack with chimpanzees. These methods can be applied to the analysis of mind as discussed in this chapter, when they are used to determine special features of the perceptual worlds of other animals. According to the evidence of its brain the dolphin should surprise us with its answers.

They should suggest different dimensions of cognition and unusual elaborations of those dimensions. These should be as unusual as the elaboration of the auditory-vocal dimension of the human mind, that is a species-typical adaptation involved in the representation of human reality. We call it language, and we also use it to communicate with one another.

The general conclusion is worth repeating: behavioral capacities developed in adaptations correlated with encephalization are most likely to be related to sensory/perceptual and cognitive information processing, since that is the only kind of processing known to require very large amounts of neural tissue. The capacities are, therefore, likely to be related to the reality constructed by a species. The evolutionary perspective emphasizes the specificity of adaptations of species to their niches, and this specificity is consistent with the idea that different species create different realities, and, furthermore, that the different realities can be based on comparable grades of processing capacity. There should, therefore, be a variety of 'intelligences' evident in the evolution of mind in animals. The human mind may serve as the model for mind in other species, but the greater challenge is to imagine and study all manifestations of higher levels of intelligence in other species.

References

Attneave, F. (1960) In defense of homunculi. In W. Rosenblith (ed.) *Sensory Communication*. Cambridge, Mass.: MIT Press.

Bitterman, M. E. (1975) The comparative analysis of learning. *Science 188*: 699–709.

Blough, D. S. (1958) A method of obtaining psychophysical thresholds from the pigeon. *Journal of the Experimental Analysis of Behavior 1*: 31–43.

Bridgman, P. W. (1959) *The Way Things Are*. Cambridge, Mass.: Harvard University Press.

Carterette, E. C. and Friedman, M. P. (1974) *Handbook of Perception*, vol. 1: *Historical and Philosophical Roots of Perception*. New York: Academic Press.

Craik, K. J. W. (1943) *The Nature of Explanation*. London and New York: Cambridge University Press. Reprinted in 1967, with postscript.

Darwin, C. (1871) *The Descent of Man*. London: Murray. Reprinted (1936) in C. Darwin. *The Origin of Species and The Descent of Man*. New York: Modern Library (Simon & Schuster).

Diamond, I. T. (1979) The subdivisions of the neocortex: a proposal to revise the traditional view of sensory, motor, and association areas. *Progress in Psychobiology and Physiological Psychology 8*: 1–43.

Eccles, J. C. (1979) *The Human Mystery*. New York: Springer-Verlag.

Gallup, G. G. Jr (1979) Self-awareness in primates. *American Scientist 67*: 417–21.

Gould, S. J. (1976) Grades and clades revisited. In R. B. Masterton, W. Hodos and H. J. Jerison (eds) *Evolution, Brain and Behavior: Persistent Problems*, 115–22. Hillsdale, NJ: Erlbaum.

Gould, S. J. (1980) Is a new general theory of evolution emerging? *Paleobiology 6*: 119–30.

Griffin, D. R. (1976) *The Question of Animal Awareness*. New York: Rockefeller University Press.

Held, R. (1965) Plasticity in sensory-motor systems. *Scientific American 213 (5)*: 84–94.

Herman, L. M. (1980) Cognitive characteristics of dolphins. In L. M. Herman (ed.) *Cetacean Behavior: Mechanisms and Functions*. New York: Wiley.

Herman, L. M., Richards, D. G. and Wolz, J. P. (1984). Comprehension of sentences by bottlenosed dolphins. *Cognition 16:* 129–219.

Hodos, W. and Campbell, C. B. G. (1969) *Scala naturae*: Why there is no theory in comparative psychology. *Psychological Review 76*: 337–50.

Humphrey, N. K. (1978) Nature's psychologists. *New Scientist 78*: 900–3.

Huxley, J. (1942) *Evolution: The Modern Synthesis*. New York and London: Harper.

James, W. (1890) *Principles of Psychology*, 2 vols. New York: Henry Holt.

Jerison, H. J. (1973) *Evolution of the Brain and Intelligence*. New York: Academic Press.

Jerison, H. J. (1976) Paleoneurology and the evolution of mind. *Scientific American 234 (1)*: 90–101.

Jerison, H. J. (1982a) The evolution of biological intelligence. In R. J. Sternberg (ed.) *Handbook of Human Intelligence*, 723–91. New York and London: Cambridge University Press.

Jerison, H. J. (1982b) Problems with Piaget and pallia. *Behavioral and Brain Sciences 5*: 284–7.

Jerison, H. J. (1983) The evolution of the mammalian brain as an information processing system. In J. F. Eisenberg and D. G. Kleiman (eds) *Advances in the Study of Mammalian Behavior*, 113–46. Special Publication No. 7, American Society of Mammalogists.

Jerison, H. J. (in press). Issues in brain evolution. *Oxford Surveys in Evolutionary Biology 2*.

Jones, E. G. and Powell, T. P. S. (1970) An anatomical study of converging sensory pathways within the cerebral cortex of the monkey. *Brain 93*: 793–820.

30   Brain and Mind

Klüver, H. (1933) *Behavior Mechanisms in Monkeys*. Chicago: University of Chicago Press.

Lande, R. (1979) Quantitative genetic analysis of multivariate evolution, applied to brain: body size allometry. *Evolution 33*: 402–16.

Mackintosh, N. J. (1974) *The Psychology of Animal Learning*. London and New York: Academic Press.

MacLean, P. D. (1970) The triune brain, emotion, and scientific bias. In F. O. Schmitt (ed.) *The Neurosciences: Second Study Program*, 336–49. New York: Rockefeller University Press.

Macphail, E. M. (1982) *Brain and Intelligence in Vertebrates*. Oxford: Clarendon Press.

Martin, R. D. (1983) *Human Brain Evolution in Ecological Context*. James Arthur Lecture on the Evolution of the Human Brain. New York: American Museum of Natural History.

Mason, W. A. (1976) Environmental models and mental modes: representational processes in the great apes and man. *American Psychologist 31*: 284–94.

Masterton, B. and Diamond, I. T. (1973) Hearing: central neural mechanisms. In E. C. Carterette and M. P. Friedman (eds) *Handbook of Perception*, vol. 3: *Biology of Perceptual Systems*, 407–48. New York: Academic Press.

Maynard Smith, J. (1978) The evolution of behavior. *Scientific American 239 (3)*: 176–92.

Merzenich, M. M. and Kaas, J. H. (1980) Principles of organization of sensory-perceptual systems in mammals. *Progress in Psychobiology and Physiological Psychology 9*: 1–42.

Mountcastle, V. B. (1978) An organizing principle for cerebral function: the unit module and the distributed system. In G. M. Edelman and V. B. Mountcastle. *The Mindful Brain*, 7–50. Cambridge, Mass.: MIT Press.

Ostrom, J. H. (1976) *Archaeopteryx* and the origin of birds. *Biological Journal of the Linnaean Society 8*: 91–182.

Parker, S. T. and Gibson, K. R. (1979) A developmental model for the evolution of language and intelligence in early hominids. *Behavioral and Brain Sciences 2*: 367–408.

Passingham, R. E. (1982) *The Human Primate*. San Francisco: W. H. Freeman.

Plotkin, H. C. (1983) The functions of learning and cross-species comparisons. In G. C. L. Davey (ed.) *Animal Models of Human Behavior*, 117–34. New York: Wiley.

Posner, M. I. (1978) *Chronometric Explorations of Mind*. Hillsdale, NJ: Erlbaum.

Premack, D. and Woodruff, G. (1978) Does the chimpanzee have a theory of mind? *Behavioral and Brain Sciences 4*: 515–26.

Rensch, B. (1959) *Evolution Above the Species Level*. New York: Columbia University Press.

Richards, D. G., Wolz, J. P. and Herman, L. M. (1984) Vocal mimicry of computer-generated sounds and vocal labeling of objects by a bottlenosed dolphin, *Tursiops truncatus. Journal of Comparative Psychology 98*: 10–28.

Rockel, A. J., Hiorns, R. W. and Powell, T. P. S. (1980) The basic uniformity in structure of the neocortex. *Brain 103*: 221–44.

Russell, I. S. (1979) Brain size and intelligence: a comparative perspective. In D. A. Oakley and H. C. Plotkin (eds) *Brain, Behaviour and Evolution*, 126–53. London: Methuen.

Simon, H. A. (1974) How big is a chunk? *Science 183*: 482–8.

Simpson, G. G. (1953) *The Major Features of Evolution*. New York: Columbia University Press.

Sperry, R. W. (1952) Neurology and the mind-brain problem. *American Scientist 40*: 291–312.

Szentágothai, J. (1978) The neuron network of the cerebral cortex: a functional interpretation. *Proceedings of the Royal Society of London B201*: 219–48.

Van Valen, L. (1974) Two modes of evolution. *Nature 252*: 298–300.

von Uexküll, J. (1974) *Streifzüge durch die Umwelten von Tieren und Menschen*. Berlin and New York: Springer-Verlag. Translated in C. H. Schiller (ed.) *Instinctive Behavior: The Development of a Modern Concept*, 5–80. New York: International Universities Press, 1957.

2 Representations of the physical and social world

Keith Oatley

What kind of adaptation to the world is the human one? It is an adaptation that succeeds in transforming the environment. It involves social cultures which shape social selves by their rules; cultures which are themselves shaped by changes in the rules that people create. It's an adaptation nowadays in which the members of society continually give accounts to each other, orally, in newspapers, in novels, of what they and others are up to, and of the relation between the actions of individuals and the society in which they occur.

Oakley (1979) has argued that the traditional idea that the large size of the human brain is related to our superior learning abilities is not supported by much evidence. Rather he supposes that the distinctively human cerebral cortex might have evolved to subserve polysensory representations of the world. In this chapter I will argue that a major function of the human brain is indeed to sustain complex structures of knowledge of the physical world, and also of plans and purposes in the social world. It is the ability to create these structures, which I will call schemata, to make inferences within them, and to reuse them symbolically for new purposes in metaphors, that provides the foundation for our peculiar human adaptation.

Our constructions of the physical and social world are not static. They continue to change. Part of our mental ontogeny might even be affected by the study we make of it. As an analogy one might imagine a computer program whose function is to rewrite itself in the light of its discovery of how it is working. This recursiveness is, I will argue also, an important aspect of conscious mind. In order to do justice to the brain and its mechanisms we need to have an account of such schemata which can, as Bartlett (1932) puts it, turn round upon themselves – which consider their own constitution and transform themselves.

In the first half of the chapter I will explore the ideas of mental schemata and metaphor, employing as part of the understanding which I am trying to create some metaphors from technology and computing, including the metaphor of representation. For the second half, available technological metaphors become less adequate, so I will use another important device by which our constructive ability is extended, the comparison and contrast with experiences different from our own; in this case with the experiences of people at the beginning of European history and of children at the beginning of individual history.

Representational theory

At least since classical Greece it has been common to see a relatedness between the nature of people and the structure of the cosmos. The microcosm of an individual mind is animated by the same principles as the macrocosm of the universe. The idea of representation in cognitive psychology, often credited to Craik (1943), is a perspective on this ancient theme from an anthropocentric viewpoint. It is that the logic by which we perceive and understand our world depends upon schematic models which parallel the structure and workings of the world. To understand is to construct and inhabit a symbolic representation of a certain kind. In other words, we perceive and understand our world largely through analogies and metaphors.

A metaphor is a kind of intellectual bridge, though 'bridge' is a less good metaphor than I need here. It allows us to understand something we do not know and do not have very adequate intuitions about. This metaphor of the bridge, implying the possibility of journeying across a divide from where we are to where we would like to be, is spatial. It has qualities which are partly what Lakoff and Johnson (1980) call orientational, such as 'from' and 'towards' which derive from our own experiences of movement, which we can take as direct and not metaphorical. Partly it is ontological, deriving from familiar 'things'. One of these things is the structure of a prototypical bridge. Another is the human action of a journey, which is also conceptualized as a thing.

Many of our most serviceable metaphors are spatial in this sense, deriving from our most familiar experiences of actions and things extended in space. They are immediate and evocative because, as embodied people, we move and exist in space. Consequently many basic representational structures have to do with spatial reasoning. So Plato would allow nobody ignorant of geometry (the formalization of spatial knowledge) to enter his academy; mnemonic systems used the method of placing images of things-to-be-remembered in niches in a familiar building that one can mentally walk round (Yates, 1966); scientists communicate results as graphs; and Papert (1980) introduces the ideas of computing to young children by means of a toy vehicle which they can drive with the programs they write, and imitate with their own body movements.

But just as the bridge is not quite the metaphor I need for the idea of metaphor, so purely spatial metaphors are inadequate for our understanding of mental processes, which after all are not extended in space. Lashley (1951) argued that in brain research theories have tended to follow technological fashions. So there were hydraulic theories in Descartes' time, more recently telegraph theories, and now theories 'based on computing machines and automatic rudders'. In just the same way, Lashley pointed out, the content of paranoid fantasies keeps up with current technology. Indeed I met someone recently complaining about having had microchips secretly implanted in his brain and abdomen to monitor and control his thoughts and feelings.

By introducing the metaphor of technological analogy as paranoid delusion Lashley could denigrate a certain kind of theorizing. My argument is that we often understand what we do not know in terms that at first belong to something other than itself, but of which we happen to have more intimate knowledge. So in the same way that my paranoid acquaintance made some sense of the disturbances of thoughts and feelings that he was experiencing, in terms of having them controlled and monitored remotely, so we can try to make sense of unfamiliar principles of mental operations in terms with which we are more familiar.

New ideas tend to come from the latest technology. This is fashion, but not just fashion. It is one means by which we extend our knowledge.

Many technological advances give us new ways of experiencing ourselves in the world. How must the invention of the plough and of sowing seed have given people a new sense of themselves. It was one of the changes that led to civilization, the art of living in towns as fixed communities. The invention of the clock, as Weizenbaum (1976) has argued, allowed another change; helping us to see ourselves in an essentially mechanical universe. It was a major step too in our independence from nature. The invention of the computer is arguably the beginning of an equally radical transformation of our world and of the way we see ourselves.

An argument of the first half of this chapter is that if brains are representational, then we can gain insights into this via the metaphor of experiencing computation, which is also the making of symbolic representations. With the attempt to design intelligent processes of conversation, perception and problem solving, come metaphors which extend our conception of mentality beyond the spatial. Ideally this needs experience of creating and working with computational representations oneself. However, many of the principles are comprehensible without the actual writing of programs, since the steps and logic can be followed by following instructions to a computer as if they were instructions to oneself. Other principles can be conveyed by more familiar metaphors which nevertheless relate to computational ideas.

Craik's famous idea in his book of 1943 was that the brain symbolically parallels the structure and principles of the environment. He argued that thought consists first of translating a problem into symbolic terms, then manipulating these symbols within a model of the world to see 'what would happen if . . .', and then translating the derived symbols back into terms of the world — into actions, for instance.

The principle works not just for human thought, but in many living systems which seem designed to operate in particular environments. Such systems work by having embodied in them representations of aspects of that environment.

An example of this kind of system is the circadian clock which produces periodic rhythms, e.g. of sleep and wakefulness, and which keeps in time with the daily alternation of light and darkness.

In a circadian clock, a set of biological processes has come to represent the alternation of night and day. By controlling waking and sleep according to this symbolic alternation, rather than directly according to the immediate brightness of the environment, several advantages are gained. An animal living in a dark hole can wake up at dawn without having to forgo the benefits of being out of immediate reach of the external world. Sets of related physiological and behavioural processes can be meshed together in cooperative fashion to prepare for the different phases of activity and inactivity, and keep in time with one another.

Mechanical clocks were early recognized as models of the rotation of celestial bodies, and they became preferred to the direct observations available from sundials. The analogy of biological with mechanical clocks is a productive one: just as clockwork is a model of celestial rotations, so biological clocks represent periodic aspects of the environment in which they operate.

Properties of being able to represent the alternations of light and darkness emerge from ordinary biological control processes. I have shown (Oatley, 1974, 1975), that any control system in which there are several steps, a time delay and a negative feedback in which some product of the process inhibits an earlier step in the chain, is capable of producing oscillations. Control processes producing hormones, for instance, have this property, which is then capable of serving symbolically as a biological rhythm. In other words, under conditions with quite broad specifications, common feedback systems are pressed into a new service to represent something which they are not. Lorenz (1969) has pointed out that this kind of serendipitous possibility of processes having alternative functions is probably necessary for evolution to take place at all.

A new function can be thought of as an emergent property. Just as an oscillation is not contained in any of the parts of a negative feedback system, but emerges as a property of the interaction of parts, so the representational properties of an oscillation constitute a second phase of emergence. An oscillator becomes a representational model when the oscillation comes to have some means of keeping in time with the alternation of light and darkness in the environment, and when it starts to affect some behaviour or physiological process in time with the environmental alternation.

The linking with day and night is one of the crucial aspects of the circadian clock. Mechanical clocks are able to represent celestial rotation because they can be made to oscillate as regularly as terrestrial rotation. Adjustments are made by human resetting. Biological clocks are not intrinsically accurate, but they keep time with the external environment by being linked automatically with it. The way in which this occurs illustrates the technological metaphor and enables us to understand how this emergence of symbolic property has occurred.

The important observation was published by Huygens in 1665. He found that two clocks hung on separate walls would keep rather different time. Clocks then were not very accurate. But if clocks were hung on the same wooden partition, when set to the same time one day, they would still be in time with each other the next. The small pressure pulses of each clock ticking were capable of jogging the escapement mechanism of the other, mutually synchronizing the clocks.

This property, called entrainment, has subsequently been shown to be general for non-linear oscillators, that is oscillators that have a rate which is not constantly proportional to fixed parameters throughout their cycle. Biochemical control systems are non-linear in this sense. Their rates of reaction vary in proportion to the changing amount of inhibitor present. Entrainment works here by one of the chemical reactions in the chain being speeded up by light. So during the light the oscillator will be advanced in phase, reaching a particular point in its cycle earlier than if there were no light. Phase advance continues to a point where it is just balanced by the slowing of reaction by the inhibitor. At this equilibrium the oscillator will run entrained on the external lighting cycle in a particular phase relation. It will re-entrain if reversals of the light-dark cycle occur, and will also entrain on longer and shorter day lengths. These properties are exactly those shown by biological clocks.

So entrainment is an emergent property of non-linear oscillators, and it has been pressed into symbolic service by a variety of living things in which it is important to have different kinds of activity in the day and night.

Conscious awareness and unconscious inference in perception

Even some plants have circadian rhythms. So though we might want to say for our own understanding that in a certain sense knowledge about the environment is embodied in such systems, there is nothing conscious about them. The idea of representation is an important step towards understanding consciousness, but evidently it is not sufficient.

We might however wish to attribute consciousness of a kind that is shared by people and other mammals to the next stage of sophistication of representation. In this stage sets of inferences are made within a model or representation. That the conclusions of perceptual inferences become the contents of awareness, was first proposed by Helmholtz (1866), though he did not stress the representational bases. He did show, however, that the perceptual phenomena of which we are aware go far beyond the evidence presented to the arrays of receptors in our sense organs. We are never aware of the process of making an inference, only of the conclusion. So if with a finger we lightly rub the right corner of our closed eyelid while looking toward the left, we will see a moving brightish patch on the left. The patch is seen in the direction that light would normally have to come from to affect the receptors we are pressing, but we do not see pressure on the right. We infer and see a bright spot on the left, which moves as we move our finger. The visual system constructs percepts from evidence which is not always reliable.

Consider what is necessary to see objects extended in space and having specific shapes and sizes. According to Craik we need a model of some aspect of the world of spatially arrayed objects. I will take as an example a world sometimes called the 'blocks world', containing only plane-sided opaque objects with straight edges. Although this is a small subset of the world in which we live, its geometrical properties allow us to characterize some of the knowledge required for a model of its structure and properties.

On the retina will appear images which are two-dimensional projections of this world. The task for a perceiver is to infer from such projections what objects there are, and how they are disposed so that they might be picked up, or avoided, etc.

When we see a picture from this world, such as Figure 2.1, we see it as something like two stairs. The percept is not given, however, but inferred. The lines on the paper in a domain of two-dimensional images can be described as defining four parallelograms and a re-entrant hexagon. Yet we see a three-dimensional object. A good deal of work in computational vision has involved making representations of the three-dimensional world so that inferences about this world can be made from two-dimensional evidence.

When we look at Figure 2.1 and see it as two stairs, we see some of the lines as concave edges, like the edge between a ceiling and a wall in a room, or like line *a* in Figure 2.1. Others we see as convex, like the

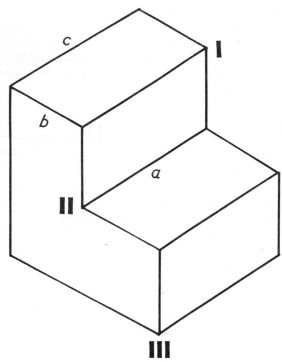

Fig. 2.1   When seen as two stairs fixed to a floor this diagram shows a concave edge at *a*, a convex edge with both meeting surfaces visible at *b*, and a convex edge in which one of the meeting surfaces is occluded at *c*. Continuing to see it in the same way the diagram also illustrates three of the corner types used by Clowes (1971). The Roman numeral I indicates an all convex corner, in this case with only two of the meeting surfaces visible. The numeral II indicates a corner with two convex and one concave edge, and the numeral III a corner with one convex and two concave edges. In these two last cases all three of the meeting surfaces are visible. These three quite different three-dimensional interpretations are represented in the two-dimensional picture by the same kind of junction — an arrow. The interpretations of corners can change during viewing, for instance when the figure reverses as described by Schroeder (1858).

edge of a block of wood. Of the lines seen as convex edges, some join regions which depict surfaces of the same object, like line *b* in Figure 2.1. Others depict edges where only one of the surfaces meeting there is visible, like line *c*. This latter type of edge is called an occluding edge.

The opacity of the object obscures one of the surfaces from the viewpoint of the picture.

In order to understand how inferences about three-dimensional structure can be made from this kind of two-dimensional evidence, Clowes (1971) and Huffman (1971) independently proposed similar schemes for making interpretations of lines as edges. Clowes proposed that a model adequate for making such interpretations would consist first of knowledge of what kinds of three-dimensional corners can exist in the blocks world. He restricted the world so that only three surfaces could meet at any corner. In this world there are four kinds of corner. Three of them are illustrated in Figure 2.1 when it is seen as stairs, and are indicated there by Roman numerals. A type I corner is the meeting of three convex edges. In a type II corner two convex edges and a concave edge meet. A type III corner is seen if the object is stuck to the floor and two concave edges meet a convex one. In a type IV corner, which is not illustrated, three concave edges meet, as they do where two walls and a ceiling meet in a room.

In the domain of the picture, however, there are no corners, only junctions. There are three main types of junction, called L, arrow, and fork, which are illustrated in Figure 2.2. So the task of seeing 3-D objects where the evidence is only of lines and junctions is in part to infer what kind of corner is depicted by each junction. This is not straightforward. It would be if each junction type always depicted the same kind of corner, but a junction type can depict several kinds of

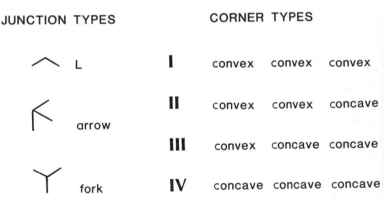

JUNCTION TYPES	CORNER TYPES		
L	**I**	convex	convex	convex
arrow	**II**	convex	convex	concave
	III	convex	concave	concave
fork	**IV**	concave	concave	concave

Fig. 2.2 The three types of two-dimensional junction (L, arrow and fork) and the four types of three-dimensional corner (designated with Roman numerals and with edges that are, respectively, all convex, two convex-one concave, one convex-two concave, and all concave) used by Clowes (1971).

corner. In a picture the appearance of a particular kind of junction is always ambiguous. It can only be disambiguated by the context of its neighbouring junctions, as interpreted by means of a model of the three-dimensional world.

So for instance in Figure 2.1 arrow junctions depict in one instance a type I corner with only two of the surfaces that meet there being visible; in another instance a type II corner with all three surfaces visible; in another instance a type III corner with all three surfaces visible. The question for any perceiver is how might one infer which is which.

It requires a model of at least some relevant structural aspects of the blocks world. The important aspect that Clowes found he had to work with was that in the blocks world an edge has the same property all the way along its length between two corners. So this meant that in interpreting lines, a line interpreted as a concave edge at one end must also depict a concave edge at the other, and so on. Clowes's program starts by making any legal interpretation of one junction, say an arrow junction as a type I corner with two surfaces visible. The centre line of the arrow is labelled as convex, and this contextually constrains the interpretation of the junction at the other end of that line. By constraining junction interpretation in this way all round the picture, mutually compatible sets of junction interpretations are discovered. Each complete set then corresponds to a possible three dimensional interpretation of the whole drawing, consistent with the rules of the model of the blocks world. For Figure 2.1 there are several complete sets, and each set defines one of a group of ambiguous interpretations of the whole. So the object might be two stairs on a floor. It might be stairs suspended in some way that is invisible from the viewpoint of the picture, so that the two lowest lines in the picture are occluding convex edges, rather than the concave edges of an object joined to the floor. Alternatively it might be stuck to a back wall, so that now the junction labelled I in the figure would not be a type I corner with an invisible surface, but a type III corner with all surfaces visible. Yet again it might be an object stuck to the wall on the left. A further ambiguity exists as the staircase reverses and looks like the underside of a staircase, with lines that had been labelled as convex edges being labelled concave. So Clowes' program provides an explanation for the reversing staircase first described by Schroeder (1858): both the normal and the reversed staircase are compatible sets of junction interpretations. The idea of compatible sets is therefore a working microtheory, or model of an aspect of the construction of the physical world, and its projection onto two-dimensional surfaces. Within this model inferences are made which are analogous to the conclusions we experience when seeing physical objects.

One application of this kind of perceptual theory to the understanding of brain mechanisms is, as I have argued (Oatley, 1978), in the understanding it affords of Lashley's (1929, 1960) theories of mass action. In perceptual programs we can see some of the ways in which knowledge must be incorporated in models or theories of the physical world to make even the most straightforward inferences. Building up structures of inference, such as Clowes has done, allows one to see perception as making sense of the visual world by evidence or cues such as junction types, addressing and guiding the beholder's models or theories.

The Clowes program makes one kind of inference about edges. The same junction cues have been shown to allow other inferences about the number and arrangement of separate objects in a scene cluttered with objects (Guzman, 1969). With programs which embody more elaborate hypotheses about what kinds of object might be encountered, similar cues have allowed visual conclusions to be reached about the sizes and shapes of objects (Roberts, 1965; Falk, 1972), even when parts of the line drawing are missing or imperfect. So with an arrangement in which a cue is able to select a number of different kinds of hypothesis, and a schema is guided by a number of cues, we begin to meet the conditions described by Winograd and Cowan (1963) for reliable computation of a whole system, despite malfunction of some of its parts, or even when pieces of evidence are missing. This fits the picture that Lashley was concerned to draw of the cortex as obeying laws of mass action and equipotentiality. It also implies that the same schema could easily be addressed from different sensory modalities, and this then provides the basis for the polysensory representations stressed by Oakley (1979).

If in perception we see not cues like line junctions, but conclusions of projected theory such as corners, and if the same schema can be addressed by gestalts made up of cues, then almost any part of an object might be obscured, and we will still be able to see the object. Parts might be obscured by the opacity of the object itself, by something else interposed between it and the viewer, or by degradation in the process of forming an image. Detectives or palaeontologists, by virtue of the theories they hold about human behaviour on the one hand, or comparative anatomy on the other, can form constructions of what kind of criminal is being sought or what an extinct animal looked like, from a very few pieces of scattered evidence. In the same way, when seeing we construct visual conclusions from evidence which can be sparse, with no particular cue being necessary, and a number of different routes of inference being possible.

This means that the knowledge in mental schemata has to be wide and various. It is by virtue of this that neural embodiments in intelligent animals are complex and redundant. What is provided by this kind of representational theory is a set of metaphors which enable us to understand how animals and people might be able to operate even when large parts of the brain have been destroyed, and how we might recognize something when only a small part is visible.

The emphasis in understanding perception is not so much on the evidence of the senses. This consists only of fleeting patterns of neural excitation. It is on the implicit models or schemata by which we apprehend this evidence, models which allow us to leap the gap from the neural excitations of sensory surfaces to the solid world of our perceptual experience. As Taine (1870) has said, it is not so much that hallucinations are disorders of perception, but that perception is a hallucination, the projection of an internal theory, but one which happens to be guided by some evidence.

Reflective self-consciousness

In biological clocks one thing, an oscillator, represents another, the alternation of night and day. In perception we see something 'as we interpret it', to use Wittgenstein's (1953) phrase. Both these are in a sense metaphorical. One thing which is a part of the organism is used to connect meaningfully with something not part of it.

The metaphor proper, however, only comes into its own in human thinking. So, for instance, Lakoff and Johnson (1980) show how we understand and experience argument as a fight: 'They attacked me mercilessly'; as a journey: 'He reached his conclusion in a roundabout way'; as a building: 'Her ideas aren't founded on anything very substantial', and so on. In thought and understanding the model of the world is a structured gestalt of a familiar activity, process, or thing which can be applied to something more abstract, less familiar.

In this chapter, for instance, I have used metaphors to reach out towards abstract ideas of representation: clocks as models of terrestrial rotation, the projection of schemata or theories onto evidence to describe perception. In similar terms understanding can now be thought of as the construction of new models or representations, in terms of those which are old or more familiar.

These three stages, simple representation, perception and understanding, can be thought of as stages of evolutionary emergence. The differences between simple representations like biological clocks, and those of perception can be characterized in terms of a continuum between fixed function at one end and flexibility, achieved by configurations of cues addressing inferential schemata, at the other. The difference between perception and understanding is that in perception our schemata for spatial relationships, objects, substances, bodies, events like causation and so on are purpose built. When an adequate configuration of visual cues elicits and modifies a schema of this kind we see; and we call this direct experience. To understand, however, is to detach these schemata, or as Lakoff and Johnson call them 'gestalts of experience', from their normal configurations of cues and apply them to similar configurations in different domains. Eventually such applications also become experience. We do experience argument as fight, attacking the other and defending ourselves, as a journey with a path towards a conclusion, as a structure like a building which can be made solid or flimsy.

This third stage might be called the stage of reflective consciousness. It is a stage in which we are aware not just of a perceptual world, but of ourselves in it (Oatley, 1980). We don't just modify our behaviour in relation to the immediate structure of cues, but we construct worlds not immediately present.

Jaynes (1976) has argued that what we call consciousness is a kind of metaphorical space in which we can represent ourselves as we are, or were, or might be. It is not the world of which we are immediately aware, but an analogical world in which we can depict actions, construct reasons, tell stories. In this world the spatial intuitions with which we grow up by virtue of having bodies which move in space are, as it were, re-represented. We can shut our eyes and see an image of ourselves from a viewpoint that we could never have had – from outside and above ourselves for instance. Try imagining yourself in this way: the last time you went walking by the water's edge, or sat in a deck chair. Within this metaphorical space, Jaynes argues, we construct a version of the world in which we can excerpt and narrate events of our lives, selecting and weaving them into more or less plausible stories suitable for our purposes. We each of us do privately what novelists and playwrights do for a more public view.

This metaphorical domain is both spatial and social. It is a re representation of visual and acoustic representations of our spatial and social world, although like the simulations embodied in games ranging from chess to space-invaders it lacks many of the physical constraints of the actual world. It is a world of dreams, of stories, of imagination. We can imagine with Jaynes that it is this inner world that makes us distinctively human. It is in this metaphorical world that we reason, understand and create what was not there before.

Perception and understanding consist in part of the projection of a theory, a metaphor, a schema onto the evidence, and then a comparison. Whether one uses the term theory, metaphor, or schema depends on the context, so that scientists talk more about theories, literary critics about metaphors, psychologists about schemata. In so far as a current schema, theory, etc. makes a match with the evidence, we grasp the evidence in terms of that schema. In so far as there is a mismatch or contrast, we infer that either our schema or what we take as evidence should change, and we can infer something about the way in which it should change, even if adequate new theories or schemata are not available.

In trying to understand our self-reflective consciousness, computational metaphors start to fail. With the possible exception of Sussman's (1975) program, which simulates learning a skill in a program that rewrites parts of itself in response to its mistakes, metaphors from the computational domain cease to be adequate.

Just at the point where experience seems most like a representation, where we as people can summon up a mental image, re-presenting to ourselves something no longer there or never there, the metaphor of representation starts to fail. The idea of representations has been popular at least since the seventeenth century study of optics (see Rorty, 1980). It has been given new impetus by artificial intelligence where knowledge is represented in procedures and in data bases. The idea of representation almost inevitably implies an observer, for instance a programmer looking at a program. But we know there is no homunculus in the brain to whom knowledge is represented, and who observes and manipulates it, even though it may be useful at times to think of procedures or sets of rules in homunculus-like terms.

From an observer's perspective, such as is taken in natural science, we can usefully employ the metaphor of representation as I have done so far in the course of this chapter. It is, however, inadequate for expressing these issues from the perspective of the person as such. With the possible exception of contemplating a mental image, we do not usually experience ourselves as split: an observer and a representation, a traveller and a map. Indeed to experience ourselves habitually in this way would in our society lead to being diagnosed as psychotic. Mostly we just see, or think, or act. The world presents itself to us as we construct it, and as we participate in it. This shift away from the representational metaphor is similar to that of Wittgenstein's shift from his representational theory of language in the *Tractatus* (1922) to his newer (1953) theory of language as rule-governed like a game, and as a form of life.

So too as we try to understand self-reflective consciousness, it ceases to be enough to elaborate metaphors of self reflection as a certain kind of recursiveness, though this is important and has been undertaken by Johnson-Laird (1983). Nor, despite Bartlett's (1932) image of the schema turning back on itself, does this recursiveness take the form simply of an observing process looking at itself. Instead, to travel the last stage of the journey of this chapter I will stop talking of representations, properties perhaps of the system of 'scientist studying the human brain', and enter more explicitly the domain of the mental. Here I will offer not metaphor as such, but contrast of the kind which occurs where a mental schema is applied to some data which it does not quite fit, in what Bateson (1970) calls a difference which makes a difference. In other words I will stop elaborating the metaphor of representation by which I have hoped that the reader's understandings of mental schemata might be elaborated. Instead I will invite you to contrast the experience of your own culture with that of two other cultures, in particular with a culture at the dawn of history, and with another alien culture, that of childhood. In this way mismatches might make a difference to ourselves and our schemata in our reflections, by seeing how mind is metaphor.

From the evidence of the first written texts of European literature, Jaynes (1976) argues that the metaphorical mindspace of consciousness is a recent human development, and that until about 3000 years ago people were not conscious in our sense. Consciousness is cultural, dependent on language, the primary conveyer of metaphor among us, enabling hearers to construct in their own mindspace perspectives analogous to those of a speaker or congruent with the rules of the society in which they live.

Before the emergence of this kind of consciousness, Jaynes supposes that people had bicameral minds. Bicameral means 'having two chambers', like two chambers of government. People of this mind were ruled both by individual motivations comparable to those of higher primates, and socially by verbal injunctions of leaders of tribes or social groups organized as hierarchies. The importance of these social injunctions is that they allowed a new evolutionary step to be taken, that of social control beyond the mainly non-verbal cues of face to face interaction. Tribal injunctions could then be passed down from generation to generation, by a kind of royal succession, with each ruler uttering the commands of ancestors, and the socially cohesive messages being passed down the hierarchy. Verbal commands can be remembered and continue to exercise an influence even in the absence of the person uttering them though invoking at the same time a sense of that person. Just as ploughs and spades were tools making it possible to begin agricultural settlement, so spoken injunctions start to make it possible to live in towns and work fields co-operatively.

Jaynes's central hypothesis is that such injunctions were heard by bicameral people as auditory hallucinations, perhaps as present day schizophrenics hear peremptory voices commanding them to do this or that. Voices would be heard particularly in times of decision, or if anything problematic or stressful arose.

Thus Jaynes argues that Homer's *Iliad*, written about 850 BC, is a text portaying people in this bicameral state. So applying Jaynes's idea to the text, we see Achilles at the beginning of the narrative becoming angry with King Agamemnon. He half draws his sword to kill him, but is restrained by the sudden appearance of the goddess Athene. She commands him: 'give up this strife, take your hand from your sword'. That a voice of a goddess is heard by Achilles, and only by him (the text specifically says that no-one else was aware of her), is not just a poetic device. It is a description of how those people actually experienced an aspect of the world. Because heard injunctions continue to be heard after the death of tribal leaders, they are called gods: voices and visions outlasting the body of their originators. We should not forget that 'hierarchy' means sacred rule.

In the centuries before the oral ballads from which Homer constructed his epics were written down, there were wars between neighbouring city states, each with their own leaders and gods. The Trojan war was an example. There had been a huge natural disaster around

1500 BC when the island of Theira erupted with an earthquake and tidal wave which devastated the Eastern Mediterranean. Inter-city trade had begun. There were social upheavals and social migrations. Jaynes proposes that amid this unrest a new kind of consciousness began to emerge where the previously simple means of social control suited to stable closed communities was no longer adequate. Achilles was one of the last survivors of the older, bicameral state. He was a sort of social robot, or perhaps more like a well-behaved child, without the power to make his own decisions. Despite their fierce and warlike portraits in Homer, such heroes were badly fitted for a life amid social disintegration, wanderings or meetings with other people subject to other gods. Only people developing the ability to reason for themselves and make their own plans would be capable of doing very well. The second Homeric epic, the *Odyssey*, is the account of such a man. He is a wanderer, meeting peoples of other lands. Although still subject to the commands and whims of gods, he makes his own plans, and is cunning and deceitful. He can present himself to others as he is not: early evidence of a mind not directly tied to the immediate or to remembered commands. Constructing for himself the other's probable reactions he, for instance, makes the Cyclops drunk in order to put out his eye with a red-hot olive bough. Later, though he experiences the plan as having come to him from Hermes, he evades Circe's attempt to drug him. He threatens her to get her to release his men who she has turned into pigs. Then he makes love with her.

Some of Jaynes's proposals seem questionable, particularly the idea of a quite rapid transition into consciousness in Europe about 3000 years ago. Anthropological evidence from groups of people still living in conditions of hierarchical tribal structure can be brought to bear here. Contrary to what might be expected if Jaynes were correct, there is no suggestion of bicameral societies in current or recent anthropology. While accepting some of the spirit of Jaynes's idea, it seems more likely that language and consciousness evolved together and more slowly than he suggests.

Whether one accepts Jaynes's argument in full or not, it is certain that consciousness has changed during the 3000 years of European literature. Perhaps the best way of seeing this is that each text expresses a theory of psychology and of contemporary society, or of a supposed society of an earlier age. Thus it is an expression of the reflection of reality of the writer, an expression of his or her mindspace in that culture. Others besides Jaynes have offered commentaries on these changing theories of selves and societies, and their transformations, e.g. Snell (1953), Auerbach (1953) and Medcalf (1981). No doubt the invention of writing itself wrought a large change of consciousness. It allowed laws to be promulgated, rather than injunctions heard and rehearsed. It made the break with oral traditions and practices.

One critical change in the culturally held theories of the ancient Greeks which contrasts sharply with our own, and which is pointed out by both Jaynes and Snell, is the theory of human motivation and choice. The Homeric epics attribute human motivations to sources outside the self. To use Snell's metaphor: although the action of life takes part on a human stage, its causes and motivations are determined elsewhere, on a sort of upper balcony of the gods. To describe some important injunction ('take your hand from your sword and do not kill the king') as an authoritative voice, as if the person speaking were standing there, can be thought of simply as a different theory of how things come to mind. Perhaps with the theory that such motivations are external, the injunctions are heard as external. In Shakespeare's age the voice of conscience whispered in one's ear, and in a post-Freudian era we might now experience the voice of our super-ego in our head. For the 3000 years during which such injunctions have been written about there seems to have been a progressive internalization and ownership. But if our experienced world depends on the constructions of our implicit theories, we might not be too surprised that attributions of source can vary from outer to inner, or as Medcalf (1981) shows, can achieve as they did in the Middle Ages in Britain a solidity in which inner and outer are as one in the sight of God.

After all, images, voices, things we say or think or want do just come to mind. For a matter so fundamental but so impenetrable as the source of all these mental events, it is hardly surprising that different cultures will have different theories. Each theory will shape the way in which various things that come to mind are experienced. So an ancient Greek poet, like Sappho, knowing that poetry is the voice of gods, will indeed experience the creation of her poetry as muses speaking through her. 'Prosperity that the golden muses gave me was no delusion: dead I won't be forgotten' (Barnard, 1953). The idea that the muse, or language speaks through us is not such a bad theory. Today we might say that utterances are constructed by schemata, and this would express something more in tune with the society in which we live. With either theory, how an utterance comes to us individually is unbeknown to us, not given to us in consciousness. It remains unbeknown for us as for an ancient poet.

Personal, as well as cultural theories, shape experience too. My paranoid acquaintance (of an earlier section) experiences indifferent events as having special significance for him, and many interactions with others as persecutory. Occasionally he hears hallucinations of denunciatory commentaries on his actions. One idea about such paranoid schemata – see, for example, Colby (1981) – is that they are expressions of an implicit personal theory that others are trying to humiliate and devalue the paranoid person, a theory perhaps derived from the culture of a family where he was derided in many pervasive ways and had irresistible influences brought to bear on him.

Development of consciousness in childhood and society

Theories and practices of a culture run (as it were) as programs on individuals, who experience the world through their mental constructions or theories and who then become able to reconstruct those constructions for themselves in consciousness, and for others in language. We can ask how these cultural theories come to be created in the individual. The traditional answer is that they are passed on from parent to child, almost from the moment of birth. There seems to be a kind of programming. I do not have a better metaphor – I use this one to emphasize not a kind of determinism, though that can exist perhaps, as in the case of the paranoid person – but as a metaphor of transmitting a structured theory into an embodiment, who will one day experience that theory as 'self'.

This programming takes place upon a substrate of close interpersonal interaction. Condon (1979) has shown how from the day of birth babies move in synchrony with adult speech sounds. In adult conversation, too, speech sounds are accompanied by synchronized body movements, both of speaker and hearer. Transposing the term from the theory of non-linear oscillators, Condon calls this 'entrainment'. Tatam (1975) has shown two-month-old babies to be sensitive to whether their mother is attentive and responsive to them. Using a one-way mirror he could fade out the baby from the mother's visual field, letting her see a different person, whereupon the baby, who was still able to see its mother, became quite distressed.

Superimposed on the structure of this close interpersonal responsivity we can observe in our culture the untiring efforts of parents to interpret the gestures, cries, and gurgles of their babies as wants and intentions: wanting to be fed, cuddled, changed, laid down to sleep, etc. Their theory is that people behave purposefully. So, from the beginning, the culture into which a Western child is thrown has representatives who engage with it in empathetic entrainment, who interpret its behaviour as proto-actions designed to achieve ends, and who will act, to start with at least, as the instrument for the achievement of these ends. The major additional step in growing up in our culture remains to be able to achieve culturally approved ends for oneself — to tie one's shoelaces, to earn one's living.

As adults in such a culture it is scarcely surprising that we should see our actions as determined by our own purposes and our thoughts as our own.

After the foundations of our own purposeful behaviour have been laid, the image our culture passes on to us is of separate selves in relation with other selves, all acting purposefully. So following the analysis of Mead (e.g. 1934) the sense we have of a conscious self is a coherent set of roles (son, employee, man, helpful person, faithful friend, etc.) each of which can be described in terms of purposes and the strategies they require for fulfilment, together with images or models of the other to whom these intentions and strategies are directed. So in growing up with a mother who wants me to admire her, I might have the goal of maintaining her love, and construct a strategy for doing this by looking at her in a certain kind of way, listening attentively to what she says, offering praise, and so on. A case of someone having grown up in such a way is treated by Horney (1942). If I had had such a mother I might have felt rewarded by feeling accepted and in synchrony with her, and might have grown up with an image of myself as acceptable or even lovable when behaving in this way. In later life I might then be attracted towards further relationships with people who are generous to those within their circle of influence who will admire them. Quite possibly I might then find people as friends and lovers who would be representatives in the outer world of my inner image of the admirable person, people who I could interact with in my well rehearsed way.

A characteristic interaction in our culture then becomes a matter of creating complementary sets of roles with others: admirer — admired, buyer — seller, helpful person — someone who needs help. By fulfilling the known cultural requirements for these kinds of role, I can experience myself as a self. I experience what Mead calls 'me'. 'Me' is the aspect of self distilled from the expectations and attitudes of others towards myself. It can be an object of contemplation, distinguished by Mead from the 'I' of direct experience, which by definition cannot be experienced, cannot be an object to itself. So I experience 'me' as a person of a particular kind, and I can maintain the sense of this person, by the roles I engage in. Mead supposed that this distiliate of social attitudes is mediated by language, and can be seen in development in children's games. First children play particular roles: fireman, mother with a doll, doctor, etc. Later, in more elaborate games, not only are there roles, but also rules which constitute the game and which define meaningful actions. Then in the socially constituted game of adult society I will take myself to be worthy of respect or contempt for acting in the ways defined by the rules of my social group.

In an earlier section, perception of physical objects was described as depending on schemata embodying knowledge of the parts of the physical world and the structural and functional connections among them. Perception in the social world is similar. It requires us to have a schematic theory of social parts and the connections among them. In the case of our culture the theory is that social parts are actions, and that actions are connected together by plans. So in seeking to perceive another we seek to infer his or her intentions and plans, particularly in the ways that they will bear on our own. This perception of the other is vital for maintaining our sense of ourself, so we experience an interaction as satisfying if what we take to be the other's actions and purposes complement our own, and sometimes devastating if they do not. The experience of actions interpreted by means of the rules of our implicit social theories can be profound. It takes on, as Goffman (1961) puts it, 'the thickness of reality', and says Goffman 'there seems to be no agent more effective than another person in bringing a world for oneself alive or, by a glance, a gesture, or a remark, shrivelling up the reality in which one is lodged' (p. 41).

Human consciousness then, involves the creation of a reality partly composed by the rules of our particular culture. If ideas or conclusions just come to us, perhaps cued by an association or analogy, then to tell it to another or oneself involves adapting it to the theory and rules that we know, to make it acceptable and appropriate. We might even think, as Harré (1981) has put it, that privately we think in poetry. Images and phrases just come to us, as cues select schemata or as the muse speaks, whereas logical thinking is a public activity, turning these images into communicable forms, putting them into prose, creating plans, procedures and commentaries acceptable to others and to ourselves.

If we are to speculate about the relation of this mindstuff to the brain, we can argue that it is social functioning that brings pressure for the enlargement of the cortex. The major behavioural implication of being a mammal is, after all, that one grows up in dependent social interaction with another. A step which is documented by the palaeontologists is that plausibly at the same time as human society grew yet more interdependent, i.e. during the beginnings of language, people started to operate on the world with tools. Indications dating from two to three million years ago indicate that tool making was undertaken by groups of people rather than individuals. Social interdependence and operating instrumentally on the world also coincide in that most human of activities, preparing and sharing food together.

Vygotsky (1979) has described an interrelation among these three elements: tool use, speech and sociality, in infant development. When trying to solve a problem that requires tools, such as stools to stand on or sticks to reach with, young children talk out loud. Speech accompanies the 'vicissitudes of problem solving'. If the child is not allowed to talk, this may result in not being able to solve the problem. At later stages in development the child's speech comes to precede action, and to involve creating a plan; indeed the speech is describable as planning. At this stage speech can be directed to others to involve them in the plan, but then interpersonal speaking, used at first to address adults, is 'turned inward . . . children develop a method of guiding themselves that had previously been used in relation to another person . . . they organize their own activities according to a social form of behaviour' (p. 27).

Much of human technical ability and social interaction revolves around plans which are enactments of purposes. Planning a meal, a journey or something we are going to make is often assisted by creating a symbolic form: a list, a map or a diagram. We then speak of any of these as a plan. Each is an external extension of the symbolic plan we might form in mindspace, in a mental list, map or diagram.

Child's speech is used now as symbolic elements in a plan, now as communication to another, now as communication to self. In adulthood too the speaking to others and oneself about problems still goes on. The focus here is often on our more difficult problems, on the social world, as we adjudicate the actions of ourselves and each other according to the rules of our group.

Vygotsky notes that it is where a problem is most difficult that the child speaks most. Mead (1913), thinking along the same lines, says of adulthood that we are not usually conscious of our highly organized self. Only when 'some essential problem appears there is some disintegration of this organization and different tendencies appear in reflective thought as different voices in conflict with each other' (p. 147). It is at these points of stress and of the problematic that Jaynes (1976) too notes that in the Homeric epics people are beset by bodily sensations (changes of breathing, pounding of the heart and the like) and voices telling them what to do. Many of the events which we now describe as emotions are discrepancies between our schemata and the constraint of an outside world (Katz, 1980), giving rise to feelings such as pounding of the heart and problems that we work out in inner debate.

Consciousness, then, is largely a social consciousness, though used for technical purposes too. It is Jaynes's metaphorical mindspace occupied by symbolic people, their doings and the ways in which they impinge on us. Perceptual schemata of physical knowledge needed a great deal of computational structure, with schemata being addressable by many cues from different sensory modalities. Constructions created by the freeing of symbols from their immediate cues, and applied as metaphor or analogy might require even more computational structure, especially in the incalculable world of interpersonal relationships.

Selves arise as objects within this introspected mindspace. They have, as Mead (1909) remarks, 'no existence outside that introspected field, and other selves are only projects and ejects of that field. Each self is an island, for who knows what mirages may arise above this analogical sea' (p. 107). Despite this we all try to know what other selves are up to, and succeed to some degree. Humphrey (1979) may be correct in arguing that an important function of introspective consciousness is that we can imagine how we might feel in circumstances that we see others in. We can use our own sense of self to simulate the other, and thereby to infer what that other might be thinking or feeling. If the 'me' that one introspects is, as Mead has argued, a distillate of attitudes and rules in the society in which we live, then for humans at least, it may be as good a representation of the generalized other as can be found without too much trouble. At the same time we can note that this method of inferring the intentions and feelings of another has shortcomings. It risks both wholesale projections of our own idiosyncrasies, and the treatment of others as ciphers; perhaps adequate for acquaintances, but scarcely for friends.

This method of perceiving and interacting in the social world is, for all its shortcomings, more complex than methods required for physical perception and much everyday instrumental action. In physical perception the structures of inference from multiple cues allow redundancy, so that perception can occur successfully even when brain damage has occurred or the evidence of the visual field is fragmentary. In social perception evidence is even more fragmentary and fleeting than in the physical world. So in the social domain the system may be operating nearer the edge of its performance limits. In animal studies, for instance, though brain lesions may give rise to barely detectable or circumscribed deficits in physical performance in the laboratory, effects on animals' social interaction in the wild can be devastating. Though some people suffer extensive brain damage and remain socially competent, changes in personality detected by friends and loved ones can be disastrous, and society constructs categories of non-competence for people whose life is made difficult when such damage has occurred.

Our theories of social perception and interaction remain problematic for us, as implied by the obsessive interest we take in elaborating our understanding of human action and social rules, in novels, at the cinema, in gossip, and in emotionally charged inner debate. This might be taken to indicate that the matters at issue are very difficult to make reliable inferences about, even with the powerful device of an introspected 'me' to simulate the other.

Understanding another, an individual whose own intentions and experience are quite different from our own, not just as a complement to a role we are taking, and not just as a generalized other with corrections made for immediate context, is very difficult for us. We might say that for the most part such computations are hard to accomplish in the present state of evolution of our society. To revert to an older metaphor, in the words of George Eliot: 'The difficult task of knowing another soul is not for young gentlemen whose consciousness is chiefly made up of their own wishes' (*Middlemarch*, Chapter 12).

One can perhaps imagine cultures more evolved than our own in which people's implicit theories about others revolve less egocentrically round their owner's wishes. In the creation of such societies consciousness will have transformed itself again, and experience will have taken on new forms. In the 10,000 years of permanent settlement and civilization we have transformed our physical environment radically. At the same time social hierarchy, which at one time was the major structure of inter-relationships in urban living, is perhaps not so prevalent. It is unlikely that the structure of the brain limits further evolution of our social and interpersonal theories. So perhaps the means of further transformation depends at least in part on a reflectiveness on our personal and cultural theories, just as it did for the young gentleman in George Eliot's novel.

Acknowledgements

I am grateful to Michael Yocum for his careful reading of a draft of this text and for convincing me of the limitations of the representational metaphor. I am grateful too to Philip Johnson-Laird and David Oakley who read the text and made helpful suggestions. Others too have contributed to these ideas in conversation, and I would like to thank them, most especially Max Clowes, Brian Goodwin and Stephen Medcalf.

References

Auerbach, E. (1953) *Mimesis*. Princeton, NJ: Princeton University Press.
Barnard, M. (1958) *Sappho: A New Translation*. Berkeley: University of California Press.
Bartlett, F. (1932) *Remembering*. Cambridge: Cambridge University Press.
Bateson, G. (1970) Form, substance and difference. In *Steps to an Ecology of Mind. Collected Essays of G. Bateson*. St Albans: Paladin, 1973.
Clowes, M. (1971) On seeing things. *Artificial Intelligence 2:* 79–116.
Colby, K. M. (1982) Modelling a paranoid mind. *Behavioral and Brain Sciences 4:* 515–60.
Condon, W. S. (1979) Neonatal entrainment and enculturation. In M. Bullowa (ed.) *Before Speech: The Beginnings of Human Communication*. Cambridge: Cambridge University Press.
Craik, K. J. W. (1943) *The Nature of Explanation*. Cambridge: Cambridge University Press.
Falk, G. (1972) Interpretation of imperfect line data as three-dimensional scene. *Artificial Intelligence 3:* 101–44.
Goffman, E. (1961) *Encounters: Two Studies in the Sociology of Interaction*. Indianapolis: Bobbs-Merrill.
Guzman, A. (1969) Decomposition of a visual scene into three-dimensional bodies. In A. Grasselli (ed.) *Automatic Interrelation and Classification of Images*, 243–76. London: Academic Press.

Harré, R. (1981) Talk given at the University of Sussex.

Helmholtz, H. von (1866) *Treatise on Physiological Optics*, part III, ed. J. P. C. Southall. New York: Dover, 1962.

Horney, K. (1942) *Self-analysis*. London: Routledge & Kegan Paul.

Huffman, D. (1971) Impossible objects as nonsense sentences. In B. Meltzer and D. Michie (eds) *Machine Intelligence, Volume 6*, 295–323. Edinburgh: Edinburgh University Press.

Humphrey, N. K. (1979) Nature's psychologists. In B. Josephson and V. S. Ramachandran (eds) *Consciousness and the Physical World*. Oxford: Pergamon Press.

Huygens, C. (1665) Sympathie des horloges. In Societé Hollandaise des Sciences (ed.) *Oeuvres Completes de Christian Huygens*, vol. 17, 183–6. La Haye: Nijhoff.

Jaynes, J. (1976) *The Origin of Consciousness in the Breakdown of the Bicameral Mind*. London: Allen Lane.

Johnson-Laird, P. N. (1983) *Mental Models: Towards a Cognitive Science of Language, Inference and Consciousness*. Cambridge: Cambridge University Press.

Katz, J. M. (1980) Discrepancy, arousal and labelling: towards a psycho-social theory of emotion. *Sociological Inquiry 50 (2):* 147–56.

Lakoff, G. and Johnson, M. (1980) *Metaphors We Live By*. Chicago: University of Chicago Press.

Lashley, K. S. (1929) *Brain Mechanisms and Intelligence*. Chicago: University of Chicago Press.

Lashley, K. S. (1951) Discussion at 'Symposium on the Brain and the Mind', American Neurological Association. Cit. S. Cobb, A salute from neurologists. In F. A. Beach, D. O. Hebb, C. T. Morgan and H. W. Nissen (eds) *The Neuropsychology of Lashley*. New York: McGraw-Hill, 1960.

Lashley, K. S. (1960) *The Neuropsychology of Lashley*, collected papers ed. F. A. Beach, D. O. Hebb, C. T. Morgan and H. W. Nissen. New York: McGraw-Hill.

Lorenz, K. (1969) Innate bases of learning. In K. H. Pribram (ed.) *On the Biology of Learning*, 13–93. New York: Harcourt, Brace & World.

Mead, G. H. (1909) What social objects must psychology presuppose? *Journal of Philosophy, Psychology and Scientific Methods 7:* 174–80. Reprinted in A. J. Reck (ed.) *Selected Writings of George Herbert Mead*, 105–13. Indianapolis: Bobbs-Merrill, 1964.

Mead, G. H. (1913) The social self. *Journal of Philosophy, Psychology and Scientific Methods 10:* 374–80. Reprinted in A. J. Reck (ed.) *Selected Writings of George Herbert Mead*, 142–9. Indianapolis: Bobbs-Merrill, 1964.

Mead, G. H. (1934) *Mind, Self and Society*. Chicago: University of Chicago Press.

Medcalf, S. (1981) Inner and outer. In S. Medcalf (ed.) *The Later Middle Ages*, 108–71. London: Methuen.

Oakley, D. A. (1979) Cerebral cortex and adaptive behaviour. In D. A. Oakley and H. C. Plotkin (eds) *Brain, Behaviour and Evolution*, 154–88. London: Methuen.

Oatley, K. (1974) Circadian rhythms and representations of the environment in motivational systems. In D. J. McFarland (ed.) *Motivational Control Systems Analysis*, 427–59. London: Academic Press.

Oatley, K. (1975) Clock mechanisms of sleep. *New Scientist 66:* 371–4.

Oatley, K. (1978) *Perceptions and Representations*. London: Methuen.

Oatley, K. (1980) Representing ourselves: mental schemata, computational metaphors, and the nature of consciousness. In G. Underwood and R. Stevens (eds) *Aspects of Consciousness*, vol. 2. London: Academic Press.

Papert, S. (1980) *Mindstorms: Children, Computers and Powerful Ideas*. Brighton: Harvester Press.

Roberts, L. G. (1965) Machine perception of three-dimensional solids. In J. T. Tippett *et al.* (eds) *Optical and Electro-optical Information Processing*, 159–97. Cambridge, Mass.: MIT Press.

Rorty, R. (1980) *Philosophy and the Mirror of Nature*. Oxford: Blackwell.

Schroeder, H. (1858) Cited and discussed in Helmholtz, H. von (1886) *Treatise on Physiological Optics*, Part III (286–88). Edited by J. P. C. Southall (1962). New York: Dover.

Snell, B. (1953) *The Discovery of the Mind*. New York: Harper & Row.

Sussman, G. J. (1975) *A Computer Model of Skill Acquisition*. New York: American Elsevier Publishing Co.

Taine, H. (1870) *De l'Intelligence*. Extracts reprinted in A. Cresson *Hippolite Taine, Sa Vie, Son Oeuvre*. Paris: Presses Universitaire de France, 1951.

Tatam, J. (1975) Reported in C. Trevarthen, Early attempts at speech. In R. Lewin (ed.) *Child Alive*, 76–7. London: Temple Smith.

Vygotsky, L. F. (1978) *Mind in Society: Development of Higher Psychological Processes*, ed. M. Cole, V. John-Stenier, S. Scribner and E. Souberman. Cambridge, Mass.: Harvard University Press.

Weizenbaum, J. (1976) *Computer Power and Human Reason*. San Francisco: W. H. Freeman.

Winograd, S. and Cowan, J. D. (1963) *Reliable Computation in the Presence of Noise*. Cambridge, Mass.: MIT Press.

Wittgenstein, L. (1922) *Tractatus Logico-Philosophicus*. London: Routledge & Kegan Paul.

Wittgenstein, L. (1953) *Philosophical Investigations*. Translated by G. E. M. Anscombe. Oxford: Blackwell.

Yates, F. A. (1966) *The Art of Memory*. London: Routledge & Kegan Paul.

3 Is consciousness the gateway to the hippocampal cognitive map? A speculative essay on the neural basis of mind

John O'Keefe

Introduction

Much discussion of consciousness centres around putative differences between its properties and those of the apparently non-conscious objects of the material world. Are these two domains really different from each other? If so, do they interact in a causal or a non-causal fashion? Are the differences only apparent, and if so, which is the 'real' domain and which the mirage? Are both perhaps the same, identical thing, or are they both surface reflections of some third metaphysically deeper domain?

In this paper I do not propose to deal with these questions. It is my belief that these issues will only be settled when we have a plausible theory of the brain which incorporates a role for consciousness. My suspicion is that in the face of such a demonstration the 'logical' objections to the identification of consciousness with some aspect of brain function will rapidly evaporate.

What should a theory of consciousness explain?

A complete theory of consciousness should consist of a psychological model at its core and linkages between the model and at least five domains of knowledge: introspection, neuroscience, ethology and behavioural psychology, the theory of evolution and the sociology of institutions.

The core of the theory must consist of a psychological model which describes the creation, manipulation and storage of mental representations of the physical world, as well as of the self in a social world (see chapters 2 and 4 of this volume). This reflects my conviction that consciousness has more to do with this aspect of the brain's function than with its role in vegetative functions, such as control of blood sugar level, or the generation of simple motor behaviours, such as habits or reflexes. The psychological model would consist of a set of subsystems each performing a different function and would describe the information flow within and amongst these subsystems. This, of course, is nothing more than a restatement of the aims of that branch of psychology called cognitive science. Consciousness would be equated with the operation of some aspect of this model, perhaps the activation of a subsystem or the control of information transfer from one subsystem to another. Consciousness is unlikely to be associated with the entire operation of the cognitive areas of the brain.

The first domain of knowledge which must be linked to this psychological model is our ideas about consciousness derived from *introspection*, intuition, and the more scientific study of illusions, mental imagery and mental chronometry. Self-awareness and the belief in the existence of awareness in others form such a central part of every aspect of human endeavour that it is hard to understand, much less accept, the attempts of behaviourists to deny them a role in psychology. The aspect of the psychological model identified with consciousness should have the properties which are commonly attributed to consciousness, such as continuity and integrity, and should account for the contents of consciousness and its apparent role in some, but not all, behaviours. Perhaps most importantly these properties should be an integral aspect of the function of the subsystem, and not merely an *ad hoc* or arbitrary addition to the model.

The second domain of knowledge which must be connected to the psychological model is the *neurosciences*. This follows from the assumption that consciousness is associated with some aspect of brain function, although probably at a level higher than that of the individual nerve cell. Consciousness is to be found at the systems level of brain function. But brain systems are composed of individual brain cells, and the properties of the system must be derived from the activities of the individual cells and their interactions. I have never understood the idea of emergent properties, in which the whole has properties which are greater than or different from the sum of its parts (see, for example, Sperry, 1952). A system is the sum of its parts and their multi-level interactions, and I do not see how the brain can be any different. It is another question to ask how crucial to the function of a system are the properties of its components. Granted that the operations of brain systems, and in particular those systems related to consciousness, can be derived from the properties of nerve cells and their interactions, could the same functions be carried out by entirely different components? Could a machine constructed of transistors perform the functions of a biological brain? Could it be conscious? The answer is . . . 'perhaps'. It depends on the importance of the specifically biological properties of individual neural elements to the functioning of the brain systems related to consciousness. If the important interactions are at the information processing level, e.g. simultaneous activity in two elements results in activity in a third, then the computer could be conscious. Alternatively, if the interactions consist of (presently unknown) force fields set up under extremely specific conditions between elements with precise anatomical and physiological (e.g. carbon-based) properties then it may not be possible to achieve these conditions in artificial systems in the foreseeable future. The confidence of those artificial intelligence scientists who proclaim the irrelevance of biology to cognitive sciences may be based on oversimplified notions of brain function and cognitive processes.

The third area of knowledge to which a theory of consciousness must address itself is that of the *behavioural sciences*. How is consciousness related to the organism's behaviour? Do the parts of the brain associated with consciousness influence or generate behaviour? Are behaviours performed under conscious control different from those which are unconscious? Furthermore, behaviours generated or influenced by the 'conscious' parts of the brain must be biologically important for the organism's survival in the course of its interaction with a particular ecological niche. It follows that the postulated physiological mechanisms related to consciousness must be ones which could have evolved under environmental pressures. Here it is assumed that consciousness and the brain circuits with which it is associated did not appear suddenly in the human but are common features of the animal kingdom. The theory should outline how this evolution takes place. One corollary of this assumption is that an adequate theory of consciousness should draw the line between conscious and non-conscious species.

Finally, a complete theory of consciousness should explain the central importance which consciousness holds in many *human institutions*. Religion, law and the arts take certain attributes of consciousness (e.g. free will) as central to their existence. An adequate theory of consciousness should reflect this fact and should consequently contribute to our understanding of these institutions.

In this essay, I do not propose to do more than outline a programme to meet these requirements. I will concentrate primarily on relating the properties of a particular brain system, the hippocampal system, to the introspectively derived properties of consciousness. I will briefly outline how such a system might incorporate additional features which would bridge the gap between the properties of the system in the rat and that in the human. Perforce this section will be almost totally speculative. I will say nothing here about the sociological relevance of the theory of consciousness I am putting forward.

Introspective properties of human consciousness

By consciousness I mean both the process of awareness and the contents of that awareness. Many writers, in trying to arrive at a concise theory of consciousness emphasize one or the other attribute of consciousness, minimizing or denying the existence of others which do not easily fit into their theory. To take a few examples, Sperry (1952) and Shallice (1972) have concentrated on the role of consciousness in voluntary action, while Barlow (1980) and Humphrey (1980) have emphasized its role in interpersonal relations. It seems to me that to emphasize only one aspect of consciousness is a mistake, and I will try to avoid it.

My goal in this section will be to try to set out as many of the major attributes of consciousness as I can and to discuss the interrelations amongst them.

Perhaps the best way to begin to analyse the attributes of consciousness is by examining a segment of consciousness. Hebb (1981) has warned against the dangers of introspection, in particular the dangers of confusing quasi-hypothetical guesses about the contents of consciousness with 'pure' introspection itself. I will try to avoid this criticism by making only the weak claim that what follows is a plausible reconstruction of a typical sequence of consciousness. My account draws heavily on the work of William James (1961) who still provides the best description of mental processes available today.

I can reconstruct the following scenario of mental events which took place during the writing of a short passage of this essay. Throughout the short period of time, there was a constant but dim presence of the surrounding environment, the table, paper, music from the radio, trees outside the window, traffic noise, position of my body on the chair, constant drone of tinnitus in my ears, etc. Similarly forming the background was the shadow-like sense of a cluster of vague ideas as to the content and purpose of my writing. Set against these backgrounds were a series of phasic mental episodes, some of them constructed from material which had briefly emerged from the shadows of the background into clearer view front of stage, others irrelevant interlopers disrupting the business at hand. Such a sequence of foreground phasic events might be as follows: (a) a sense that a particular sentence didn't quite catch the meaning I had wished to convey, a feeling of mismatch between an unstated intention and the accomplishment: I make a note to try a rewrite later; (b) a short passage from the Elgar symphony that is playing on the radio breaks through and I listen for a few seconds; (c) nose scratch; (d) a few more lines written; (e) the trees outside the window momentarily emerge from the constantly present background, their bareness summoning up the image of their summer coat of leaves; (f) the sharp intrusion that I have to finish this paper within the next week since the deadline is long past – this latter accompanied by a slight pang of anxiety and embarrassment (vague autonomic sensations here); (g) 'must resolve to pace workload better' says the bland voice of inner speech above the tinnitus; (h) must get back to the business at hand; (i) pause to reread the previous page of writing and half-way through my mind wanders off on a new tangent: perhaps this passage might better be pushed forward to the previous section; (j) when my attention returns to the written page before me I find that my eyes have moved down the page from the point where I left off; I am vaguely aware of having gone through the mechanics of reading in the interim but clearly I have not taken in what I have read; (k) crash! from outside the window – 'the builders still working next door?'

It seems from this and similar reconstructions that consciousness consists of a stable framework which acts as the setting for a sequence of episodes which vary in duration, content and elaborateness. Each episode, no matter how brief and insignificant, is a portal into an extensive story or narrative, either because it provides an extension to an existing narrative or because it is pregnant with the possibility of a new one. Episodes can vary in length from the momentary notice of the unclad trees or the transient scratch of the nose to the extended reverie of the daydream. Each episode consists of an individuated entity or set of entities, some referred to the external world, others to one's internal subjectivity. Although differing vastly in content, and connecting to very different narratives, these episodes are not entirely independent of each other. They are connected by the fact that they are experienced as a succession occurring within the same framework (the same consciousness) and that consciousness has a single proprietor (myself).

The properties of consciousness which an adequate theory should explain are as follows.

(1) The varied, evershifting nature of the contents of consciousness

A constellation of perceptions and subjective states crowd onto the stage of my consciousness, each one trying to push forward into the centre of the stage, each one clamouring for its moment in the spotlight. As the spotlight shifts onto an entity it rapidly acquires a frame and then with continued attention becomes part of an episode. Those entities and frames which are not currently at the centre of attention do not necessarily disappear but become vague and hazy in the background.

The most prevalent contents of my consciousness are: (a) the multimodal constellation of objects set in a three-dimensional world seen from a particular perspective: my hand writing, the trees outside the window, the music on the radio; (b) the words of inner speech as I form phrases to write, cajole myself, rehearse speeches, hold imaginary conversations; (c) subjective feelings (anxiety), inchoate thoughts, bodily sensations (tinnitus, stiffness in my arm), and (d) intentions to act. In contrast, there are many things of which I am seldom, if ever, conscious: my rhythmic breathing, the tapping of my foot to the music, the movements of my eyes during reading. It is now clear that considerable cognitive processing can occur in the absence of conscious awareness, as can be demonstrated in tasks such as automatic writing (e.g. Spelke, Hirst and Neisser, 1976) or binaural shadowing (Lackner and Garnett, 1973), which depend on divisions in attention, as well as in the phenomenon of subliminal perception (Dixon, 1981). The classic example here is one's ability to drive a car while carrying on a reasonable conversation. (This particular example is sufficiently classic in fact to appear also in chapters 6, 7 and 8 of this volume.)

What then, distinguishes those things of which we are conscious from those of which we are not? One possibility that I would like to suggest is that we are conscious of those things which can be seg- mented and considered as individual entities. We are aware of this piece of paper, this word, this performance of this symphony, this pain, and not of paper, words or music, as abstractions or classes of entities. Consider breathing. Usually this is controlled by unconscious mechanisms but can become conscious under certain conditions. One of these is laboured breathing. One becomes aware of each breath as an individual and in particular the success or failure of catching each breath. Furthermore that breath is set within a framework which connects it to the place and time where it occurred and to other circumstances associated with it.

The question of how much attention is necessary to drive a car may have a similar analysis. As long as the behaviour of the car and the external world can be predicted and controlled on the basis of con- tinuous patterns of optical, tactile, auditory and vestibular stimu- lation, consciousness need not be involved: the road, other cars, the terrain, all meld into a continuously varying but predictable sensory pattern. At an intersection or when a car suddenly changes lane, how- ever, the level of uncertainty rapidly increases and the course of events are no longer predictable from the ensemble and portions of the sensory array must be segmented out of the total and treated as individuals. 'That red Ford cut me off a while ago so I'd best keep a close eye on it; where's the sign for the airport?'

(2) The unity, stability, and continuity of consciousness in spite of the constantly varying contents

Introspectively one has the strong sense of an enduring framework or container which provides spatial and temporal continuity to the stream of consciousness. Whence does this sense of a framework arise? I think that there are at least three different sources: (1) the short- term stability of the background; (2) the ability to knit together a set of experiences in spite of intrusions or gaps, or to relate the current episode to a stored narrative, and (3) the sense of 'me-ness' which tinges most or all of the contents of consciousness.

Whereas the foreground focus of consciousness hops about incessantly and can only remain on one subject for any period of time with the utmost effort, the contents of the background can remain relatively stable for long periods. When they do change they do so in a reasonably smooth and predictable way. The background physical world, the topic of conversation, the intention of this essay, all provide a short-term stability (cf. Gibson, 1950, with reference to the stability of the visual world). I will return to the difference between the foreground and background in a later section. The second source of stability, the ability to leap across the breaks in experience, the temporal gaps left by sleep and anaesthesia, the spatial gaps left by overconcentration on the matter in hand, obviously relies on memory and the ability to connect up experiences on the basis of narrative pattern. It feels like someone weaving a carpet who puts it down to put a few stitches into a shirt, but who can easily return to pick up where he left off without losing the flow of the pattern.

The third source of stability for consciousness is the sense of possession which attaches to the contents of consciousness. These are *my* thoughts, *my* percepts. In the case of perceptions part of this proprietory sense might arise from the association to a particular body. It is always the same nose, hands, etc. in the visual field which accompany the visual inputs. In a related fashion the sensory transducers label the different sensory inputs in a characteristic way: the visual image derived from the left eye is more blurred and slightly dimmer than that of the right, the familiar tinnitus, etc. Perhaps the strangest source of the mineness of my consciousness is the phenomenon of self-awareness, the awareness of being aware. This quasi-mystical notion, with its constant threat of tumbling the introspector into the chasm of infinitely-nested awarenesses (I am aware that I am aware that I am aware . . .), has seemed the least likely of all attributes of consciousness to admit of a scientific explanation. An adequate theory of consciousness should provide a role for it.

One note of caution. The strong sense of unity and continuity is no guarantee that consciousness, or its neural substrate, is unified or continuous. These are not the sorts of things one can know from the 'inside'. A theory of consciousness should explain the sense of unity without necessarily demonstrating that it is unified. (The plurality of mental processing which underlies this subjective illusion of unity is considered further in chapters 7 and 8 of this volume.)

(3) Consciousness is not homogenous but consists of a variable foreground and background

At any given moment, some item or items of consciousness will be in 'sharper focus' than others. These others do not disappear but remain in the background. James referred to them as the 'fringe'. Intense concentration on the foreground item(s) can make virtually every-thing else disappear but this is the exception rather than the rule. More often consciousness consists of a succession of foreground epi-sodes against a relatively stable background. One interesting aspect of the foreground items is their tenuousness and short lifetime. The focus of consciousness is always on the move. It appears to be ex-tremely difficult (if not impossible) to concentrate on the same item for more than a few seconds, to freeze the frame, so to speak. Very quickly the strain becomes enormous and resistance is overcome. Attention shifts to different aspects of the same item, to the difficulty of maintaining attention, to the object of the experiment, and finally to something else entirely. The foreground of consciousness is not reserved for one actor delivering an all-night monologue. And yet the contents of the foreground are not totally random. As we shall see in the next section the sequence of items within an episode, and even to some extent the sequence of episodes themselves, can be controlled in accordance with some plan or other strategic framework.

(4) The origin and control of the contents of consciousness

Items in consciousness are referred to the external world (perceptions) or to an internal generator (emotions, images, thoughts). They gain entrance either by dint of some attribute of their own (loud noises, foul smells, pleasurable reveries), because they are unexpected, or because they are invited or admitted in accordance with some plan or other superordinate schema. The actual stream of consciousness, then, would seem to be the result of a competition between these different classes of items and indeed within classes. Often in attempt-ing to follow an orderly line of thought in accordance with some plan or interest the mind has to fend off intrusions from strong stimuli and unexpected events, as well as from competing plans and interests. The temptation to daydream or indulge in reveries would fall into this latter category. The more difficult it is to pursue a line of thought the more easily does one succumb to the temptation.

Although the plan itself is usually only dimly perceived it can become the subject of consciousness, especially if there is a conflict between several plans. As we shall see in the next section, consciousness is involved when decisions between different courses of action are necessary. What relationship obtains between the plan which controls the path of consciousness and the description of the plan which enters consciousness, is not clear. This latter is of the form 'need to write that paper', which suggests there are paper writing plans which call up the elements of the paper and organize them into a sequence. The called up, but not presently focused, items would form part of the background fringe for paper writing. Other activities would have different plans. I will discuss the role of consciousness in voluntary behaviour in a subsequent section.

The picture we are left with is that of a device which can accept inputs from several different sources, and where the items which gain access can be under the control of some planning device. Information about the planning device itself can also enter consciousness. Presumably in the latter case control is under the aegis of a different plan, although one can write a paper about writing a paper.

(5) Consciousness is intimately related to some aspect of long-term memory

Apparently many parents habitually read to their children without consciously processing the material read. At the end of their session they have little or no recall of the content of the narrative. It seems quite likely that the written material which I absentmindedly scanned was processed up to some level, in spite of my inability to encode its meaning or to remember its content. On the other hand, Hebb (1961) has shown that the memory for strings of numbers longer than the immediate memory span can improve with repetition, despite the fact that the subject may not be aware of the repetition. I suggest that consciousness is only necessary for the encoding of episodes and narratives into long-term memory. If this is the case, then it prompts the further question: what is the role of consciousness in the storage and retrieval of narratives? At this stage one can do no more than suggest that it might have something to do with organizing the material into the appropriate form. When the material has its referent in the external world the appropriate form is a spatio-temporal one; when the material is linguistic the appropriate form is a narrative one.

(6) Consciousness is involved in some actions and not others

Consciousness can be involved in the control of behaviour at the level of the individual action and at the more molar level of the plan. William James (1961) discussed the relationship between the conscious intention to move and the movement itself, and believed that once a clear image of the intention was formed the movement followed automatically. On the other hand, many well-learned skilled actions can proceed without conscious involvement. Why is consciousness necessary for the original learning of skilled movements? What is the conscious content during skilled movements?

The role of consciousness during skilled movements seems to be the generation of the goal or subgoal of the movement and the calculation of the mismatch between that goal or subgoal and the present situation. The actual movements are not coded. It is as though consciousness was part of the system which transmitted the goals of the action to the motor systems, monitored the outcome of the action and scored the result, but had no direct influence on the motor programmes. Consciousness is also involved in the control of actions in two other ways. The first occurs when some aspect of the action goes wrong and control shifts from automatic to conscious; the second occurs when there are reasons which oppose the action. Let us briefly consider each in turn.

Control of an action sequence passes to consciousness when either the outcome of a movement deviates from the expected result or the sensory information controlling the action falls below a certain level of predictability. The standard example here is the shifts in attention which occur during motor car driving and conversing. Little or no conscious control of driving is required when travelling along a predictable highway and conversation on relatively difficult topics is possible. Erratic behaviour by another driver or the approach of an intersection or roundabout forces a shift in attention and the cessation of the conversation: 'Let me just pay attention here for a moment'. As we have already seen, novelty and unpredictability are powerful determinants of the control of consciousness. The present considerations suggest that this is the case when action is involved as well as when it is not. If this analysis is correct, the question translates into the rather different one: what is the source of predictability in the situations which do not require conscious attention, and how does consciousness help to cope with the unpredictability? In the case of the driving example, it seems that one needs consciousness to predict the behaviour of other cars if it is necessary to attribute agency to them. For example, at a roundabout it is necessary to predict where each driver is trying to go in order to avoid collision, and these predictions may not be possible on the basis of the immediately preceding behaviour. A driver trapped on the outside lane may want to take the next exit and may change several lanes at the last moment. But even in instances where agency is not involved conscious control may be necessary, as for example when the road suddenly becomes winding. The general rule then seems to be that consciousness is required in those situations where reliable predictions cannot be made on the basis of the immediately preceding information and where other factors such as agency need to be taken into account.

Our third situation in which consciousness is involved in action involves the resolution of conflict: consciousness is the arena within which reasons and impulses struggle for control of behaviour. The most obvious case here is the internal struggle a person experiences between a base impulse or habit and the reasons which his or her conscience offer for resisting that impulse. One banana-split is indulgence, the little voice says, two is gluttony and you will undoubtedly get stomach cramps. In general the promptings of reason and rationality are based on the larger, more inclusive view of the situation. What is the effect of this action on my overall goals? What will happen tomorrow, next week, the following year? Remember the last time I did the same thing! Deliberation is the frustration of the habit or impulse until due consideration has been given to these questions. The process has much in kin with the attempt to concentrate on the job at hand in the face of distractions (see p. 67). Perhaps one reason why bodily states are given access to consciousness is just so that they can be recognized as the well-springs of action and subjected to this type of consideration and debate.

Less often, but perhaps more importantly, consciousness is the forum for debate between different rational courses of action. Shall I be a doctor or an engineer? Here the process is not one of obstructing a course of action but constructing an overall plan which will integrate large areas of information into a consistent schema. This schema, then, can be consulted in specific instances (e.g. in the face of an impulse), and used to influence behaviour at any moment in accordance with long-term goals.

Sketch for a Cartesian theory of mind

Whereas consciousness or some aspect of consciousness seems to be localizable at a gross level (somewhere inside the head), it is not so obvious that consciousness can be localized to a finer level (e.g. at the level of the single neurone). Localization at this level would appear to depend on the particular theory of consciousness entertained. At the most general level the brain can be thought of as a device for the manipulation and transmission of information by the activation of neurones in different anatomical areas. Theories can be classified according to which aspect of this process each relates to consciousness. In the first theory, which I shall call the *searchlight theory*, consciousness is equated with the physiological process of activation; the second theory (the *filter theory*) locates consciousness in an anatomical area of the brain; the third (the *dual aspect theory*) identifies it with some types of information and not others. These theories are not mutually exclusive and the theory to be presented towards the end of this section incorporates aspects of each of them.

The *searchlight theory* equates consciousness with a particular physiological state of activation in different sets of neurones. The physical analogy is that of the beam of a searchlight which moves across a set of representations illuminating now one, now another. The act of illumination changes the representation, endowing it with radically different properties from those of the darkened state. Thus the same anatomical elements may or may not participate in consciousness at different times. The direction and spread of the searchlight are the analogues of the selection and focus of consciousness. The putative action of the reticular activating system on the neocortex is a good example of this type of theory (Delafresnaye, 1954).

The second model for consciousness uses the analogy of the filter, gate or valve. I refer to this as the *filter theory*. The best known example is the influential theory of attention proposed by Broadbent (1958), though this particular version has since been modified in the light of experimental evidence (e.g. Treisman, 1964). Here consciousness is a rate limiting aspect of a transmission line, or a selection mechanism which allows passage of a subset of messages while blocking others. On this analogy, the filter or transmission element is the container, and the control which selects the properties of the filter or the setting of the gate corresponds to the controlling features of consciousness: a narrow setting of the filter would coincide with a highly focused state of attention. This model suggests an anatomical location for consciousness through which the information or representations flow. The same information passes into and out of consciousness as it passes through the filter. Information outside the filter is never conscious.

The third theory of the relationship between consciousness and the brain holds that the difference between conscious and unconscious correlates of brain function resides in the representations themselves. I have called this theory the *dual aspect theory* since it resembles in some respects the classic theory originally proposed by Descartes and suffers from some of the same difficulties.

Descartes' notion was that there are two fundamentally different types of process underlying behaviour and these operate on very different principles. One process was mechanical in nature and explicable in principle according to purely mechanical laws. These reflex processes were similar to those which operated the hydraulic statues in the royal garden. These statues were normally hidden but were activated by valves strategically placed under the pathways. Unsuspecting visitors were confronted with these 'reflex-activated' creatures while walking around the gardens and marvelled at their intelligent behaviour. By analogy, Descartes argued that the intelligent behaviour of animals, and at least in part of humans, might also be attributable to reflexes.

In contrast, a second system which he called the soul operated on different principles and was responsible for the non-reflexive aspects of behaviour. To this second system Descartes attributed the properties of thought, originality and the self-referential aspects of language. Since he could not imagine any mechanical device which could accomplish these feats, he assumed that this second system was non-material. In these days of intelligent machines, however, no such difficulties would arise. I would imagine that if he were alive today Descartes would be happy with two material systems.

The dualist model, then, views the conscious aspects of the brain as consisting of different entities and operating on different principles from the rest of the brain. The big problem for this theory is how these different systems interact. Two solutions have been proposed: one envisages a transducer, which converts an activity in one system into a form suitable for use in the other; the other postulates an inductive process, where activity in one system indirectly influences activity in the other by some process which does not involve the direct transfer of substance. The transducer model specifies an anatomical location for the point of contact between the two systems, but this is not necessary for the induction model. Descartes' theory appears to be a combination of the two. He thought that the soul and the reflex mechanical system interacted at the pineal gland but that there was no actual interchange of substance between the two. Either system could cause slight movements of the gland which would influence the other. In the case of the mechanical reflex system this influence would be exerted by slightly deflecting the animal spirits into different brain pores where they would produce a different action. The organization of the soul was not specified, nor was the way in which movement of the pineal gland affected it.

A version of Cartesian dualism which relies on something like induction seems to be advocated by Eccles (1980). He argues that consciousness is non-material but interacts with the neocortex to integrate its activity and to reinforce the activity of certain areas as against others – a sort of invisible searchlight. On the face of it there seems no reason to suppose *a priori* that the two systems might not both be material but operate on such different principles that a transducer or inducer was necessary for them to interact.

The theory espoused in this article has elements of each of the three theories, and has five major assumptions. (1) It starts from the Cartesian dualist view that there are two major brain systems, which represent information in different ways and which operate according to different principles. (2) Communication between these two systems takes place via a set of neural structures which act as interfaces, each transforming information coming from one system into a form suitable for the other. Candidates for these interface systems are the septo-hippocampal system, the amygdala and the striatum. (3) Consciousness is identified with the operation of one of these interfaces, the septo-hippocampal system. (4) The theory takes from the searchlight theory the notion that consciousness is to be equated with a particular type of activation of the neurones in the system, in this case the theta mode (slow rhythmical activity ranging from 4 to 12 Hz). (5) Finally, since one of the functions of the theta system appears to be the selection and organization of information, the theory shares certain affinities with the filter theory as well.

The two major brain systems are the phylogenetically older brainstem core (in which I include the hypothalamus) and the more recently developed neocortex. An important assumption of the present theory is that these two systems of the brain operate on fundamentally different principles.

The models generated by the brainstem operate on the assumption that changes in the environment take place in a continuous cyclic fashion. The most common model for these processes is a sinusoid, whose period approximates that of the process modelled. The most obvious regularity modelled in this way is the circadian rhythm of the sun. In animals such as the rat many behaviours are time-locked to particular phases of this rhythm. For example, motor activity, eating, drinking, body temperature, and corticosteroid secretion are all synchronized to this cycle (see Rusak and Zucker, 1979, and Zucker, 1983, for reviews). Female sexual behaviour in the rat is strongly cyclic, with a period approximately four times that of the diurnal cycle (Zucker, 1983), and is presumed to be dependent on the same internal clock.

Even circannual behaviours such as hibernation and migration may be indirectly dependent on circadian rhythms. Experiments by Meier and his colleagues (summarized in Meier and Fivizzani, 1980) suggest that both the behavioural and physiological changes occurring during migration, in animals as diverse as the white-throated swallow and the gulf killifish, are controlled by the phase relationships between two independent hormonal rhythms. In both animals the release of the hormones prolactin and corticosterone varies with a daily rhythm, and the relative timing of these two rhythms determines the animal's responsiveness to the amount of daylight. In the spring, when the peak release of the two hormones occurs twelve hours apart, the conditions associated with spring migration are induced: fattening, increased gonadal weights and migratory restlessness in a northerly direction. During the summer there is an eight hour separation between hormonal peaks, an inhibition of fat stores and decreased gonadal weights (the post-migratory phase). Finally, during the autumn the phase lag between the two rhythms is only four hours, and the conditions associated with autumnal migration (fattening, absence of gonadal growth, orientation in a southerly direction) prevail. These effects were observed both during the normal circannual cycle and when the hormones were injected with the appropriate time intervals. The primary difference between the fish and the bird is that the rhythms of the former are more dependent on temperature than are those of the latter.

The most likely neural location for these rhythmical models of the environment is the hypothalamus. Lesions of the suprachiasmatic nucleus disrupt many of these circadian rhythms, including locomotor activity and drinking (Stephan and Zucker, 1972), corticosteroid hormone release (Moore and Eichler, 1972), body temperature, and sleep/wakefulness cycles (see Rusak and Zucker, 1979, and Zucker, 1983, for reviews). One intriguing possibility that has not been properly explored is that some of the effects of hypothalamic lesions may be due to the disruption of the *interaction* between different circadian rhythms. For example, the restlessness and fattening of the ventromedial hypothalamic syndrome may point to a role for the VMH in migration and hibernation (see Mrosovsky, 1971) rather than to a role in the control of food intake *per se*. The hypothalamus may be the locus for the interaction of different oscillators (as in the corticosteroid/prolactin involvement in migration) as well as for parts of the oscillators themselves.

The second way in which the brain models the environment can be characterized as discrete, individuated and non-recurrent. Whereas the brainstem is concerned with smoothly changing repetitive inputs and outputs, this system is interested in abrupt transitions in the sensory array and discrete movements of individual body parts, and embodies a linear non-repetitive principle of time. The primary location for this more recently evolved system is the neocortex.

Recent ideas about the anatomical organization of the posterior neocortex in different mammals suggests that it consists of a set of discrete, relatively independent modules, each of which receives its own thalamic input and each of which is involved in the analysis of a different aspect of the sensory array (Zeki, 1978; Merzenich and Kaas, 1980; Diamond, 1979). In the visual domain, cortical area VI may provide the information about oriented lines (Hubel and Wiesel, 1963) required for the identification of corners and edges and an important feature in the recognition of objects (Marr, 1982), while other areas may create the notion of colour (Zeki, 1978). Although it has often been assumed that neocortical function is primarily involved in higher psychological processes, such as memory and cognition, some of the behavioural deficits following decortication do not support this view. For example, decorticate rats have difficulty in sticking out their tongues to obtain food, although they have no problem licking and eating food placed in their mouths (Whishaw and Kolb, 1983). They also fail to manicure their toenails properly

(Whishaw, Kolb, Sutherland and Becker, 1983). These deficits suggest that if there is a common function for the neocortex, it cannot adequately be described as cognitive. Rather it would appear to have something to do with the segmentation of input or output into individual entities: the identification of a sharp boundary in the sensory array, the isolation of a foreground object from the background, the subdivision of the world into visual edges, discrete sounds located in specific places, words, objects. On the output side, the neocortex is concerned with the movement of individual limbs or digits, the manicuring of an individual toe nail, the generation of a non-repetitive sequence of movements.

One of the major problems which the vertebrate brain has to solve, then, is communication between these two different systems. How does a system which models the physical world in terms of discrete entities with sharp edges, interact with a system which is designed to ignore sharp transitions and to assume that variables change in continuous analogue fashion? How does the neocortical information that there is an edge at a particular position of the visual array guide the subcortical cyclic pattern generator underlying walking? Conversely, how does the activation of such a pattern generator enable the neocortical system to predict the occurrence of a sound coming from a particular ego-centric direction?

The answer, I propose, is a set of interfaces designed to translate information from one format into the other. These interfaces are the hippocampus, the amygdala, and perhaps the striatum. In this paper I will concentrate on the hippocampus and its relation to consciousness. It is not obvious to me that the amygdala and the striatum are related to consciousness, but I do not wish to rule out that possibility.

The cognitive map theory of hippocampal function

Nadel and I (O'Keefe and Nadel, 1978) have proposed that the hippocampus acts as a cognitive mapping system, which identifies different environments and locates the animal's position within those environments. Furthermore the system encodes the location of objects in an environment. The construction of maps appears to take place on the basis of exploration, a cognitive motivation generated by mismatches between the information contained in the current map of an environment and the sensory information sent to the mapping system at that time. In our previous work Nadel and I proposed a model of the

hippocampal mapping system which was consonant with our understanding of the anatomy and physiology of the hippocampus. In this
article I would like briefly to sketch my latest ideas for a model of the
mapping system. In particular I will emphasize those aspects of the
model which relate to the functions of consciousness.

Several recent findings suggest that information about an environment is stored in the hippocampus in a manner similar to that used in
optical holography. In this section I will give an outline of these principles, and point out the parallels with hippocampal physiology. (A
simple introduction to the construction of holograms is the classic
Scientific American article by Leith and Upatnieks (1965); a more
technical summary of recent developments is the book by Abramson
(1981).)

Holographic representations differ from ordinary photographic
pictures in several ways. Perhaps the most important of these is that
they do not represent an object in a topographic manner. In the
normal photographic process the light waves reflected from a point on
an object are focused onto a point on the recording medium. Thus the
image stored is a topographic point-to-point representation of the
physical object in two dimensions. In contrast, the holographic technique does not attempt to reproduce the image of the object on the
recording medium. Instead the wave patterns reflected from an object
are recorded outside of the focal plane, at a point where the light waves
reflected from many points on the object are mixed-up with each
other. The resultant image on the recording medium does not represent the object in a topographic way but contains the information by
which the object can be reconstructed. The information is contained in
the form of interference fringes, whose contrast and spacing code the
interaction of the light waves from the various points on the physical
object. The interaction of the waves depends on their relative ampli-
tudes and phases. Since the recording material cannot directly retain
information about the temporal phase relations of the waves, this is
done indirectly by interfering the reflected light with a reference light
of known amplitude and phase from a laser. Where the reflected waves
are in phase with the reference wave there will be bright fringes, where
they are out of phase they will cancel and there will be dark ones. Thus
the holographic image contains both the amplitude and phase information necessary to reconstruct the original scene.

Reconstruction of the scene is accomplished by illuminating the
hologram with the same frequency monochromatic reference wave as

was used to construct it in the first place. The light waves captured by the hologram continue on their way with little sign that they have been interrupted. The original scene can be reconstructed by a suitable lens system. There are several aspects of this information storage process which I think might find parallels in the physiology of the hippocampus. The information about a part of the physical scene is not concentrated at one point in the recording medium but is spread across the entire record. Conversely, the information to reconstruct the entire scene is contained in each small portion of the hologram. Illumination of that small portion with the reference beam does reconstruct the entire scene but it is poorly resolved. Increasing the area of the hologram that is illuminated increases the resolution of the reconstructed scene but decreases the depth of field. When a large area is illuminated only the objects or parts of objects at the same depth are in focus. Change in the lens focus can also move different objects in and out of focus. Movement of the lens in a plane parallel to the plane of the hologram produces parallax effects enabling one to look around the sides of objects in the foreground. If a hologram is constructed with waves of one length, and reconstructed with waves of a longer length, the image will be magnified. This was in fact the original goal of the inventor of the hologram, Dennis Gabor (1949).

Several scenes can be independently stored on the same holographic plate, using two different techniques. In the first, two scenes are illuminated with laser lights of different wavelengths, and these different wavelengths are used to retrieve the different scenes. In the second method the angle between the wave patterns from the reference beam and those reflected from the scene are changed for the two scenes. In this latter case the different scenes are separated at the reconstruction stage by viewing the hologram from a different angle.

More recently holographic techniques have been used to measure slight movements of one of the objects in a scene, or the deformation of parts of an object. If the same scene is photographed twice on the same hologram, before and after a small movement of an object, the reconstructed picture shows the object covered with fringes, which can be related to the amount and direction of displacement.

These properties of holograms have striking counterparts in the physiology of the hippocampus. Some of these have previously been pointed out by Landfield (1976), who to my knowledge was the first to suggest an analogy between hippocampal physiology and holograms, although not in the context of the cognitive map theory.

Nadel and I have suggested that the hippocampus is the centre of a brain system which acts as a spatial map (O'Keefe and Nadel, 1978). The theory was designed to account for two domains of experimental data. We wished, on the one hand, to suggest functions for some of the important anatomical and physiological features of the hippo-campal system while, on the other, to explain the effects of lesions of the hippocampal system on animals' behaviour. In the next sections, I will briefly summarize the main points of the theory. Readers interested in more details should consult O'Keefe and Nadel (1978).

The hippocampal system appears to consist of three sheets of iden-tical cells, the granule cells of the fascia dentata and the pyramidal cells of CA3 and CA1 (Figure 3.1). Within each sheet the cells appear to be highly interconnected in a random net-like fashion (Braitenberg and Schüz, 1983). Between sheets, connections take place in a highly

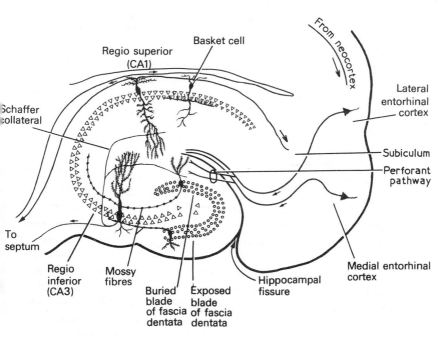

Fig. 3.1 Schematic diagram of the internal hippocampal connections. The section is in a horizontal plane through the right hippocampus. The small circles represent the cell bodies of the dentate granule neurones; the triangles represent the cell bodies of the pyramidal neurones. (Modified from O'Keefe and Nadel, 1978.)

organized fashion, dividing the hippocampus into a set of lamellae (Andersen, Bliss and Skrede, 1971). Thus the upper layers of the entorhinal cortex pick up sensory information from widely diverging areas and project it onto the granule cells of the fascia dentata; these in turn project to the next sheet of cells in the CA3 field, and these in their turn to the CA1 field. Interestingly, one of the ultimate target areas of the final stages in this hippocampal circuit are the deeper layers of the entorhinal cortex itself, the original source of the sensory information to the circuit. As seen from the point of view of the entorhinal cortex, the whole complex hippocampal circuit is a long detour for information travelling from the upper to the lower layers of the entorhinal cortex.

The business of this circuit seems to be the construction and manipulation of information about the animal's location in an environment. Information about the function of a circuit can be obtained from an examination of the behavioural or psychological correlates of the neurones in that circuit. In the hippocampus of the freely moving rat two types of neurone have been distinguished: the place cell and the theta cell (Ranck, 1973; O'Keefe, 1976). The most prevalent type of cell found in the hippocampus proper (fields CA1–4) of the rat is the place cell (Kubie and Ranck, 1983; O'Keefe, 1976; Olton, Best and Branch, 1978; see O'Keefe, 1979 for a review). These neurones fire maximally when the animal is in a particular part of a familiar environment. Figure 3.2 shows a picture of the field of one of these neurones. The activity of the neurone, together with the position of the rat, was recorded for twenty-five minutes while the rat was gently coaxed around a small (40 cm × 40 cm) platform. The figure shows the places where the firing rate exceeded three arbitrarily selected levels. It is clear that the cell fires maximally along one edge of the platform and that the rate falls off as the animal moves away from this area. Interestingly, the place field does not end abruptly but gradually declines at the edges. Other place cells would be active in other parts of the platform. Some would have larger fields while others would only be interested in minute areas of environment, for example when the rat poked its nose into one of the corners. Taken together these fields would cover the entire area of the platform and appropriately linked together they would form a map of the area.

These place cells are not simply sensory cells, responding to particular smells or sights. For example, if one rotates the platform through 180 degrees almost all of these neurones continue to fire in

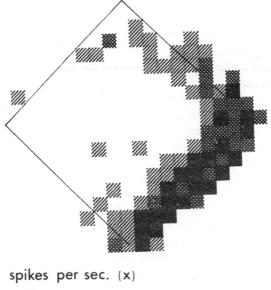

spikes per sec. (x)

■   x > 3·5

▦   2·1 < x ≤ 3·5

▨   0·4 < x ≤ 2·1

Fig. 3.2 The firing rate of a CA1 place cell while the rat was on a small elevated platform. The firing rates in each small square are classified into one of three levels and shaded appropriately. Areas with a rate less than 0.4 spikes/sec. are left blank. The cell fired when the animal was along the south-east edge of the platform. (Modified from O'Keefe, 1983.)

the part of the platform as defined by the distant room cues (see also Olton *et al.*, 1978). Similarly, turning out the lights usually does not markedly affect the field of the neurone. This finding, taken together with the fact that many of these neurones will become active regardless of the direction in which the animal is facing within the place field, indicates that the neurones are not responding to specific visual inputs alone, as these would very likely be effective only when they fell upon a small portion of the retina. In a formal test of the multi-modal nature of the sensory convergence on these place cells, Conway and I showed that some of them could identify the appropriate part of an environment when only two of the normal four cues were available. For example, if the rat was originally trained in an environment where the cues for location were a fan, a light, a white card and a buzzer, the neurone continued to identify the appropriate field when only two of the cues were present (O'Keefe and Conway, 1978). This suggests that these cells receive information from many sensory modalities and can identify places in an environment on the basis of portions of the total information. In addition to place cells, 'misplace' cells have been identified which increase their rate of firing when the animal encounters a change in a previously explored environment. This increase in firing might result, for example, from the presence of a novel object or the absence of a familiar one, and would lead to renewed exploration.

Attempts to gain an idea of the way in which an environment is represented in the hippocampus strongly suggest the absence of any topographic isomorphism between the map and the environment. For example, cells recorded next to each other in the CA1 pyramidal layer are as likely to have their major fields in different parts of the environment as in neighbouring parts. Furthermore, it appears that a small cluster of neighbouring pyramidal cells would map, albeit crudely, the entire environment. This observation, taken together with the ease that many experimenters have had in finding place cells with arbitrarily located electrodes in the hippocampus, suggests that each environment is represented many times over in the hippocampus, in a manner similar to a holographic plate. In both representational systems the effect of increasing the area of the storage which is activated is to increase the definition of the representation.

A second major similarity between the way in which information can be stored on a holographic plate and the way environments can be represented in the hippocampus is that the same hippocampal cells can participate in the representation of several environments (O'Keefe and Conway, 1978; Kubie and Ranck, 1983). In the Kubie and Ranck study the same place cell was recorded from the hippocampus of female rats in three different environments: an 8-arm radial maze, in which the animal was trained to retrieve pellets from each of the 8 arms without returning to a previously visited arm; an operant chamber, in which the animal was trained on a DRL 20 schedule; and a home box, where the female built a nest for herself and a litter of suckling pups. Each of the 28 non-theta cells had a place field in at least one of the environments, and 12 had a field in all three environments. The elevated radial arm maze enjoyed the greatest representation of cells with place fields (23 of 28), in contrast to the enclosed home box (17 of 28), and the operant chamber (15 of 28). There was no systematic relationship amongst the fields of the same neurone in the different environments. One can conclude that each hippocampal place cell can enter into the representation of a large number of environments, and conversely, that the representation of any given environment is dependent on the activity of a reasonably large group of place neurones.

The third major similarity between the holographic recording technique and the construction of environmental maps in the hippocampus is the use of interference patterns between sinusoidal waves to determine the pattern of activity in the recording substrate (see Landfield, 1976). In optical holography this is done by splitting a beam of monochromatic light into two, reflecting one beam off the scene to be encoded and then interacting the two beams at the plane of the substrate (see p. 77). In the hippocampus something similar might be happening. (There follows a detailed account of the anatomical pathways which form the basis of the putative hippocampal holographic system. Some readers may prefer to go straight to the final paragraph of this section (p. 88) for a summary of the anatomical arguments before continuing with the next section.)

The beams are formed by the activity in the fibres projecting to the hippocampus from the medial septal nucleus (MS) and the nucleus of the diagonal band of Broca (DBB).

Anatomical studies indicate that the projections of these nuclei are extensive, and include not only the hippocampus proper and the fascia dentata but closely related structures, such as the subiculum, parasubiculum and entorhinal cortex, the anterior cingulate cortex and extensive brainstem regions in the lateral hypothalamus and midbrain (Swanson and Cowan, 1979). In this paper I will concentrate on the function of the projections to the hippocampus and immediately adjacent tissues, such as the entorhinal cortex and subiculum, but the mechanisms of information processing suggested may apply to a much larger area of the brain.

Pioneering work by Petsche, Stumpf and their colleagues (Stumpf, 1965) showed that the function of the MS and DBB nuclei was to translate the amount of activity ascending from various brainstem nuclei into a frequency modulated code. Neurones in the MS/DBB complex fire in bursts, with a burst frequency which varies from 4–12 Hz. Increases in the strength of brainstem stimulation produce increases in the frequency of the bursts but not necessarily in the number of spikes within each burst (Petsche, Gogolak and van Zweiten, 1965). It is now widely accepted that this bursting activity in the MS/DBB is responsible for the synchronization of the hippocampal theta rhythm.

Much of the information about this EEG pattern and its relationship to cellular activity, on the one hand, and the animal's psychological and behavioural processes, on the other, has been set out in detail elsewhere (O'Keefe and Nadel, 1978, pp. 141–80; Gray, 1982, pp. 77–101; 184–95). In this article I will summarize only those aspects which are relevant to my claim that the neural system which generates hippocampal theta may be related to the neural substrate for consciousness.

The first relevant piece of information is that the theta mechanism acts to 'gate' the firing of cells in the hippocampus. Examination of the firing patterns of both the theta cells and the place cells shows that they exhibit considerable phase-locking to the EEG theta rhythm. The primary difference between the two classes of neurone is that the theta cells will fire in this pattern whenever the theta rhythm occurs, regardless of the animal's position in the environment (Figure 3.3). The place cell, on the other hand, will only become synchronized to the theta pattern when the animal is in the place field of that neurone.

Ranck, Fox and their colleagues have been studying the relationship between hippocampal theta and the firing patterns of the two cell types in a careful systematic way. They find that all cell types in the hippocampus tend to fire at a particular phase of the theta cycle (although not necessarily the same phase), and that the excitability of these cells (the ease with which they can be activated by an afferent input) also varies with the theta cycle. The theta mechanism then, acts as a gate which defines the point in time during which an input to the cell can activate that cell (Fox, Wolfson and Ranck, 1983).

The second important piece of information about the theta mechanism stems from the work of Vanderwolf, Whishaw, Robinson and their colleagues. They have suggested that there are two different theta systems, which relate to different aspects of the animal's behaviour and which are sensitive to different drugs. The first theta occurs when an animal runs, swims, sniffs, rears, or otherwise explores its environment; the second theta occurs during the same behaviours and, in addition, in response to arousing or alerting stimuli in an animal such as the rabbit, but under less clearly defined circumstances in the rat. For convenience I will refer to this second theta

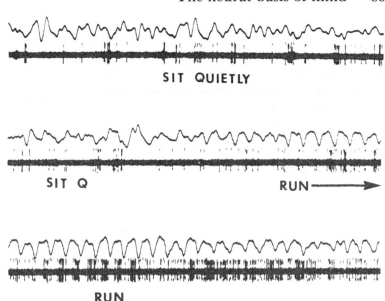

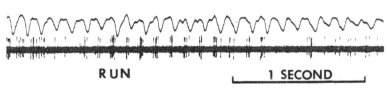

Fig. 3.3   Hippocampal EEG (top trace) and the activity of a theta cell from the same microelectrode (lower trace). The EEG shows the theta pattern and the theta unit fires in a phase-locked bursting pattern when the rat runs. (From O'Keefe and Nadel, 1978.)

system as the non-movement theta system. The best evidence for the existence of two independent thetas is that certain drugs and/or lesions selectively affect one or the other system. For instance, atropine, which blocks muscarinic cholinergic synapses, eliminates the non-movement theta but seems not to affect the movement-related theta (Vanderwolf, 1975). Conversely, the anaesthetic urethane blocks the movement-related theta but leaves an anaesthetized animal with non-movement hippocampal theta, which can be blocked by atropine. More recently Vanderwolf and Leung (1983) have shown that the system which generates movement-related theta probably enters the hippocampus through the entorhinal cortex, since lesions of this area leave only atropine-sensitive theta.

Although the evidence is not very strong yet, there is some indication that the two theta systems have different distributions within the hippocampus and that they might have slightly differing frequencies. For example, following entorhinal cortical lesions theta activity could no longer be recorded dorsal to the CA1 field of the hippocampus, and the theta recorded in the dentate gyrus during movement was slightly (but not significantly) slower in frequency. On the basis of extensive studies of single unit and EEG activity in the hippocampus of freely moving rats, Buzsaki, Leung and Vanderwolf (1983) have suggested that the theta pattern is generated by two different inputs: one input comes from the entorhinal cortex onto the dendrites of the CA1 pyramidal cells and the dentate granule cells, and a second input arrives at the somas of these cells via inhibitory interneurones. The effect of this circuitry would be to produce an interaction of the two theta systems on each cell.

If there are two independent theta mechanisms, and they each act as gates which determine the time period when afferents to a section of the hippocampus can activate the cells in that section, then the simultaneous operation of these two systems would act as a kind of logical AND gate, whose properties depended on the interactions between the two systems. Only when the two theta waves had the correct phase relationship would a particular set of afferents have preferential access to a particular cell. Following Landfield, I suggest that the direct non-movement theta input acts as a reference beam, while the indirect (via the entorhinal cortex) movement-related theta acts as a reflected beam, i.e. as a carrier signal, which has superimposed on it the amplitude and phase relations representing the sensory information in the entorhinal cortex. One problem with theta as a wave carrier is its low frequency and consequent low information capacity. It should be noted, however, that it is not the theta wave itself that is being suggested as the carrier but the activity in the individual theta cells. Another unexplored possibility is that the carrier is the higher frequency 'ripples' (80–120 Hz) which have been described in the hippocampus (O'Keefe and Nadel, 1978, 150–3).

The role of the reference wave is to maintain the phase relations between the activity of different parts of the hippocampus with each other and with other parts of the brain. It acts to keep anatomically distant areas in synchrony. It is also important to note that in the present model subcortically generated theta is not invariant over time but is modulated by activity within subcortical regions. In this way it introduces information based on subcortical analog processing into the hippocampal circuitry. Theta thus serves as a source of rhythmic activity, forming the reference and reflected waves, and as an information input channel in its own right.

On this model, the features of the environment impinging upon the animal at a particular environmental position are represented in the entorhinal cortex. Features in the neocortex are stored in spatially distinct anatomical loci and it is reasonable to assume that the projections of these features onto the entorhinal cortex preserves this discrete spatial form. The projection from the entorhinal cortex comes from layers 2 and 3 (Steward and Scoville, 1976). These are the layers which contain theta cells, according to Mitchell and Ranck (1980). It seems reasonable to assume that the cells of projection through the perforant path are theta cells and the information that they carry is contained in the amplitude modulation of the theta waves projected on the dentate granule cells. Rose has recently proposed that the granule cells are theta cells (Rose, 1983).

The interference patterns (which record the relative phases of the theta wavefronts) would be formed either in the dentate granule cells or in the CA3/4 pyramids by the interaction of the direct theta projection from the MS/DBB with the reflected wave pattern from the entorhinal cortex. There is a major anatomical projection from the CA3 pyramids to the CA1 field via the Schaffer collaterals, and from the CA1 field to the subiculum and thence to the entorhinal cortex (cf. Figure 3.1). These additional areas are probably used for comparing the current image of the environment with that stored in the preceding areas. Recall that in holography the effect of movement of an object relative to others is to produce an interference pattern superimposed on the image of that object when the two holographic images are superimposed and focused to produce a point-to-point photographic image. Perhaps some such comparative mechanism as this is being reflected in the increased firing of the misplace cells following a change in a familiar environment (see O'Keefe, 1976). The CA1 field is also probably where the maps are manipulated. Preliminary evidence from our laboratory strongly suggests that maps can be rotated to bring them into register with the current environment (O'Keefe, 1983). Although it is not clear how this could be accomplished, it might involve a global transform on the representation of the environment, rather than a piecemeal breaking and making of individual nerve connections.

As an interface between the neocortex, which stores information in discrete categories, and the brainstem, which operates on the basis of continuous analog models, the hippocampus not only combines information from both but projects to and influences both. The projection from CA3, and to a lesser extent CA1, onto the hypothalamus via the lateral septum must be the primary path by which the hippocampus controls the brainstem, although the direct pathway from the subiculum to the mammillary bodies (Swanson and Cowan, 1975) might also be involved. The projection from CA1 to the subiculum and thence to the parahippocampal cortex and other neocortical areas (Van Hoesen, 1982) must be the pathway for the display of the hippocampal image on the neocortex. It is quite likely that the hippocampal representation of an environment needs to be transformed in different ways to interact with the neocortex and the brainstem. Interposed in the pathway to the neocortex there would have to be the neural equivalent of a lens system, to transform the holographic representation into an isomorphic image appropriate to the neocortical form of representation. A different type of transform would be necessary to interact with brainstem structures. It is unfortunate that we have virtually no detailed information about the behavioural correlates of lateral septal, subicular, or entorhinal cortical neurones.

Hippocampal cells appear to code for places in an environment regardless of whether an animal is using a place hypothesis or not. Place cells have been recorded in studies where no task has been deliberately taught (e.g. as the rat was gently coaxed around the small platform shown in Figure 3.3), in studies where place strategies were irrelevant (e.g. on the forced choice radial arm maze used by McNaughton, Barnes and O'Keefe, 1983), in studies where place strategies may have been used (e.g. the cue-controlled environment of O'Keefe and Conway, 1978, and the free choice radial arm maze used by Olton et al., 1978, and Kubie and Ranck, 1983), and in studies where place hypotheses were definitely being used (the cue-controlled environment memory studies described by O'Keefe and Conway, 1980, and O'Keefe, 1983). No studies have been done yet to assess whether there are any differences between the place fields where the animal is using a place hypothesis and the place fields where it is not.

In summary then, it has been suggested that the known anatomy and physiology of the hippocampal complex can be described by an analogy to photographic holography in the following way: a common source of theta activity deriving from brainstem nuclei is passed via the diagonal band of Broca and the medial septal nucleus towards the hippocampal complex. In addition to being a source of rhythmic activity, the theta wave incorporates information derived from processing which is taking place in subcortical sites. Part of the rhythmic input (so-called non-movement theta) serves as a reference beam and goes directly to the hippocampus. The remainder of the input (movement-related theta) is projected as the carrier beam to the more superficial layers of entorhinal cortex where it can be influenced by information arriving from neocortex, before being reflected back to the hippocampus. The two beams interact in the hippocampus to form a 'holographic' image of the neocortically derived information in the dentate granule cells or cells of CA3. Holographic maps formed in this way are projected to area CA1 for storage, comparison and manipulation. Suitably transformed versions of the information contained in the hippocampal holograms can then be projected back, either to neocortex via subiculum and the deeper layers of entorhinal cortex, or to subcortical sites via the lateral septum and hypothalamus. (A second route for subcortical projection has also been suggested, passing from CA1 via subiculum to the mammillary bodies.) A system of this sort would not only give an account of the formation and storage of multi-modality cognitive maps in the hippocampus but would identify the hippocampal complex as the interface for information deriving from, and passing to, neocortical (discrete, categorical) systems on the one hand, and subcortical (analog) systems on the other.

Consciousness and the hippocampal cognitive map

I am now in a position to propose a biological theory of consciousness. According to this theory, *consciousness is identified with the activation of the theta system, which organizes the neocortical and entorhinal inputs into the hippocampus and which synchronizes all three structures for the construction, correction and manipulation of maps of the environment.* On this model, consciousness is equated with a particular type of activity, in several forebrain structures, at the same time. The different properties of consciousness discussed earlier (pp. 64–71) are identified with the following aspects of this theta activation.

(1) The unified and holistic nature of consciousness is identified with two aspects of the system: (a) the distributed nature of each map

in the hippocampus such that the entire environment is represented at the same time across the whole surface, and (b) the participation of each hippocampal neurone in numerous environments. These two properties mean that the hippocampus acts as the unifying container for all environmental representations and provides continuity from one representation to the next. Since the entire system is used in an integrated fashion for each representation it is not possible to maintain two different representations in an active state at the same time, as would be possible in a system in which different representations were located in different anatomical regions (e.g. the neocortex acting on its own).

It is not clear that the rat hippocampus incorporates a temporal dimension but at some stage in evolution such a dimension was added to the map. This might have involved an ordered list of all changes occurring in each map. Such an addition would increase the unity of the mapping system since search for items could be based on temporal relations between maps as well as on spatial relations within maps.

(2) The contents of consciousness are multi-modal because it is the function of the hippocampus to integrate sensory information from the different modality-specific sensory areas of the neocortex into a multi-modal place representation.

Normal activation of the neocortical-hippocampal system provides the contents of the background fringe of consciousness, while the foreground, or selective attention component, is generated by mismatch signals produced in the hippocampus.

The two modes of controlling consciousness (internal and external) are mirrored by the two modes of activating the theta mechanisms, one driven from the brainstem and the other from the hippocampus itself. The input from the brainstem directs the theta on the basis of problems external to the mapping system. The second source of theta is the output of the misplace system in the hippocampus itself. On receipt of an unexpected sensory input, the misplace system generates a mismatch signal, which drives the exploratory system and produces behaviour designed to evaluate the mismatch and, if necessary, change the representation to incorporate the novel input. A more sophisticated type of mismatch occurs when an animal first enters an environment and searches its hippocampus for an extant map which fits the incoming sensory data. This process appears to involve both the retrieval and manipulation of maps, in an attempt to get them to 'fit the data'. This matching procedure may involve 'rotations' and other types of manipulations such as scaling (Kubie, Muller and Ranck, 1983). The identification of attention, or the foreground component of consciousness, with the mismatch signal explains why it is difficult to attend to any particular item in consciousness for very long: as it becomes incorporated into the current map, the mismatch signal is reduced or removed.

The second source for selective activation of part of a map comes from outside the hippocampal system. Circuits external to the system can selectively activate a neocortical representation and probe a particular map with this input. This probe will activate all of the locations of this representation within the map. In the rat this type of activation might be used when the animal wants to find food in a particular environment. There is however no direct evidence on this point.

(3) Consciousness, on this model, is related to access to long-term narrative memory because such memories are stored in the hippocampal complex, and theta is the system which allows information access to it and organizes and codes the information in an appropriate form. There is evidence that some hippocampal place cells modify their activity during a spatial memory task (O'Keefe, 1983).

(4) The need for conscious involvement in some behaviours and not others derives from the fact that the same problem can be solved by means of several different hypotheses, some dependent on the hippocampus, others not. Thus the model sees the transition from conscious to unconscious control of behaviour as a switch from hippocampal to non-hippocampal control of the motor system. We have suggested that the same task, e.g. moving between two fixed points in an environment, can often be accomplished by non-place as well as place strategies. Initial learning is often controlled by the mapping system, with its rapid incorporation of environmental information and flexible control of the motor system. After criterion, control is ceded to the less flexible orientation system with the resultant rigidity of behaviour. This account is supported by: (a) evidence from the studies of Hicks (1964) and Mackintosh (1965) which showed a switch from place to response strategies with overtraining on a T-maze; (b) the evidence from our own studies that both the place and orientation hypotheses can co-operate (or compete) for the control of the animal's motor behaviour (O'Keefe, 1983). Notice that the hippocampus continues to monitor the environment during behaviours which are under the control of a non-place hypothesis and can override this

control upon receipt of unexpected sensory input. The analogue with the interruption of automatic control of motor car driving, when a deviation from environmental regularity or an unanticipated event occurs, is obvious.

(5) Several aspects of human consciousness do not seem, at first glance, to be easily accommodated within this scheme. The most obvious are those contents of consciousness which are not spatial: awareness of internal body states, linguistic entities and self-awareness.

Nadel and I (O'Keefe and Nadel, 1978) have suggested that a major change in the functioning of the human hippocampal system from that of the infrahuman one is due to the development of language. Whereas both infrahuman hippocampi are wholly dedicated to the construction of maps of the physical environment, only the right hippocampus performs this function in the human. Damage to the left hippocampus leads to loss of memory for verbal material. The left hippocampus in humans appears to function as a semantic map for the storage and manipulation of narratives. Narratives are seen as the deep structures underlying stories and consist of linguistic items, i.e. the names for concrete physical entities and abstract entities such as truth, and their spatial, temporal, possessional and circumstantial relationships to each other. Consequently, consciousness is necessary to organize words into narrative structures. Other aspects of language usage, such as the retrieval of meanings from the neocortical lexicon, can take place without conscious involvement.

Another aspect of human consciousness which appears to differ from that of the rat, and which therefore requires an extension of the theory, is self-consciousness. There seems no reason to believe that a rat is aware of itself as a conscious organism, and no evidence from hippocampal studies which would lend itself to this interpretation. In contrast, human conscious experience is that of an awareness that is aware that it is aware. Can the model incorporate this idea?

The solution involves the incorporation of three additional features into our model of the mapping system: agency, self-reference, and the association of internal autonomic stimuli with certain features of the self-representation within the map. The first notion — agency — assumes that one of the ways that the human brain categorizes entities is into those which are self-motivating and those which are not. The latter cannot change their position within a map in the absence of another external cause. Conversely, agents are those entities whose behaviour cannot be understood on the basis of external events alone. Internal events such as thoughts, wants, desires, etc. need to be taken into account as well. The activities of these internal entities and their interrelationships constitute the mind. The second important addition to the mapping system is the notion of the self. This is a representation of one's own body as an object, and underlies the ability to look at oneself as others do. Evidence that chimpanzees and orangutans might have this ability has been provided by the experiments of Gallup (1983). He showed that both of these great apes could recognize themselves in a mirror, as evidenced by the fact that they tried to remove a red spot painted on their foreheads when they saw it in a mirror. Gorillas and monkeys failed to do this, in spite of prolonged exposure to mirrors. According to the present theory the representation of the self in the mapping system would take the form of a third person marker, similar to that used to represent other entities. Furthermore it is likely that this representation would be coded as an agent. Therefore in the same way that the map of an event would include hypotheses about the intentions and motives of other agents, so also would it incorporate hypotheses about the internal processes of the representation of the self. The organism which represents itself as an object can also entertain hypotheses about the causes of its own behaviour (see also chapter 5 of this volume). The way in which subjects attribute causes to their own behaviour and to that of others has been described within the context of social attribution theory (see for example Jones *et al.*, 1971).

The final addition to the mapping system is the introduction of inputs conveying information about the internal autonomic states of the organism and the development of pathways which would enable these to become linked to the representation of self and, in particular, to the representations of the self's internal processes. This suggests that the association of internal stimuli with states of fear, happiness, etc. is a learned one which is derived from the attribution of these states to others (see also chapter 4 of this volume).

This would explain why one can experience fear, hunger, and other bodily states but cannot remember the bodily state − only the fact of having been in that state at a particular time and place. On this model, the association between internal body signals and a particular mental state would not be an invariable one.

Self-consciousness then is the result of the existence of a representation of a conscious entity, which is referred to one's own body, and the association of internal bodily states with certain aspects of the representation of the mental activities of this representation.

Conclusions

Introspection suggests the existence of a brain system which serves to integrate large amounts of multi-modal information into a three-dimensional framework or into a narrative sequence. Within this framework, the focus of attention incessantly shifts from one item to another. Access to long-term narrative memory seems to depend on this system. Only some types of behaviours require conscious involvement.

On the basis of recent findings on the anatomy and physiology of the septo-hippocampal system I suggest that it may operate on principles similar to those of a holographic storage system. The most striking parallels are: (a) information about an environment is stored across the entire surface of the hippocampus, (b) each hippocampal neurone may be involved in the storage of more than one and very probably many environments, and (c) two sinusoidal waves of similar frequency are involved in the storage, retrieval and manipulation of information from the system.

The parallels between some of the characteristics ascribed to human consciousness and the properties of the rat septo-hippocampal system suggest that, with suitable modifications and additions, the latter might act as the neural substrate for the former. Some of the changes necessary would be the development of the notion of agency, the incorporation of a model of the self within the mapping system, and the association of internal somatic stimuli with various aspects of the representation of the self within the map.

Acknowledgements

Research described in this article was supported by the Medical Research Council of Britain. I would like to thank Patrick Wall and David Oakley for comments on a previous version.

References

Able, L. P. (1980) Mechanisms of orientation, navigation and memory. In S. A. Gauthreaux Jr (ed.) *Animal Migration, Orientation, and Navigation*, 283–373. New York: Academic Press.

Abramson, N. (1981) *The Making and Evaluation of Holograms*. London: Academic Press.

Andersen, P., Bliss, T. V. P. and Skrede, K. (1971) Lamellar organization of hippocampal excitatory pathways. *Experimental Brain Research 13*: 222–38.

Barlow, H. B. (1980) Nature's joke: a conjecture on the biological role of consciousness. In B. D. Josephson and V. S. Ramachandran (eds) *Consciousness and the Physical World*. Oxford: Pergamon Press.

Braitenberg, V. and Schüz, A. (1983) Some anatomical comments on the hippocampus. In W. Seifert (ed.) *Neurobiology of the Hippocampus*, 21–37. London: Academic Press.

Broadbent, D. E. (1958) *Perception and Communication*. Oxford: Pergamon Press.

Buzsaki, G., Leung, L-W. S. and Vanderwolf, C. H. (1983) Cellular bases of hippocampal EEG in the behaving rat. *Brain Research Reviews 6*: 139–71.

Delafresnaye, J. F. (ed.) (1954) *Brain Mechanisms and Consciousness*. Oxford: Blackwell.

Diamond, I. T. (1979) The subdivisions of neocortex: a proposal to revise the traditional view of sensory, motor and association areas. *Progress in Psychobiology and Physiological Psychology 8*: 1–43.

Dixon, N. F. (1981) *Preconscious Processing*. Chichester: Wiley.

Eccles, J. C. (1980) *The Human Psyche*. Berlin: Springer International.

Fox, S. E., Wolfson, S. and Ranck, J. B. (1983) Investigating the mechanisms of hippocampal theta rhythms: approaches and progress. In W. Seifert (ed.) *Neurobiology of the Hippocampus*, 303–19. New York: Academic Press.

Gabor, D. (1949) Microscopy by reconstructed wavefronts. *Proceedings of the Royal Society (London), Series A, 197*: 454–87.

Gallup, G. G. (1983) Toward a comparative psychology of mind. In R. L. Mellgren (ed.) *Animal Cognition and Behaviour*. Amsterdam: North Holland Publishing Co.

Gibson, J. J. (1950) *The Perception of the Visual World*. Boston: Houghton Mifflin.

Gray, J. A. (1982) *The Neuropsychology of Anxiety*. Oxford: Clarendon Press.

Hebb, D. O. (1980) *Essay on Mind*. Hillsdale, NJ: Erlbaum.

Hicks, L. H. (1964) Effects of overtraining on acquisition and reversal of place and response learning. *Psychological Reports 15*: 459–62.

Hubel, D. and Wiesel, T. (1962) Receptive fields, binocular interaction, and functional architecture in the cat's visual cortex. *Journal of Physiology 160*: 106–54.

Humphrey, N. K. (1980) Nature's psychologists. In B. D. Josephson and V. S. Ramachandran (eds) *Consciousness and the Physical World*. Oxford: Pergamon Press.

James, W. (1961) *Psychology*. New York: Harper.

Jones, E. E., Kanouse, D. E., Kelley, H. H., Nisbett, R. E., Valins, S. and Weiner, B. (1971) *Attribution: Perceiving the Causes of Behaviour*. New Jersey: General Learning Press.

Kubie, J. L. and Ranck, J. B. (1983) Sensory-behavioural correlates in individual hippocampus neurones in three situations: space and context. In W. Seifert (ed.) *Neurobiology of the Hippocampus*, 433–47. London: Academic Press.

Kubie, J. L., Muller, R. U. and Ranck, J. B. (1983) Manipulations of the geometry of environmental enclosures control the spatial firing patterns of rat hippocampal neurons. *Society for Neuroscience Abstracts 9*: 646.

Lackner, J. R. and Garnett, M. (1973) Resolving ambiguity: effects of biasing context in the unattended ear. *Cognition 1*: 359–72.

Landfield, P. W. (1976) Synchronous EEG rhythms: their nature and their possible functions in memory, information transmission and behaviour. In E. H. Gispen (ed.) *Molecular and Functional Neurobiology*. Amsterdam: Elsevier.

Leith, E. N. and Upatnieks, J. (1965) Photography by Laser. *Scientific American*, June.

Mackintosh, N. J. (1965) Overtraining, transfer to proprioceptive control and position reversal. *Quarterly Journal of Experimental Psychology 17*: 26–36.

McNaughton, B. L., Barnes, C. A. and O'Keefe, J. (1983) The contributions of position, direction and velocity to single unit activity in the hippocampus of freely moving rats. *Experimental Brain Research 52*: 41–9.

Marr, D. (1982) *Vision*. San Francisco: W. H. Freeman.

Meier, A. H. and Fivizzani, A. J. (1980) Physiology of migration. In S. A. Gauthreaux, Jr (ed.) *Animal Migration, Orientation and Navigation*, 225–82. New York: Academic Press.

Merzenich, M. M. and Kaas, J. H. (1980) Principles of organization of sensory-perceptual systems in mammals. *Progress in Psychobiology and Physiological Psychology 9*: 1–42.

Mitchell, S. J. and Ranck, J. B. (1980) Generation of theta rhythm in medial entorhinal cortex of freely moving rats. *Brain Research 189*: 49–66.

Moore, R. Y. and Eichler, V. B. (1972) Loss of a circadian adrenal corticosterone rhythm following supra-chiasmatic lesions in the rat. *Brain Research 42*: 201–6.

Mrosovsky, N. (1971) *Hibernation and the Hypothalamus*. New York: Appleton-Century-Crofts.

O'Keefe, J. (1976) Place units in the hippocampus of the freely moving rat. *Experimental Neurology 51*: 78–109.

O'Keefe, J. (1979) A review of the hippocampal place cells. *Progress in Neurobiology 13*: 419–39.

O'Keefe, J. (1983) Spatial memory within and without the hippocampal system. In W. Seifert (ed.) *Neurobiology of the Hippocampus*, 375–403. London: Academic Press.

O'Keefe, J. and Conway, D. H. (1978) Hippocampal place units in the freely moving rat: why they fire where they fire. *Experimental Brain Research 31*: 573–90.

O'Keefe, J. and Conway, D. H. (1980) On the trail of the hippocampal engram. *Physiological Psychology 8*: 229–38.

O'Keefe, J. and Nadel, L. (1978) *The Hippocampus as a Cognitive Map*. Oxford: Clarendon Press.

Olton, D. S., Branch, M. and Best, P. (1978) Spatial correlates of hippocampal unit activity. *Experimental Neurology 58*: 387–409.

Petsche, H., Gogolak, G. and van Zweiten, P. A. (1965) Rhythmicity of septal cell discharges at various levels of reticular excitation. *Electroencephalography and Clinical Neurophysiology 19*: 25–33.

Ranck, J. B. Jr (1973) Studies on single neurons in dorsal hippocampal formation and septum in unrestrained rats. *Experimental Neurology 41*: 461–555.

Rose, G. (1983) Physiological and behavioural characteristics of dentate granule cells. In W. Seifert (ed.) *Neurobiology of the Hippocampus*, 449–72. London: Academic Press.

Rusak, B. and Zucker, I. (1979) Neural regulation of circadian rhythms. *Physiological Reviews 59*: 449–526.

Shallice, T. (1972) Dual functions of consciousness. *Psychological Review 79*: 383–93.

Spelke, E., Hirst, W. and Neisser, U. (1976) Skills of divided attention. *Cognition 4*: 215–30.

Sperry, R. W. (1952) Neurology and the mind-brain problem. *American Scientist 40*: 291–312.

Stephan, F. K. and Zucker, I. (1972) Circadian rhythms in drinking behaviour and locomotor activity of rats are eliminated by hypothalamic lesions. *Proceedings of the National Academy of Science (USA) 69*: 1583–6.

Steward, O. and Scoville, S. A. (1976) Cells of origin of entorhinal cortical afferents to the hippocampal formation of the rat. *Journal of Comparative Neurology 167*: 285–314.

Stumpf, C. (1965) Drug action on the electrical activity of the hippocampus. *International Review of Neurobiology 8*: 77–138.

Swanson, L. W. and Cowan, W. M. (1975) Hippocampo-hypothalamic connections: origin in subicular cortex, not Ammon's horn. *Science 189*: 303–4.

Swanson, L. W. and Cowan, W. M. (1979) The connections of the septal region in the rat. *Journal of Comparative Neurology 186*: 621–56.

Treisman, A. M. (1964) Selective attention in man. *British Medical Bulletin 20*: 12–16.

Vanderwolf, C. H. (1975) Neocortical and hippocampal activation in relation

98   Brain and Mind

to behaviour: effects of atropine, eserine, phenothiazines, and amphet-amine. *Journal of Comparative and Physiological Psychology 88*: 300–23.

Van Hoesen, G. W. (1982) The parahippocampal gyrus. *Trends in Neuro-science 5*: 345–50.

Whishaw, I. Q. and Kolb, B. (1983) 'Stick out your tongue': tongue pro-trusion in neocortex and hypothalamic damaged rats. *Physiology and Behavior 30*: 471–80.

Whishaw, I. Q., Kolb, B., Sutherland, R. J. and Becker, J. B. (1983) Cortical control of claw cutting in the rat. *Behavioural Neuroscience 97*: 370–80.

Zeki, S. M. (1978) Functional specialization in the visual cortex of the rhesus monkey. *Nature 274*: 423–8.

Zucker, I. (1983) Motivation, biological clocks and temporal organization of behaviour. In Satinoff, E. and Teitelbaum, P. (eds) *Handbook of Behav-ioral Neurobiology: Motivation*, vol. 6, 3–21. New York: Plenum Press.

4 Cognition and imagery in animals

David A. Oakley

Introduction

A convenient point of departure for a consideration of the evidence in
favour of cognition and imagery in animals is the controversy which
existed in learning theory in the 1930s and 1940s. At that time the
view had emerged and, in the interest of scientific respectability for
the new psychology, had gained wide acceptance, that behaviour was
best explained solely in terms of observable stimulus and response
events (see Walker, 1983, chapter 3; Bolles, 1979, chapters 1–6). This
view had developed from Thorndike's earlier crusade to rid comparative psychology not only of the then popular anecdotal approach but
of all appeals to 'mental' processes as explanations of observed behaviour. Instead he proposed an automatic process of 'stamping in' of
reflexive associations between stimuli and responses, on the basis of
the effects which the particular response produced. If the outcome
had been 'satisfying' then the bond between the current stimulus
complex and the successful response was strengthened, making that
response more likely in the same situation on future occasions. This
model of adaptive behavioural change effectively removed the need to
suggest the existence in animals of processes akin to insight, reasoning
or expectancy of outcome. The latter processes, Thorndike suggested,
were the province of primate brains and human brains in particular.
This mechanistic, reflexive view gained enormous credence from the

independent work of Pavlov on classical conditioning, which was not only seductively objective in its methodology but lent itself to a description in reductionistic terms, relating stimuli and responses with no need for an appeal to intervening mentalistic events. This mechanistic approach was finally established as the mainstream of thought in psychology generally by the 'behaviourism' advocated by Watson (1925), and the stimulus-response (S-R) psychology of Hull (1943), which adopted an elaborate mathematico-deductive stance and was intended to encompass human behaviour as well as that of other animals.

It was in this climate of opinion that Tolman (1932) expressed an increasing dissatisfaction with S-R accounts of behaviour. He found the mechanistic, incremental growth of S-R habit strength an unconvincing explanation for the sometimes rapid and apparently insightful behavioural changes he saw, not only in humans, but also in the laboratory rat. Tolman argued that behaviour was 'docile', not rigid and inflexible as S-R theory would seem to imply. What seemed to be 'fixed' was the goal of the animal's behaviour but the means of obtaining that goal were flexible. Tolman believed that his data demanded the assumption that the animal in its commerce with its environment developed representations of that environment, its rewards and its punishments, which intervened between the perception of objects or events and the output of behavioural responses. One of the most basic types of representation perhaps, or at least the simplest to comprehend, is that of the layout of one's environment in the form of a map. Tolman suggested that animals finding their way around their environment behaved as if referring to some centrally located 'cognitive map', often learned in the absence of any external motivation, and did not appear to be slavishly following routes which they had learned by the automatic linking of particular stimuli with particular responses. An early experiment by one of Tolman's students made the last point in an elegantly simple manner (MacFarlane, 1930). Training rats first to swim through a maze for food in a goal box, MacFarlane then drained the maze and observed the behaviour of rats on the first trial in the dry conditions. These animals had little trouble in fact in running directly to the goal box, despite the new response patterns required to do so and a major change in stimulus conditions. An outcome of this sort is difficult to explain in terms of rigid S-R bonds, but is what would be expected if what the rats had learned was the layout of the maze and the fact that food was available at a particular place, and if they had acquired a disposition to get themselves to the goal box in whatever way was available to them at the time.

A somewhat more elaborate, and less easily replicable, experiment by Tolman and Honzik (1930a) indicated not only that the means of achieving a goal might vary, but that rats behave in an insightful fashion in a situation which appears to demand the use of a cognitive map. Rats were first of all allowed to explore three routes leading from a common start point to the same goal box containing food. Route 1 was a short direct pathway to the goal box. Route 2 was a little longer and rejoined route 1 before the goal box was reached. Route 3 was the longest and made an independent entry to the goal box. Once the rats were familiar with the apparatus it was clear that they preferred to run along route 1 to the goal. If, however, they found the initial section of route 1 blocked they selected the next shortest path along route 2. The most interesting question concerns their behaviour if, after running route 1, they find a blockage in the later section, which it shares with route 2. On being forced to retrace straight back to the start point would they choose the next preferred route – route 2 – as S-R habit strength theory would suggest, and so re-encounter the blocked section, or would they choose the longest, least preferred route 3, which was still unblocked? Would they in other words 'know' that route 2 was also blocked? The majority of rats took route 3, suggesting that their central representation of the apparatus was sufficiently accurate as to provide the basis for an 'insightful' solution to the problem. Apparent insight by rats in a similar experimental arrangement has since been demonstrated by Deutsch and Clarkson (1959).

Tolman produced many other demonstrations of behavioural outcomes which were embarrassing to S-R theory and supportive of his own brand of cognitive behaviourism. Hull in particular responded by providing plausible alternative explanations in S-R terms, but only at the expense of introducing 'internal' events in the form of anticipatory goal responses and their concomitant stimuli. Many of Hull's S-R explanations for Tolman's results were ingenious but they became increasingly cumbersome and lost the simple elegance and popular appeal of his earlier statements. Since Tolman's day psychology has seen an increasing acceptance of the possibility that all animals, or at least all mammals, share the capacity to form representations or cognitive maps, and that descriptions of behaviour in these terms are at least as useful as S-R formulations. Even within the writings of authors representing the continuation of the Hullian animal learning theory tradition a cognitive approach is now being actively advocated (see, for example, Dickinson, 1980; Mackintosh, 1984).

Before considering some of the more recent evidence in favour of cognition and imagery in animals, it is necessary to offer some clarification of the way these terms are to be used. I take 'cognition' to refer to the existence and utilization of stored representations of that 'knowledge' which the animal has about its environment, its fellow creatures and about itself. An important aspect of representations or cognitions is that they stand between sensory input and action, and, unlike associations, do not link the two directly. In a sense representations allow the animal to step back from the immediate data and, as Bartlett (1932) suggested, to 'turn around on its schemata'. In well developed representational systems a number of representations may be organized and reorganized in a form of internal experimentation (see Oakley, 1979) providing a safe means of problem solving during a period of behavioural silence. When an animal produces a behavioural act, apparently on the basis of what it recalls of a previously encountered situation, one way of explaining this outcome is to suggest that an image of the original situation has been revived and forms the basis for current action. Beritoff (Beritashvili, 1971), for instance, described experiments in which the animal had to return after a delay to the precise location in a room at which it had previously received food. Correct performance on this test was considered to demonstrate 'image-driven behaviour'. Equally, in more formal delayed response experiments, in which the animal sees, for instance, one of two cups being baited with food and has to wait for a while with both cups hidden before being given the chance to select the baited one, a correct choice could be seen as evidence of the retention and/or retrieval of an appropriate image. Imagery in this sense seems to be coextensive with the process of storing and using representations generally. For most humans the most compelling type of imagery is both visual and conscious.

Imagery may of course involve any or several sensory modalities, and so far as imagery in animals is concerned, we have no direct way of knowing what form of consciousness is involved. In view of the unwanted associations which the term imagery produces I shall avoid it, and refer instead to the use of stored representations. The reader may nevertheless feel that a number of the examples which follow involve processes which are best described as imagery, and it is for this reason that I have retained the term in the title of this chapter. It is also important to point out that a belief in the presence in animals' brains of representations, cognitive maps and the like, need not imply any particular position on the question of consciousness (see chapter 8); it merely refers to a type of information processing where the route from stimulus to response is indirect, via an internal cognitive structure.

What is represented?

(a) Space

An obvious application for representational systems is in modelling an animal's environment and providing a continuous record of its own position within that space, in relation to all its other features. This indeed is the most literal use of a 'cognitive map' in Tolman's terms. We are all familiar with our own, sometimes less than reliable, sense of direction and place, which in a familiar environment does not seem to depend on any one or two familiar landmarks (see Downs and Stea, 1977; Moar and Carleton, 1982), though there is now evidence that at least some of this ability may depend less upon accurate mapping and more, in males at least, on the existence of a magnetic sense (see Baker, 1981). It turns out, however, that the laboratory rat has a superbly developed spatial ability, which a number of recent studies have explored.

A series of experiments deriving from some of Tolman's experiments on place learning has been reported by O'Keefe and his co-workers (see O'Keefe and Nadel, 1978, and chapter 3). In one such experiment rats were trained in a cross-shaped maze which was enclosed in a two-metre square room, with curtain walls on which were hung six distinctive cues, which always bore the same spatial relationship to each other and to the location of a food reward. The food might, for instance, always be at the end of the arm which terminated between a white card and a light bulb. The rat's task was to run to the same food location irrespective of which of the other three arms it was placed in. The majority of rats learned this task very rapidly, and control manipulations indicated that they were basing their performance on the six extra-maze cues, and not on unintended cues either outside the curtained enclosure or within the four-armed maze itself. The most important question now is whether the rats were using a map-like representation or were simply running towards a particular cue, such as the white card, which did not require any sense of location. The fact that, provided some of the original cues remained, any of the other cues could be removed without disturbing performance, suggested that a multi-cue map with high internal redundancy was involved. Even more convincing, however, is that placing all six cues at the end of the goal arm, so giving another set of rats the opportunity to solve the problem exclusively by stimulus approach strategies, seemed to make the task far more difficult, and learning under these conditions was much slower. This suggests that rats are able to scan a familiar environment for a variable subset of cues and then run to a particular place within that environment, and to do this more readily than they will perform the apparently simpler task of moving towards a particular stimulus, or set of stimuli, on each trial. This experiment was also conducted under conditions which required the rat to retain a representation (or image) of its own location in space in relation to the six cues. This was achieved by placing the rat in any of the three non-goal arms and allowing it to survey the six cues around it. The cues were then removed and after a delay the rat was released from its start-arm and had to go to the place which had been identified as the food location during the brief inspection period. Somewhat surprisingly, perhaps, the rats were able to perform accurately on the basis of their spatial memory with delays of up to thirty minutes, and could maintain accuracy even if they were forced to make a surprise detour en route to the goal location.

Olton (1979) has described performance by rats in a radial, eight-arm maze in which each arm is baited with a single food pellet. Rats placed in a maze of this sort rapidly remove all the food, entering arms in an apparently unsystematic order but with very few, if any, re-entries to already visited arms. This performance again appears to depend on a mapping capacity based on extra-maze cues. In a similar way, rats placed in a circular tank of water readily learn the location of a small submerged safe platform even though the platform is painted white and made invisible to the swimming rat by the addition of milk powder to the water (Morris, 1981; Sutherland, Kolb and Whishaw, 1982). The cues used to solve the problem once more appear to be those outside the boundaries of the apparatus itself, as solution requires that these remain in the same relative locations with respect to the platform. Once the rats had learned the location of the platform

from a fixed start point they could immediately swim towards it irrespective of where they were subsequently placed in the tank (Morris,
1981). If the platform were to be moved, rats would be seen searching
diligently in its original location, occasionally squealing and diving
below the surface in the appropriate sector of the tank (Sutherland,
Kolb and Whishaw, 1982). It is possible to argue that the rats in these
studies were performing on an S-R basis and approaching particular
extra-maze cues. Morris (1981) points out, however, that rats have no
difficulty finding the platform from a novel starting position, despite
the fact that the extra-maze cues not only look different but may bear
a different relationship to the goal with reference to the rats' own
bodies. A cue which appeared to the left of the platform from the
original start point, for example, may appear to the right of the goal
from a new start point. He concludes that evidence of this sort makes
an interpretation in terms of cognitive mapping the more plausible
one. In particular it would be expected that once a cognitive map was
formed it could be accurately read irrespective of the point of entry
and would immediately and accurately generate a novel route to the
goal.

The readiness with which rats form spatial representations suggests
that this is, in an evolutionary sense, a prepared function based on
high biological utility. The relationship between performance on a
radial-arm maze and foraging strategies has been discussed elsewhere, and it is possible to see accurate performance in this apparatus
as a reflection of win-shift strategies in animals whose food resources
are widely distributed and not rapidly replenished (see Oakley, 1983).
Recent studies of wild populations of animals also offer some support
to the notion that activity within a home range is more indicative of
cognitive mapping than it is of the development and utilization of set
routes, though of course favoured routes are in evidence on many
occasions. One such set of observations, using a radio-transmitter
system with foxes in the Chizé forest in France, has recently been
reported by Fabrigoule and Maurel (1982). These authors concluded
that the high levels of variability seen in the paths taken during foraging in their own study, combined with earlier evidence that foxes
when pursued by dogs run in circular paths within their own territory,
and that tame foxes can find their own caches of food on over 96 per
cent of occasions, support an interpretation in terms of spatial mapping. The question of rediscovering hidden food has been investigated in greater detail in marsh tits, which hide several hundred food

items per day in order to take maximal advantage of local abundances, and then recover most items within twenty-four hours. It would appear that this rate of recovery depends on a well developed spatial memory and not on chance re-encounters during the course of normal foraging, as has previously been suggested (see Cowie, Krebs and Sherry, 1981). The marsh tit's performance further suggests an interpretation in terms of spatial memory in that it displays a recency effect and has the characteristics of huge capacity and persistence over time, which are similar to those described for the spatial memory system in the laboratory rat (see Shettleworth and Krebs, 1982).

Under semi-natural conditions, Menzel (1978) has described the development and use of a cognitive map in relation to food localities in wild-born chimpanzees presented with the 'travelling salesman problem'. For this test one of the animals was carried around a familiar one-acre field by one experimenter and was allowed to watch as a second experimenter hid 18 items of food in randomly selected locations. Two minutes later the 'informed' animal and his five companions were released into the field. The animal which had been shown the food locations was seen to run accurately from one location to another using the most economical route, collecting food as it did so. The fact that the route chosen for collecting the hidden items was not the one used during the demonstration by the experimenter, suggests a reorganization of the original information within a map-like cognitive structure. This was even more apparent when the co-experimenter had hidden 9 fruit items and 9, less preferred, vegetable items in a random order. In this situation the 'informed' animal was able to use a least-distances route to collect the fruit first, and only later to collect the hidden vegetables. Over a series of such tests the experimental 'informed' animal found, on average, 12.5 items per test and the control animals found 0.21 items each. On several tests, examples of sudden recall were noted, in which the informed animal, after collecting 10 or so piles of food, would fall asleep satiated, only to wake some 30 minutes later and rush off straight to a hidden piece of food 20 to 30 metres away. It was rare for the 'informed' chimpanzee to recheck a place it had already visited on a given test, but common for it to visit a location already cleared by one of the other animals. The latter further indicates the representational basis for the behaviour, rather than the use of local cues deriving from the presence of food itself.

(b) Environmental events and relationships

A representational system need not be limited to relating a series of locations to each other in space but can operate upon behavioural and environmental events, organizing them in terms of the temporal and/or causal relationships which exist between them. As with spatial representations, an important consequence of this sort of mapping is to introduce flexibility in the solution of problems and to allow internal reorganization within the representational systems to produce novel solutions to an existing problem. If the animal were to learn to solve a problem on the basis of S-R associations alone, performance would be rigid and similar on each occasion. If, on the other hand, performance is based on a representation of the relationship between salient events and actions, then the animal's behaviour should display some evidence of this underlying knowledge. An example of this distinction can be drawn from some of Lashley's work on the solution of latch box problems by rats (Lashley, 1935). In the simplest of these problems the rat had to depress a lever protruding from a partition, in order to open a door within the partition and so gain access to a food compartment on the other side. On the first trial the lever was typically operated by the animal's hind limb in the course of its attempts to climb up the partition wall. In S-R terms the animal should associate the hind leg movement in the particular stimulus complex with the subsequent availability of food, and might be expected to repeat that action on future trials. What in fact was seen was that within one or two trials the rat was operating the lever by placing one forepaw on it and pressing down sharply. This seems to be more consistent with the animal having a representation of the lever's movement and the subsequent escape into the food compartment. Rats with large neocortical lesions, however, performed in the same situation in an S-R manner, and even at the end of training were still climbing onto the lever, falling in front of the door and then scurrying through into the food compartment, suggesting a lack of representational capacities as a result of the lesion (see Oakley, 1983b).

Similarly in a chain-pull box, where escape to the food compartment could be effected by pulling a chain suspended from a bar attached to the partition, initial escape appeared as an accidental accompaniment to exploration. Most rats escaped by climbing upon the projecting bar, tangling their hind feet in the chain and releasing the catch whilst dropping to the floor to extricate themselves from their predicament. Subsequently the normal rats, often on the next trial, would grasp the chain in their teeth or paws, and pull. Moreover, on subsequent trials these two responses were likely to be used interchangeably. Cortically lesioned rats, true to S-R form, continued to climb onto the bar and operate the chain in the same inefficient, stereotyped manner. Lashley noted, somewhat ruefully, that the high levels of behavioural flexibility and evidence of motor equivalence in the normal animals were suggestive of central processes akin to 'insight', 'intelligence' or 'initiative'. He concluded that with a little experience of the latch box the rat was able to identify the movable latch as a distinct object connected with the opening of the door, and was able to apply any one of a variety of behaviours to achieving the appropriate movement. This description is far removed from conventional S-R formulations, and implies cognitive structures which represent the salient aspects of the experimental situation and their relationships and which form the basis for flexible action.

Lashley's suggestion that the normal rat acquires a representation of the latch 'as an object to be manipulated in a certain way' is, as he admitted, close to the view that it had been identified as a tool to achieve a particular end. Once the physical and functional properties of an object have been represented in a cognitive structure new relationships can be explored centrally, giving rise to novel solutions to environmental problems. When an object is incorporated into the solution of a problem as a means of extending the animal's own capacities it becomes classifiable as a tool, and there are a number of examples of tool use, and of tool construction, in animals (see reviews by Beck, 1980; Passingham, 1982; Warren, 1976).

By far the majority of reported instances of tool use have been for primates. Non-human primates have, for example, been observed to use rocks and sticks in aggressive behaviour, to use branches as ladders and bridges, to stack boxes and similar objects in pursuit of otherwise inaccessible food, to use twigs as toothpicks and to use leaves as toilet paper for wiping fruit juice, blood, urine and faeces from their bodies, and to use wads of leaves to soak up drinking water from crevices or to clean out the last scraps of brain tissue from the skull of a prey animal. The majority of these observations derive from the study of chimpanzees and other apes, but some involve monkeys. A number of explanations have been offered for these behaviours, ranging from their early interpretation as examples of reasoning to more recent attempts to see the origins of tool-using behaviours either in the animal's natural repertoire or as products of simple S-R learning (see Warren, 1976). Whilst not wishing to deny the importance of the last two sources of behaviour, there would appear to be sufficient evidence of novelty and flexibility in the literature on tool use in primates to justify the tentative conclusion that representational processes are involved, and to concur that the associated behaviours are evidence of such less objectifiable cognitive attributes as 'intelligence' (Passingham, 1981) and 'insight' (Warren, 1976).

The classic observation that captive chimpanzees will stack boxes one on top of another to reach a banana suspended from the ceiling of the cage was accompanied by the additional information that, if no boxes were available, the animals would use stones, wooden blocks, tins and coils of wire, as well as the back or shoulders of another chimp, or of the researcher himself, as a footstool to reach their goal (Köhler, 1925). Once the relevant properties of the box had been represented in the course of interaction with it, the basis would appear to have been laid for the recognition and exploitation of the same properties in other objects. In some instances chimpanzees appear to modify the existing properties of objects to match the functions required of them. Chimpanzees tackle the somewhat hazardous job of collecting driver ants for food by dipping a stick into the nest and waiting until about 300 of the aggressive ants have climbed on. With the stick held vertically the ants are then transferred, as a mass the size of a hen's egg, directly into the mouth by sliding the other hand up the stick. The specifications of a suitable implement for this purpose are quite precise, and sticks are carefully selected and trimmed to an ideal form 'presumably based on some kind of cognitive model' (McGrew, 1974).

The evidence for tool using in mammals other than primates is slim, and apart from isolated instances of horses, bears and dolphins using tools in captivity, the only widely accepted example of tool use by a mammal in the wild is that of the sea otter, which uses a stone held against its chest as an anvil to assist in extracting mussels from their shells (Beck, 1980). There are more, though still not many, cases of tool use in birds. Egyptian vultures, for example, drop stones onto eggs to crack them, and the woodpecker finch uses thorns or twigs to remove insects from the bark of trees. It is not clear to what extent the sea otter's anvil or tool use by birds should be taken as evidence of underlying representational systems, implying insight, or whether they should be seen in the context of biologically predisposed behaviours which have been specifically selected. Though the woodpecker finch has been seen to shorten overly long probes, the uniformity of distribution of the tool-using behaviours within the species of mammals and birds in question suggests an innate basis for them.

More idiosyncratic tool-using behaviours have been described in captive birds, though even here a non-representational explanation may be adequate. To take one example, a young captive rook is reported to have adopted the behaviour of inserting a plug into an outflow hole in the floor and so flooding a small section of its aviary (Reid, 1982). This bird and three adult rooks were seen to use the flooded section for communal bathing, which was not otherwise possible. The experimenter repeatedly removed the plug, whereupon it was regularly replaced by the bird. Of several plug holes the plug was inserted selectively into the ones which would block the available water flow, and the incidence of plug replacement was far greater on warm sunny days when presumably the opportunity to bathe was more reinforcing for the birds. Reid offered an account of the plug placing behaviour in terms of normal food hiding activity, with the plug being used as if to conceal a cache in the plug hole. This action, he suggested, was reinforced by the accumulation of water as a pool and secondarily reinforced by the cessation of the sound of water draining away. In the absence of other evidence this explanation may have to suffice, and overall it would seem that insufficient evidence exists on tool use to suggest that it is based on representational processes in animals other than primates. It may be that the well developed representational systems needed to support truly innovative tool use do not occur with less neocortical development than is achieved in primate brains. It is perhaps of some significance in this context that tool use, as reflected in the ability to use a stick to retrieve food, has been reported to be lost after temporal lobe lesions in a Cebus monkey, though judgements of relative length and distance were apparently not disturbed (Klüver and Bucy, 1939).

(c) Other animals

An important part of the environment for the majority of animals consists of other animals, and salient characteristics of these other creatures are potentially available for inclusion into representational frameworks. In principle all other animals which were encountered by a cognitive modeller could be represented, and the resultant model would include conspecifics, symbionts, predators and prey. For the purposes of this section, however, I will consider only members of the same species so that the representations in question can be seen as social models. These models incorporate the overall structure of the animal's immediate group, the characteristics of group members in general and of particular individuals, the relationships which exist between the modeller and his companions, and their relationship with each other. The advantages for the individual are once more in flexibility of response, the ability to anticipate the outcome of different interactions and to select the most appropriate course of action. It would also follow that the success of the group as a whole, as well as that of the individual, would depend on the accuracy of the social modelling which occurs.

From the little that is known of the social behaviour of the laboratory rat and its wild counterpart it seems clear that the ability to live effectively within a social group is acquired through experience (see Lore and Flanelly, 1977). This is most easily seen in situations where a single 'intruder' rat is introduced to an established colony. If the intruder is a socially naive animal it is likely to be attacked by the residents, but this is much less likely to occur if the intruder has gained social experience in another colony. One explanation for this is that the socially sophisticated animal has learned to emit appropriate ultrasonic submission calls if threatened. Attack on an intruder is also more likely if the resident colony consists of twenty animals or less, and this has been taken as an indication that in this size of colony the members recognise each other individually and so detect an intruder more easily. In mixed-sex colonies it is usually the males who attack a male intruder but if the males are absent, or if they are rendered anosmic so that they do not show intruder attack, the females take over the aggressive/defensive role. The composition of the group would thus seem to affect the behavioural roles adopted by individual animals.

Competition for food within colonies of rats rarely leads to aggressive encounters and there seems to be no strong correlation between aggressive dominance (the ability to win fights) and feeding precedence. Indeed in systematic observations of mixed-sex colonies the females controlled the single food source for 59 per cent of the time. In a newly formed, mixed-sex colony of rats with a proven liking for sweet tastes, a single piece of chocolate was dropped into the communal cage each day. Over a period of time it was clear that one animal, usually a female, was responsible for eating the chocolate on over 70 per cent of occasions. For the most part the other members of the colony simply did not move as the chocolate was dropped even though they must have known it was there. This seems to suggest a well-defined system of feeding priorities accepted by all colony members. It is of course possible that all of these observations could be accounted for in terms of simple trial and error learning or by phero-monal communication of dominance, feeding precedence and so forth. I would simply like to raise the possibility here that expla-nations in such terms may prove inadequate to account for the complexity already evident, and for the greater complexity which may yet be discovered, in rat social behaviour. The rat may have a more structured representation of the group in which it lives than we have suspected.

A stronger case could perhaps be made at present for seeing the inter-individual relationships in social carnivores (see Wilson, 1975, chapter 25) as based on representations or social modelling. In the African wild dog, for instance, there is a hugely complex social system based on pair bonding, and a communal commitment to feeding the elderly and infirm. In the hunting pack the behaviour of individuals clearly anticipates and depends on the behaviour of other members of the group. Similarly in the wolf, the ambush tactic for capturing caribou depends on a group of animals driving the prey towards another member of the pack lying in wait. This would seem not only to require good spatial mapping but also a representation of other pack members and their likely behaviours in relation to the prey and each other. The ability of any one member of the pack to change tactics in response to variations in the behaviour of either the prey or its fellow hunters, whilst maintaining the goal of the group, appears to demand a continually updated working model of the entire situ-ation and its likely development over time.

The ability to anticipate the actions of others and their likely outcomes in relation to personal goals is even more apparent in the interactions of chimpanzees, described by Menzel (1978). When two chimpanzees are involved in a chase, for instance, and the animal in front runs behind a barrier, the second animal will quite reliably run ahead so as to arrive at the far side of the barrier as his companion emerges, indicating not only object permanence but an ability to represent the actions of another animal in time and space and to extrapolate to future situations. In the wild this type of behaviour is seen also in the fact that the animal acting as the leader will often initiate a move to a new part of the range but other animals in the group will then roam far ahead to arrive at the goal in advance of the leader. In more elaborate test situations Menzel found that a group of six chimpanzees released into an enclosure with six stakes each topped with food, will so judge the situation on the basis of each other's movements that the majority of animals get food and do not compete for the same food supply. The relevant factors are the direction and speed of the initial movements of others, the advantages which already exist in terms of who is in the lead and the relative dominance of the potential competitor.

This capacity for extrapolation from the actions of others and evaluating several possible outcomes leads in some cases to quite elaborate food collecting strategies. In other tests reported by Menzel a single chimpanzee was allowed to watch as two piles of food were hidden in diagonally opposite locations in a field, and was then released along with five others. The 'informed' animal could initially run first to one food cache and then to the other. Within a few trials, however, his companions had detected the underlying regularity in the two food locations, and would watch the informed animal as he headed off towards the first food cache and then, whilst he consumed that, they would all bound off to the diagonally opposite location, with great accuracy in terms of angle and distance, and collect the second pile of food. In these situations the informed animal as he set out clearly imparted directional information to his companions, but usually retained an advantage in that he alone knew the precise distance and location of the first cache. In some instances, however, even that advantage was not sufficient to ensure that the informed animal arrived at the food first, and more subtle strategies were required. In a similar situation where one chimpanzee had watched as the experimenter walked 5 paces in the direction of a small, hidden food source and 15 paces towards a large one, the informed animal always ran first to the large pile. One animal, Bido, was frequently beaten to the large pile of food, however, as the other, swifter animals ran ahead on her projected course. She countered this by running first towards the large food cache and then, once the others were well on their way, would double back and pick up the smaller food pile whilst her companions shared the larger one.

These examples from Menzel's experimental observations suggest a well developed ability in the chimpanzee to form cognitive models or representations of both the current and future social situations and to act accordingly. It is likely that those familiar with the literature on chimpanzees in the wild could suggest even richer evidence of social modelling in established groups of individuals.

(d) Self

Effective modelling of a social group should include a representation of the modeller himself as his own presence and actions affect group dynamics. In this sense self-representation has been implied in many of the above examples. It is commonplace to suggest that a self-representation, or self-image, emerges from social interaction, and there is a certain uniqueness about self-representation which demands further consideration. It will become clear that appropriate evidence of self-representation in the majority of mammals is hard to come by, and my evidence in this section is restricted to primates. The next chapter is concerned with self-image in man and other primates, so only a brief treatment will be given here.

The first set of examples which highlight the importance of self-representation come once more from Menzel (1978). In a situation where a chimpanzee can see both a banana, say, and another chimpanzee, who is dominant to him but has not yet seen the banana, several strategies have been reported for the subordinate animal. First, he may do nothing, ignore the banana completely, and so avoid drawing the other animal's attention to it, until the dominant animal moves away, whereupon he can quickly claim his prize. Chimpanzees have been seen to wait up to half an hour in this situation before achieving their objective. Alternatively, if the dominant animal remains in the situation but becomes engrossed in some other activity or, better still, falls asleep, the subordinate may be seen to move out of his potential competitor's line of sight and circle round to reach the food. This seems to imply that the subordinate's representation of himself includes the fact that not only is he an object visible to others, but also, and more subtly, that his own action may cease to be observed by another animal in circumstances where he still has the other animal in sight. More ambitious animals have been observed to lead the dominant animal away from the food and to then seize the first opportunity to sneak back unseen. On other occasions the subordinate chimpanzee grooms the dominant animal until he settles down and falls asleep, before going himself for the food.

A somewhat more unusual situation, which seems to indicate a clear perception by an individual animal not only of her own status as a group member but also of changing roles and relationships within an established representation, was described by Delgado (1969). In one experiment Ali, the powerful and ill-tempered leader of a captive group of rhesus monkeys, was fitted with brain stimulation electrodes terminating in the caudate nucleus. Remote stimulation of this structure within his brain, via a radio transmitter, caused an immediate cessation of aggressive behaviour and a loss of dominance for the duration of the stimulation. A lever controlling Ali's brain stimulation was provided in the colony cage and one of the subordinate females, Elsa, soon learned of its effects. She was regularly seen operating the lever if threatened by Ali, and took full advantage of the situation not only to maintain a peaceful existence but, with one hand judiciously on the lever, to engage Ali in eye to eye staring, which her status would not have permitted under ordinary circumstances.

How is the information obtained?

(a) Exploration

For Tolman, cognitive maps developed simply as a consequence of the animal's activity within its environment, irrespective of any other motivational state or the presence or absence of conventional reinforcers. He demonstrated this by giving three groups of hungry rats 18 trials each in a 14-unit maze (Tolman and Honzik, 1930b). For one group, food was present in the goal box after each trial, and the time taken to run through the maze became steadily less as training progressed. A second group were never reinforced in the maze at all, and were simply removed when they reached the goal box. They showed a very small tendency to travel through the maze more quickly as trials passed but nothing like the dramatic change seen in the reinforced group. The most interesting group, however, was the third one, which ran for 10 trials with no reward and then on the 11th trial found food in the goal box. On the very next trial these rats ran the maze as rapidly and with as few errors as the group which had been rewarded from the outset. Tolman's explanation was that during the 10 non-reinforced trials the rats had been forming a cognitive map of the maze, which they were able to employ immediately they had a reason for getting quickly to the goal box. In other words, learning had been taking place all the time but had not been revealed until a conventional reinforcer was present. The covert learning in this and similar situations has become known as 'latent learning'. Hull and his followers made much of the small change in running times seen in the consistently non-reinforced group, to claim that some reinforcement, and hence some conventional S-R learning, was present in Tolman's maze even when there was no food in the goal box — perhaps doubling back from a barrier was aversive or being picked up in the goal box was rewarding in itself. Again the explanations in S-R terms were ingenious and plausible, but they seem less adequate than Tolman's account in explaining the dramatic changes which were seen in the latent learning group.

It seems reasonable to go a little further than Tolman and to suggest that animals with a capacity for processing information in the form of cognitive maps or representations are motivated not only to develop these representations in the first place but also periodically to update and refine them. In practical terms we should expect to see evidence of animals making particular efforts to explore the layout of their environments, the properties of objects they encounter, the relationships between events, the effects of their own actions on the environment, the capabilities and propensities of conspecifics, and the structure and dynamics of their social group. Which of these driven quests for structured knowledge we saw would, of course, depend upon the type and complexity of the representations which the particular animal was capable of forming. Under natural conditions rats spend a considerable proportion of their time exploring their home ranges, but also seem to make additional sorties over very wide distances into the surrounding areas (Ewer, 1971). Regular patrolling of familiar environments is also seen in rats under laboratory conditions, particularly in dominant males (Henry, Ely, Watson and Stephens, 1975) and in oestrous females (Martin and Bättig, 1980). Chimpanzees for the first 3—4 years of life are dependent on others for guidance around their environments but thereafter they also make long solitary excursions outside the usual home range. It is assumed that in the course of such trips a map of a very wide area of land is built up which may aid in the future exploitation of resources. In captivity also, older chimps show very active exploration of new areas, and even juveniles after a 24-hour break will detect and explore, within 15 seconds of release, a novel object placed in a one-acre field containing up to 20 previously present toys and household objects (Menzel, 1978).

Consistent with the suggested link between exploration and representational systems is the fact that damage to the septo-hippocampal system, which has been claimed to be essential for cognitive mapping in the rat, produces high levels of activity but reduced curiosity and exploration (see O'Keefe and Nadel, 1978). Lashley (1935) similarly described rats with neocortical lesions as being restricted in their exploratory activity in that they would ignore the corners and projecting edges of the box, and the cracks and irregularities in the floor, which elicited persistent investigations in the normal animals, were at best only briefly attended to. In the wild a number of advantages may result from patrolling and exploration. An up-to-date picture of potential food sources and places of refuge within the territory should maximize its safe exploitation, and an already acquired map of the surrounding region would ensure successful migration should the home range become less hospitable. It has been demonstrated, for example, that mice who were familiar with a particular environment were more successful at escaping predation by an owl than those without experience in the same environment. The experienced mice escaped into burrows which they had not previously used (Metzgar, 1967). Under laboratory conditions at least, it would appear that latent learning may take place even when an animal is highly motivated to learn about something else. Hungry rats running a straight alleyway for food reward seem to be able to learn that water is also available and can demonstrate that knowledge on later tests, even though they never drank water in the apparatus during the food reward trials (Capaldi, Hovancik and Davidson, 1979).

On a smaller scale than is implied by general exploration, rats also show strong investigatory tendencies. Lashley (1935) described how they would investigate aggressively within his problem boxes, seizing, shaking and gnawing at loose wires, the wooden frame of the box and at the latches and doors, paying particular attention to anything which yielded in response to their efforts. With a little experience in latch boxes the rats seemed actively to seek out possible means of operating the door or breaking through the partition. Rats with damage to neocortex failed to show this aggressive investigation of objects within their environment. Object investigation is even more clearly present in primates. Rhesus monkeys, for example, have been found to manipulate, and solve, even complex wire puzzles, not to mention releasing the locks on their cages, apparently simply for the pleasure of doing so (e.g. Butler, 1965). Other examples are considered in the next section, as illustrations of object-play in primates.

(b) Play

Spontaneous behaviours which appear to have no immediate goal are often classified as play. According to the above arguments the process of gathering information to create cognitive maps or representations is also goalless in this sense, and much of the play behaviour described in animals may reflect the active search for information. Such a role could coexist, of course, with other putative functions of play, such as exercise or physical skills training (for a review see Smith, 1982). The activity of wire puzzle solving in monkeys, which was mentioned above, has all the characteristics of object play, and the introduction of conventional rewards into the situation frequently has the effect of interfering with the process of solution. Schiller (1952) provided twelve chimpanzees with boxes in their home cage and noted that they sat on them, rolled them over and over, and used them as pillows. Six of the animals spontaneously stacked the boxes one on top of another, forming a tower, which they then climbed and used to reach up for the ceiling. Schiller also noted that the older chimpanzees would spontaneously manipulate sticks, shaping them and fitting them together. As all these behaviours were carried out in the absence of obvious goals they can be considered as a form of play, driven, I would suggest, by the imperative to collect information for inclusion into representations of interactive object relationships. In the case of box stacking and stick manipulation new properties can be discovered which become available for later inclusion with other representations, in pursuit of solutions to problems with clearly observable goals. Object play has also been widely reported in dolphins (Tayler and Saayman, 1976). I am not aware of any clear descriptions of object play in rats, apart from object investigation already described. Cats, however, do show play behaviour in relation to objects (leaves, balls of wool, etc.), though this seems to be very closely related to the practice of predatory behaviours rather than in learning about the objects themselves (Egan, 1976).

Play involving other animals of the same species allows the possibility of practising not only predatory and aggressive behaviours but also of developing social skills. If representations of social situations are developed in this way the effects may not only be reflected in improved social capacity later in life, as the Lore and Flanelly (1977) observations on socially reared intruders suggests, but may also improve behavioural flexibility generally (Humphreys and Einon, 1981). The implication here is that cognitive structures which are developed to cope with the complex interactive relationships which occur in groups of animals may be used later to cope with analogous problems encountered in interactions with the physical world. Indeed Humphrey (1976) has claimed that the impressive cognitive capacities of primates in particular have emerged in response to the need to survive within, and to maintain the coherence of, social groups, and have only subsequently been applied to the solution of environmentally posed problems. In the case of humans, he suggests, this has enabled us to form profitable interactive relationships with animate objects, as in agriculture, and may explain why we still interact with the physical world in a proto-social manner, even if we have abandoned, overtly at least, our ancestors' tendency to make bargains with volcanoes, the weather and the like.

(c) Observing others

In its broadest sense this category includes the act of observing the behaviour of other animals in relation to each other, to the observer and to the environment, in order to form central structures to represent the observed relationships. Activities of this kind have been referred to in several places above and I do not propose to pursue them any further here. What I would like to consider, however, is the possibility that one animal may observe another performing a particular act, especially whilst solving a problem, and may be able to imitate or copy that act. There is an important difference, of course, between simply imitating the actions of another and understanding the purpose of those actions in the particular context in which they were performed. The former could reflect an innate predisposition whereas the latter implies insight, based on already well developed representational systems. It is important to note that either of these approaches would work in some situations in speeding up the solution of problems following the observation of an experienced individual at work. Imitation would, however, depend on the reappearance of exactly the same problem to be tackled in exactly the same way for it to be effective. Insightful observational learning, on the other hand, involves the acquisition of the principle underlying the solution, allows far more flexibility in approach, and would be potentially trans-situational in its application. There are in fact even simpler effects seen in social situations which facilitate performance by an observing animal, and these should be distinguished from both imitation and insightful observational learning. (See Davey, 1981, chapter 9, and Passingham, 1982, chapter 7, for further discussion of the different types of social learning.) Social facilitation, for example, refers to the fact that in many species the sight and sound of one animal involved in a species-typical activity, such as eating, will induce others to do the same. There are also possible local enhancement effects in which the demonstrator's behaviour serves to draw the observer's attention to salient parts of the situation, to a lever or food tray for example. The observer may simply then direct its behaviour selectively towards these objects and come up with its own chance solution.

The salient feature of both imitation and insightful observational learning which distinguishes them, at least from local enhancement effects, is that the observer's subsequent performance should retain either the detail or the essence of the demonstrator's approach. Under natural conditions it has been reported that some colonies of rats living on the banks of the river Po in Italy have adopted the habit of diving for molluscs as a source of food, whereas in neighbouring colonies with equal opportunities to do the same none of the animals dived in this way (Parisi and Gandolfi, 1974). This bimodality in the distribution of the behaviour was taken to suggest that the underlying mechanism was a form of social learning, in which one animal acquired the habit as result of its own exploration and the others in the group imitated it. An attempt by Galef (1980) to replicate these observations under laboratory conditions indicated that the willingness of rats to dive for pieces of chocolate was not influenced by the presence of a trained diving conspecific. Galef suggested that the Po rats' behaviour was more likely a result of local conditions, such as a process of natural response shaping in locations where molluscs were occasionally exposed by changes in water level. Other relevant factors might be the availability of alternative sources of food and, where deep water was involved, local facilitation effects from being in the presence of other rats consuming food in association with water. Ewer (1971) carried out a number of feeding tests, including fishing for nuts in a bowl of water, on a natural colony of black rats, and found that the discovery of an unorthodox food source by an individual resulted in many others also exploiting it. She concluded, however, that what the rats learned from each other was that food was available at a particular location, but each animal still had to discover for itself how to get at it. More promising, from the point of view of imitation learning, are the observations by Will, Pallaud, Soczka and Manikowski (1974) that observer rats in a two-compartment Skinner box not only more readily acquired a lever pressing habit but in later stages of training adopted strategies of lever pressing similar to those of their demonstrators. The latter is less easy to explain in terms of local enhancement or social facilitation, though it need not imply insight.

In cats, where prey killing seems in part to be learned from accompanying the mother on her hunting trips, it would appear also that the mother's general demeanour is copied (Egan, 1976). Kittens with mothers who behave with a mouse in a quiet fashion are more likely to approach and kill mice than those whose mothers overreact and become agitated. Indeed kittens with the latter type of mother are apt to avoid mice in future. If there is a biological advantage in learning from others we might expect there to be a complementary process, in some species at least, in the provision of a motivation to teach. It is interesting in this context that cats appear to like to be watched when playing with objects (where they display predatory skills) and with actual prey. Adult cats are said to call loudly before bringing live prey back to the nest (or the kitchen) where they proceed to play with it before killing and perhaps eating it, in view of their kittens (or human caretaker).

Imitation seems to be curiously well developed in the dolphin, and the copying of a wide variety of acts performed by other dolphins, humans and other animals has been documented (see Tayler and Saayman, 1973). Captive dolphins, for instance, have been seen to swim behind skates, turtles and penguins, copying their swimming movements as closely as possible, and it is common Oceanarium lore that novice dolphins are not taught tricks but are simply left to pick them up from their more experienced companions. One of the most engaging examples of imitation in these animals, and one which would appear to imply a considerable underlying representational ability, is that of a young dolphin, Dolly, who, on looking through an observation port, was faced by a human observer who released a cloud of cigarette smoke against the glass. Immediately the young dolphin swam to her mother and returned with a mouthful of milk which she discharged, producing a similar effect to the cigarette smoke. Dolly is said to have subsequently used the same action many times as a means of attracting the attention of human observers at the portholes. Tool use in dolphins has also been reported as a consequence of imitation. In one group of dolphins a great deal of attention was paid to the human diver who used a scraper attached to a suction hose to clean seaweed from the floor of the tank. One of the group was later found holding the hose with her flippers, supporting the scraper with her head and pushing it along the floor dislodging seaweed, some of which she ate. After the scraper had been removed the same dolphin was seen using a piece of tile, which she held in her mouth, to dislodge seaweed from the floor. After watching for some time an older dolphin used first the same tile and then her own piece of tile to remove weed. Eventually the two animals worked together, scraping off far more weed than they could consume. These observations could indicate little more than a capacity for imitation, with the behaviours subsequently maintained by their reinforcing consequences. The transfer of the activity from one tool to another, especially as this was held in a different way, suggests however that the behaviour had some attributes of insightful observational learning, based on an accurate representation of the properties of scraping implements and the principles of their use. The behaviour would also appear to be intrinsically reinforcing for the animals because of the joy of exercising the products of a new cognitive structure, which parallels perhaps the mastery play of human infants (Piaget, 1951).

Perhaps the most famous instance of imitation in non-human primates was the habit of potato washing which was developed by a young female Japanese macaque and spread to other monkeys in the colony. This habit transferred from the stream in which it was first practised to the sea, perhaps because salty potatoes taste better, and was later generalized by the same female as a means of separating sand and grains of wheat. Again, once discovered the trick spread throughout the colony (see Passingham, 1982, chapter 7, for a summary of this and other examples of imitation in primates). Menzel (1972) has presented a careful account of how captive chimpanzees developed their communal skills in bridge building from an early stage of using sticks and branches as vaulting poles, to their use as bridges to climb into and plunder the observation house. The bridge building enterprises of this group culminated in the animals taking poles up onto overhead runways and making a bridge by resting one end of the pole on the narrow runway with the other end on a nearby tree above the level of a ring of electrified wires, which had been installed to deter such activities. In some instances a second animal appeared to steady the construction whilst the builder climbed into the branches of the forbidden tree. The performance of these acts of escape would seem to require a representation of the basic rules of mechanical statics, and the acts were readily copied by other members of the group. It is of course impossible, on this sort of data, to decide if the observational learning involved included insight at the time the target behaviour was first seen, or even at the time that it was reproduced by the imitator. It would be equally difficult to make the same decision for a human observer in the same situation without recourse to language to obtain an introspective commentary. The fact that the imitators were able to go on to use the bridge building principle, in other situations and with other materials, suggests that insight was not far behind the act of imitation.

A similar problem of interpretation attends the question of teaching amongst primates. Clearly, simply allowing another animal to observe one's own actions is not the same as setting out to teach it and so to aid it in the construction of appropriate central representations. We would expect to find examples of active teaching in primates, particularly between mother and offspring, even if only by analogy with our own case, but unambiguous evidence of such an intent to teach is not at present available. The fact that gorilla mothers, for instance, are reported to support the heads of their offspring as they begin to crawl and later to back away and encourage them to move forwards (Whiten, cited by Passingham, 1982), may or may not meet everyone's criterion of an intention to teach, and the behaviour itself is not cognitively demanding. Observations of this kind, as with the cat mothers, do nevertheless seem to support the notion of some sort of disposition in adult animals to behave in a way which facilitates the process of learning in their offspring.

(d) Self-observation

If an animal is to form a model in its head of the world, or parts thereof, and of its possible actions within it, an important source of its information is from the observation of the effects which its own behaviour has on that world, and of the changes in its own behaviour which accompany environmental events. This process could be restricted to the sort of information which any other observer might obtain about the individual's actions and their environmental correlates, but there is a potentially much richer source of knowledge. If an individual is able to introspect on its own experience, to examine the contents of its mind, then not only can better models be formed of the individual's own behaviour but it will be able to extrapolate those models to account for the behaviour of its fellows. The potential importance of introspection in animals, particularly in relation to social models, has been eloquently argued by Humphrey (1980), and what follows owes much to his account. We do not really know at what stage, or stages, of evolution the trick of turning in on one's own experience occurred, though we readily accept introspection in ourselves as a short-cut to determining the mainsprings of the actions of others. There seems to be no good reason for denying the existence of a similar source of information in certain animals, at least within those parts of the animal kingdom which have invested in representational systems. The proviso must be that some representational systems are better developed than others, and some specialization is inevitable, so that the depth and range of introspection which is possible must vary between animal groups.

We would be hard-pressed to understand human society if we were limited to behavioural observations of our companions. We recognize in ourselves feelings of hunger, fear and compassion and accept them as explanations of the actions of others. It is questionable that rats are better behaviourists than humans and so, unless we accept that their social organization is entirely reflexive, the most plausible explanation of their social success may be that rats, like ourselves, have access to internally generated information which allows the formation of better, more accurate, predictive social models. The importance of personal experience for forming accurate models of others is taken in humans to the point of actively seeking relevant experience. At an intellectual level anthropologists have on occasions found it important to live with and share the life experiences of their subjects in order fully to understand them. By the same argument it is unlikely that a psychiatrist can have an accurate predictive model of a drug addict unless he has experienced a similar addiction himself. Similarly the failure of males in our society to form completely accurate social models of females (and vice versa) is at least in part a product of the inaccessibility, at both a biological and cultural level, of some fundamental categories of experience.

In addition to the somewhat intellectual urge to further one's experience and so broaden the mind, Humphrey identified three major sources of experience which provide opportunities for introspection. These are play, parental manipulation and dreaming. In play, feelings of excitement, anxiety, disappointment and success accompany physical interactions with others and with the environment. Play, however, seems overloaded with the more positive emotions and it is left to parents to provide the child with negative experiences. Children, even within a loving family, are punished and deprived 'for their own good' lest they should grow up 'marred'. Parents intuitively make provision for hurting and frightening children, mystifying them, and making them suffer feelings of jealousy and guilt. To the extent that accurate social modelling is biologically adaptive these activities must be seen as part of the evolutionary role of parents. By the same token we might expect a biological disposition to accept such experiences on the part of the child, and indeed within limits human children appear to enjoy the experience of having been briefly frightened, mystified and so forth. In other animals parental rejection at weaning must serve, amongst other things, to give the infant first-hand experience of frustration, rejection, hunger and loneliness. Dreaming may provide for the experience of powerful emotions in situations which the dreamer may never have experienced in reality, as well as allowing him to rehearse and benefit from actual experiences. In addition to these natural sources of varied experience, particularly for the developing animal, human society has developed their cultural equivalents. Organized sports and games, for instance, parallel the role of play in arousing strong emotions in participants and onlookers alike. Parental abuse is institutionalized perhaps into such activities as initiation rites. Dreams find a parallel in the theatre, literature and works of art, which draw individuals into fantasies and experiences outside their normal lives, but which allow them to model the behaviour of others and understand it using introspections derived from the fantasy.

So far the discussion of introspection has centred on feelings and emotions but there are other types of experience to consider. We are all able, for instance, to introspect on our sensory capacities. We not only see but know that we can see. We use this information to conclude that others can see and infer, rightly or wrongly, that their experience of seeing is much the same as ours. We also know that our range of sight is limited. In particular we see clearly only what is in front of us, less clearly that which appears in the sides of our visual fields, and have no visual record of things which occur behind our backs. The earlier account of Menzel's subordinate chimpanzee, scheming to take possession of a banana whilst a dominant animal was present, would seem to imply exactly this type of knowledge. First of all the subordinate chimpanzee behaved as if the other animal could see, but also took account of the fact that seeing was not necessarily mutual. That is, the subordinate could be in a position of seeing the dominant animal whilst not being seen in return. It is possible that such information could have been gleaned from behavioural observation alone. It would, however, have been arrived at with far less intellectual effort if the animal was able to use its own visual experience as a basis for the model it used to generate those particular interactions.

Comparative and anatomical considerations and conclusions

So far as vertebrates are concerned I have argued elsewhere that representational systems emerged with the development and expansion of forebrain cortical structures, particularly neocortex, but also hippocampal cortex and its derivatives, in mammals and their homologues in birds and reptiles (Oakley, 1981, 1983a). There are three major consequences of this view. First, it suggests that we should see progressively more elaborate and effective representational systems with increasing grades of forebrain differentiation in the phylogeny of vertebrates. Second, it also seems likely that there is an ordering of complexity between types of representational system, so that the range as well as the sophistication of representations is likely to increase with forebrain differentiation. Specifically it would appear that spatial mapping is an early representational acquisition, and seems to be well developed in all mammals irrespective of grade of neocortical differentiation. This is consistent with the involvement of the phylogenetically older hippocampal system in its mediation, as well as its very clear presence in animals, such as the rat, with a relatively lowly grade of neocortical differentiation. Other representational systems appear to be newer acquisitions and to depend more on neocortex and its homologues. Social modelling, including representations of the self, may have only a rudimentary form in the rat compared to the more impressively neocortically evolved groups, such as primates and cetaceans (dolphins, porpoises and whales). The more sophisticated representational systems, which form the foundations of innovative tool use, insightful observational learning and other higher cognitive skills, would appear to demand a very high grade of forebrain development, and have been described convincingly only in primates and cetaceans. Language in humans is based on the most complex representational system of which we are aware and is primarily neocortically based. Given the potential advantages of enhanced representational capacities to the individual it is possible that human language developed as a means of internal discourse based on acoustic representations, and only secondarily acquired the role of communication with others (Jerison, 1976). Much of animal reasoning, particularly in primates and cetaceans, may be mediated by a similar internal discourse, though not necessarily an acoustic one.

The third consequence of my proposal takes me back to the introduction to this chapter. It seems to me that Thorndike, Hull and Tolman were all correct. Association learning, in traditional Pavlovian conditioning and instrumental learning situations, does occur in exactly the way the S-R theorists described it. The point is that it is an old form of information processing carried out by subcortical sites and is usually overlaid by later representational systems. Recent evidence, in fact, suggests that Pavlovian conditioning may take place within dedicated systems specialized for a particular response type. In the rabbit, for instance, the association underlying the Pavlovian nictitating membrane response appears to occur in a localized region of the cerebellum (Thompson, 1983; Glickstein, Hardiman and Yeo, 1983). As representational systems develop so they progressively obscure the S-R learning which is simultaneously taking place, and the animal's behaviour begins to take on the 'cognitive' flavour, which Tolman noted in his rats and which is so powerfully obvious in primates. There is good evidence that as cognitive skills emerge, both developmentally and phylogenetically, the individuals concerned perform progressively less reliably, in the way that S-R theory would predict (see Oakley, 1983b). Removing representational capacity, moreover, by removing neocortex in rats and rabbits, produces a good S-R learning preparation uncomplicated by cognitive processes, and some examples of this were given earlier when discussing Lashley's latch box experiments (for other evidence see Oakley, 1981, 1983a,b; Russell, 1980).

Accepting the hypothesis of a continuity of representational systems once they emerged in phylogeny demands that similar types of explanation for observed behaviour are attempted in humans and other animals. If we are prepared to accept the validity of a cognitive approach for human psychology then we must be prepared also to do the same when talking of other animals. This may lead those of us who work with animal subjects into unfamiliar territory even, as I have suggested, so far as to suggest that in animals, as in ourselves, a process such as introspection may be a valuable source of information upon which mental modelling may be based. If we are to take this road, however, it is essential that we also develop realistic models of information processing in actual brains which can account for the cognitive structures we propose.

References

Baker, R. R. (1981) *Human Navigation and the Sixth Sense*. London: Hodder & Stoughton.

Bartlett, F. C. (1932) *Remembering: A Study in Experimental and Social Psychology*. Cambridge: Cambridge University Press.

Beck, B. B. (1980) *Animal Tool Behavior*. New York: Garland.

Beritashvili, I. S. (J. S. Beritoff) (1971) *Vertebrate Memory: Characteristics and Origin*. New York: Plenum Press.

Bolles, R. C. (1979) *Learning Theory*, 2nd edn. New York: Holt, Rinehart & Winston.

Butler, R. A. (1965) Investigative behavior. In A. M. Schrier, H. F. Harlow and F. Stollnitz (eds) *Behavior of Non-human Primates*, 463−93. New York: Academic Press.

Capaldi, E. D., Hovancik, J. R. and Davidson, T. L. (1979) Learning about water by hungry rats. *Learning and Motivation 10*: 58−72.

Cowie, R. J., Krebs, J. R. and Sherry, D. F. (1981) Food storing by marsh tits. *Animal Behaviour 29*: 1252−9.

Davey, G. C. L. (1981) *Animal Learning and Conditioning*. London: Macmillan.

Delgado, J. M. R. (1969) *Physical Control of the Mind*. New York: Harper & Row.

Deutsch, J. A. and Clarkson, J. K. (1959) Reasoning in the hooded rat. *Quarterly Journal of Experimental Psychology 11*: 150−4.

Dickinson, A. (1980) *Contemporary Animal Learning Theory*. Cambridge: Cambridge University Press.

Downs, R. M. and Stea, D. (1977) *Maps in Minds: Reflections on Cognitive Mapping*. New York: Harper & Row.

Egan, J. (1976) Object-play in cats. In J. S. Bruner, A. Jolly and K. Sylva (eds) *Play: Its Role in Development and Evolution*, 161−5. New York: Basic Books.

Ewer, R. F. (1971) The biology and behaviour of a free-living population of Black Rats (*Rattus rattus*). *Animal Behaviour Monographs 4, part 3*: 127–74.

Fabrigoule, C. and Maurel, D. (1982) Radio-tracking study of foxes' movements related to their home range. A cognitive map hypothesis. *Quarterly Journal of Experimental Psychology 34B*: 195–208.

Galef, B. G. (1980) Diving for food: analysis of a possible case of social learning in wild rats (*Rattus norvegicus*). *Journal of Comparative and Physiological Psychology 94*: 416–25.

Glickstein, M., Hardiman, M. J. and Yeo, C. H. (1983) The effects of cerebellar lesions on the conditioned nictitating membrane response of the rabbit. *Journal of Physiology 341*: 30–1.

Henry, J. P., Ely, D. L., Watson, F. M. C. and Stephens, P. M. (1975) Ethological methods as applied to the measurement of emotion. In L. Levi (ed.) *Emotions: Their Parameters and Measurement*, 469–97. New York: Raven.

Hull, C. L. (1943) *Principles of Behavior*. New York: Appleton-Century-Crofts.

Humphrey, N. K. (1976) The social function of intellect. In P. P. G. Bateson and R. A. Hinde (eds) *Growing Points in Ethology*, 303–17. Cambridge: Cambridge University Press.

Humphrey, N. K. (1980) Nature's psychologists. In B. D. Josephson and V. S. Ramachandran (eds) *Consciousness and the Physical World*, 57–75. Oxford: Pergamon.

Humphreys, A. P. and Einon, D. F. (1981) Play as a reinforcer for maze-learning in juvenile rats. *Animal Behaviour 29*: 259–70.

Jerison, H. J. (1976) Palaeoneurology and the evolution of mind. *Scientific American 234*: 90–101.

Klüver, H. and Bucy, P. C. (1939) Preliminary analysis of functions of the temporal lobes in monkeys. *Archives of Neurology and Psychiatry 42*: 979–1000.

Köhler, W. (1925) *The Mentality of Apes*. Harmondsworth: Penguin.

Lashley, K. (1935) Studies of cerebral function in learning. The behavior of the rat in latch-box situations. *Comparative Psychology Monographs 11 (2)*: 5–40.

Lore, R. and Flanelly, K. (1977) Rat societies. *Scientific American 236 (5)*: 106–16.

MacFarlane, D. A. (1930) The role of kinesthesis in maze learning. *University of California Publications in Psychology 4*: 277–305.

McGrew, W. C. (1974) Tool use by wild chimpanzees in feeding upon driver ants. *Journal of Human Evolution 3*: 501–8.

Mackintosh, N. J. (1984) The mind in the Skinner box. *New Scientist 101 (1394)*: 30–3.

Martin, J. R. and Bättig, K. (1980) Exploratory behaviour of rats at oestrus. *Animal Behaviour 28*: 900–5.

Menzel, E. W. (1972) Spontaneous invention of ladders in a group of young chimpanzees. *Folia Primatologica 17*: 87—106.

Menzel, E. W. (1978) Cognitive mapping in chimpanzees. In S. H. Hulse, H. Fowler and W. K. Honig (eds) *Cognitive Processes in Animal Behavior*, 375—422. Hillsdale, NJ: Erlbaum.

Metzgar, L. M. (1967) An experimental comparison of screech owl predation on resident and transient white-footed mice (*Peromyscus leucopus*). *Journal of Mammalogy 48*: 387—91.

Moar, I. and Carleton, L. R. (1982) Memory for routes. *Quarterly Journal of Experimental Psychology 34A*: 381—94.

Morris, R. G. M. (1981) Spatial localization does not require the presence of local cues. *Learning and Motivation 12*: 239—60.

Oakley, D. A. (1979) Cerebral cortex and adaptive behaviour. In D. A. Oakley and H. C. Plotkin (eds) *Brain, Behaviour and Evolution*, 154—88. London: Methuen.

Oakley, D. A. (1981) Brain mechanisms of mammalian memory. *British Medical Bulletin 37*: 175—80.

Oakley, D. A. (1983a) The varieties of memory: a phylogenetic approach. In A. Mayes (ed.) *Memory in Animals and Humans*. Wokingham: Van Nostrand Reinhold.

Oakley, D. A. (1983b) Learning capacity outside neocortex in animals and man: implications for therapy after brain injury. In G. C. L. Davey (ed.) *Animal Models of Human Behaviour: Conceptual, Evolutionary and Neurobiological Perspectives*, 247—66. Chichester: Wiley.

O'Keefe, J. and Nadel, L. (1978) *The Hippocampus as a Cognitive Map*. Oxford: Clarendon Press.

Olton, D. S. (1979) Mazes, maps and memory. *American Psychologist 34*: 583—96.

Parisi, V. and Gandolfi, G. (1974) Further aspects of the predation by rats on various mollusc species. *Bolletino di Zoologica 41*: 87—106.

Passingham, R. E. (1981) Primate specialization in brain and intelligence. *Symposia of the Zoological Society of London 46*: 361—88.

Passingham, R. E. (1982) *The Human Primate*. Oxford: W. H. Freeman.

Piaget, J. (1951) *Play, Dreams and Imitation in Childhood*. London: Routledge & Kegan Paul.

Reid, J. B. (1982) Tool-use by a rook (*Corvus frugilegus*) and its causation. *Animal Behaviour 30*: 1212—16.

Russell, I. S. (1980) Encephalization and neural mechanisms of learning. In M. A. Jeeves (ed.) *Psychology Survey 3*.

Schiller, P. H. (1952) Innate constituents of complex responses in primates. *Psychological Review 59*: 177—91.

Shettleworth, S. J. and Krebs, J. R. (1982) How marsh tits find their hoards: the roles of site preference and spatial memory. *Journal of Experimental Psychology: Animal Behavior Processes 8*: 354—75.

Smith, P. K. (1982) Does play matter? Functional and evolutionary aspects of animal and human play. *Behavioural Brain Sciences 5*: 139–84.

Sutherland, R. J., Kolb, B. and Whishaw, I. Q. (1982) Spatial mapping: definitive disruption by hippocampal or medial frontal cortical damage in the rat. *Neuroscience Letters 31*: 271–6.

Tayler, C. K. and Saayman, G. S. (1973) Imitative behaviour by Indian Ocean bottlenose dolphins (*Tursiops aduneus*) in captivity. *Behaviour 44*: 286–98.

Thompson, R. F. (1983) Neuronal substrates of simple associative learning: classical conditioning. *Trends in NeuroSciences 6*: 270–5.

Tolman, E. C. (1932) *Purposive Behavior in Animals and Men*. New York: Century.

Tolman, E. C. and Honzik, C. H. (1930a) 'Insight' in rats. *University of California Publications in Psychology 4*: 215–32.

Tolman, E. C. and Honzik, C. H. (1930b) Introduction and removal of reward and maze performance in rats. *University of California Publications in Psychology 4*: 257–75.

Walker, S. (1983) *Animal Thought*. London: Routledge & Kegan Paul.

Warren, J. M. (1976) Tool use in mammals. In R. B. Masterson, C. B. G. Campbell, M. E. Bitterman and N. Hotton (eds) *Evolution of Brain and Behavior in Vertebrates*, 407–24. Hillsdale, NJ: Erlbaum.

Watson, J. B. (1925) *Behaviorism*. New York: Norton.

Will, B., Pallaud, B., Soczka, M. and Manikowski, S. (1974) Imitation of lever-pressing 'strategies' during the operant conditioning of albino rats. *Animal Behaviour 22*: 664–71.

Wilson, E. O. (1975) *Sociobiology: The New Synthesis*. Cambridge, Mass.: Belknap/Harvard.

5 Animal awareness, consciousness and self-image

David A. Oakley

Introduction

It is common to commence discussions of this kind by claiming that
there are as many definitions of awareness or consciousness as there
are writers (and readers). This, of course, allows the author to propose
his own definitions and to pursue his own particular interests. This
author is no exception, though he would claim a particular virtue in
the fact that the model of consciousness which emerges does so on the
basis of ideas which were developed for other purposes, and so may
have a more general heuristic value. The problem is that we all know
intuitively what consciousness is and, though formal definitions never
quite seem to catch its essence, our own experience of being 'conscious' quickly fills the gaps. A view expressed throughout this book is
that the development of representational systems as practical internal
models of the real world was a significant step forward in the design of
nervous systems, and this may provide a way of resolving the problem
of definition. The classification of awareness and consciousness which
follows is summarized in Figure 5.1.

First, the terms 'awareness' and 'consciousness' are frequently used
synonymously, but I would like to differentiate them. To the extent
that an animal is capable of responding to events in its environment

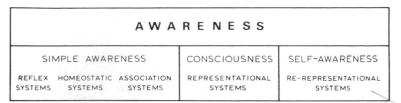

Fig. 5.1   Subdivisions of awareness and the information processing systems which underly them.

[handwritten annotation: it. aware of The ability to create a representation]

or within its own body it can be said to be 'aware' (from the Old English *ge + waer* = quite wary or heedful). Awareness thus is to be the broadest category of responsivity. Awareness in this sense may take a simple form and be based on inbuilt mechanisms and the most elementary of acquired reactions. I would then like to suggest that the emergence of neural modelling, the ability to create central representations of external events and to use them as a basis for behaviour, corresponds to the emergence of mind, and that the activity of processing information via such cognitive systems constitutes consciousness (from the Latin *conscius* = cognizant of: *cum* = with; *scire* = to know). Similar definitions of consciousness have been proposed by Jerison (1973, 1976, and chapter 1 of this volume) and Griffin (1976) and the interested reader is recommended to read their somewhat different accounts. Consciousness thus constitutes a second category of awareness.

There is a third category of awareness which must be considered. Just as we are aware of events in the world around us and respond to them, we may also become aware of the products of our own consciousness. In order to avoid the clumsiness of terms like 'awareness of consciousness' I have previously suggested 'self-awareness' to refer to this awareness of our inner world (Oakley, 1979a). I shall argue later that there were practical reasons for developing a system which re-represented items from consciousness, and that this system forms the substrate of self-awareness. It is, however, the subjective aspect of self-awareness which is for humans its most striking attribute and the most difficult to deal with when we consider animals. Indeed it is only by an act of faith that we accept self-awareness in other humans. We know from our own experience that we can only report upon mental and perceptual events which enter our current window of self-awareness, and we take the introspective reports of others as describing the same subjective domain. Perhaps, as Griffin (1976) points out, we shall have to wait until the science of 'cognitive ethology' has progressed to the point at which introspective reports can be taken from animals, before we will have a full answer to the comparative question with respect to self-awareness. Griffin also notes that until such time as this is possible, all the comparative and neurophysiological evidence of biological continuity should lead us to conclude that the mental experiences of animals are similar to our own (see also Walker, 1983). There is certainly no reason to assume that human self-awareness is a unique property of our own version of the vertebrate brain. Within the representational systems there may be developed, as discussed in the previous chapter, a representation of the individual himself or herself. The behavioural and psychological consequences of this self-representation, and in particular of its entry into self-awareness as a self-image, are considered later in this chapter.

Simple awareness

Awareness has been defined very broadly above and is implied by all forms of behavioural reactivity. Awareness in this sense is a property of all nervous systems and there is little point in itemizing particular examples of it. It is clear that animals can respond to a range of stimuli provided they are within the limits set by their sensory systems. Animals are also, it seems, aware of their own actions. Rats can for instance use the last action they performed, usually washing, rearing or scratching, as the cue to which lever of several will provide a reinforcement when it is pressed (e.g. Morgan and Nicholas, 1969). Awareness may be detected both within the confines of inbuilt mechanisms and in the form of newly acquired responses to environmental events. Behavioural reflexes, such as limb withdrawal in response to a painful stimulus, as well as homeostatic responses may be considered as innate adaptations. In the case of some inbuilt mechanisms it is reasonable to infer that they embody a model of either a desirable physiological state or of an important aspect of the external environment. An instance of the latter would be the model of the day-night cycle which underlies circadian rhythms (see Oatley, chapter 2 of this volume). This type of model allows anticipation of events in the outside world but is distinguished from true representational capacities, which are considered here as based on a system of acquired central models with dynamic and interactive potential. The processes underlying habituation, Pavlovian conditioning and instrumental learning in their pure associative form are a means of acquiring new reflexes, or, in the case of habituation, of losing an old response to a particular set of stimuli (see chapter 4). Pure association learning results in the attachment of new response outputs to stimulus inputs, either directly or via the prior association of two stimulus events, and does not involve intermediary representational processes (see Oakley, 1983, for further discussion of this).

My own view, as I indicated at the end of the previous chapter, is that the capacity to develop representations from experience is associated with the expansion of cortical systems, especially hippocampus and neocortex in mammals, and a model of the subsystems of awareness taking this into account is presented as Figure 5.2. A mammal surgically deprived of hippocampus, neocortex (neodecorticated) or both should thus still show simple awareness and so be capable of

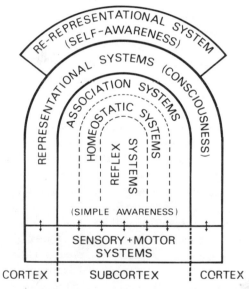

Fig. 5.2   A quasi-anatomical model of awareness in vertebrate brains. Cortex refers primarily to neocortex and hippocampus in mammals and their homologues in birds and reptiles (see Fig. 5.3). Subcortex refers to the rest of the central nervous system, including spinal cord. Sensory and motor systems have cortical and subcortical components. Double arrows show mutual exchange of information or input/output relationships.

association learning, but should demonstrate a loss of representational capacities. Neodecorticated rats and rabbits have been found in fact to show habituation (Yeo and Oakley, 1983), nictitating membrane conditioning (e.g. Oakley and Russell, 1977), autoshaping (Oakley, Eames, Jacobs, Davey and Cleland, 1981), alleyway running for food reward (Oakley, 1979b) and bar-pressing on ratios of up to sixty presses per reinforcement (e.g. Oakley, 1980). In many of these studies the association learning produced by the animals without neocortex was more reliable and more vigorous than that of normal animals, but it was also noticeably more bound by immediate stimulus and response factors. Damage to the hippocampus, similarly, does not impair the basic processes of either Pavlovian or instrumental learning (see O'Keefe and Nadel, 1978, for a review).

Abilities dependent upon representational systems, such as spatial mapping in a water maze, on the other hand, are abolished both by damage to the hippocampal system (Sutherland, Kolb and Whishaw, 1982) and by removal of neocortex (Kolb, Sutherland and Whishaw, 1983). A mammal deprived of neocortex and hippocampus can thus be said to show simple awareness but not consciousness, if the above arguments and their supporting data are accepted. It is an interesting corollary to this that it is also possible to imagine a situation in which consciousness could exist without simple awareness. Cognitive processes may perhaps continue on the basis of sensory input and stored representations provided neocortical and hippocampal systems are intact, even if reflex behavioural responsiveness and the products of association learning are absent, due possibly to diffuse subcortical damage. At the comparative level it would appear that simple awareness, in the form of the ability to form new associations in the traditional learning paradigms, is present in all animals from protozoans onwards, and is present throughout the nervous systems of those animals which have them (see Oakley, 1979a). The last point is particularly well documented in recent studies showing good evidence of instrumental learning in the isolated spinal cord in rats (Sherman, Hoeler and Buerger, 1982), and of Pavlovian conditioning of a bladder reflex in a spinal human (Ince, Brucker and Alba, 1978). In both phylogenetic and neuroanatomical comparisons, however, there is a considerable expansion in the range of behavioural reactions and associatively learned responses which are possible as central nervous systems appear and differentiate or as more rostral structures remain intact. On this basis it is possible to claim that the simple awareness shown by a paramecium is less than that of a rat, but that this is a difference of amount rather than kind.

Consciousness

Consciousness is qualitatively different from simple awareness in that it depends on different information processing strategies. If I am consistent I must go on to claim also that consciousness, in the form of a representational learning capacity, emerged after the evolution of the hippocampus and neocortex or their homologues, at some point in their subsequent differentiation. Taking the emergence of a differentiated neocortex as a criterion, strong candidates for consciousness would be the more differentiated reptiles, birds and mammals. In reptiles the dorsal ventricular ridge is considered to be homologous to neocortex, as are the neostriatum and wulst of birds, and whilst these are very differently organized structures from the neocortex, there is at present no good reason for assuming that they are not also involved in representational processing (see Figure 5.3). The relevant behavioural data are only now being gathered with the renewal of interest in a cognitive approach to animal learning abilities, and only a few comments can be offered here. It would seem that reptiles are not only capable of learning in a wide range of behavioural situations but some may also form representations of the environment. Brattstrom (1978), for instance, has claimed that the western fence lizard is capable of learning the location of heat sources during its exploration of a complex maze, and to later use that knowledge when returned to the maze after being cooled for five minutes at 10°C. If the capacity to display this type of latent (or image driven) learning turns out to be a general ability of some types of reptile then it can be taken as an example of representational ability and therefore, on my definition, of consciousness. Examples of spatial mapping which suggest cognitive structures in both birds and mammals were presented in the previous chapter and need not be repeated here. The case for attributing cognitive capacities to birds and mammals in preference to other types of vertebrates is discussed further in Walker (1983). In animals other than birds, reptiles and mammals, it is possible to find reports of spatial map formation, though this seems generally to be of a highly specific kind which does not support flexible behaviour. The sort of examples I have in mind are the abilities of digger wasps, bees and butterflies to learn the spatial layout of their territories or burrows.

Fig. 5.3 Showing the derivation of neocortex in mammals and its homologues in reptiles and birds from a hypothetical common ancestor. In the hypothetical ancestor the major structures forming the cerebral hemispheres are shown surrounding the central ventricles (in black). The primordial hippocampal cortex (hi) and pyriform cortex (p) are separated by a primordial dorsal cortex (d) and flanked by the mass of cells identified as the dorsal ventricular ridge (DVR) or (in mammalian embryology) the lateral ganglionic eminence (LGE). Neocortex (nc) is derived developmentally from dorsal cortex and cells migrating from the lateral ganglionic eminence. The homologues of neocortex in reptiles are thus the greatly expanded dorsal ventricular ridge and the relatively underdeveloped dorsal cortex. In birds the homologues of neocortex are shown as the neostriatum (N) which derives from the dorsal ventricular ridge and the wulst (W) which derives from dorsal cortex. Note that though neocortex is shown as convoluted in the placental mammal many have smooth (unconvoluted) surfaces to their cerebral hemispheres. In mammals the hippocampal cortex is folded upon itself and becomes enclosed within the hemispheres to form the hippocampus. Also shown in the figure is

(continued)

Figure 5.3—continued

the medially located septum (S) and the corpus striatum (St), which in mammals becomes incorporated within the hemispheres forming the basal ganglia (caudate, putamen and globus pallidus). The oval superimposed on the corpus striatum represents a bundle of fibres arriving from the thalamus, and the lines radiating from it indicate thalamic projections within the hemispheres. The corpus callosum (cc) is composed of fibres linking neocortical regions of the two hemispheres in placental mammals.

In amphibian brains the same general arrangement exists as is depicted in the hypothetical ancestor except that the DVR/LGE region is not represented. In fish the appropriate homologies are difficult to establish. This is particularly the case for the bony fishes (teleosts) in which the cerebral hemispheres develop in quite a different way, without the formation of a central ventricle. In the cartilaginous fish, such as sharks, a more orthodox vertebrate plan is evident in brain development, and the subdivisions of the cerebral hemispheres seem to be similar to those described for amphibians (see Macphail, 1982). It is clear, however, that fish and amphibians, irrespective of homologies, have proportionately much smaller and less differentiated cerebral hemispheres than birds, mammals and many reptiles.

For convenience only the left hemispheres are shown for birds and reptiles and only right hemispheres for the mammals. This figure is based largely on Karten (1969) and Northcutt (1978). I am grateful to Euan Macphail and to Jane Mitchell for their comments on an earlier version of the figure.

They commonly achieve this during a single orientation flight, apparently on the basis of rigid, two-dimensional 'snapshots' or eidetic images, which are quite unlike the representational mapping systems suggested above for birds, reptiles and mammals (see Collett and Cartwright, 1983, for further discussion). Other impressive spatial performances may resolve themselves, in part at least, in terms of unsuspected environmental cues such as appears to be the case for homing in salmon and the peculiar ability of the limpet to return to home base – apparently in this case by following its own slime trail (see Baker 1982; Walker, 1983).

Self-awareness

By argument from our own case, self-awareness reflects an ability to attend to, or become aware of, certain aspects of our own consciousness. We may become aware of at least some of the information arriving from our sensory systems, particularly of our complex visual world, of having feelings and emotions of various sorts, of entertaining and dismissing thoughts and of originating actions. It is evident also that there are limits to self-awareness and that we cannot admit more than a few aspects of consciousness into our window of self-awareness at any one time. John O'Keefe's account (see p. 63) of the passage of external events, thoughts and plans into and out of self-awareness (which he calls consciousness) as he sat writing chapter 3 of this volume captures well the fleetingness, intermittency and the apparent serendipity of the process. It also appears that what enters self-awareness is determined at times by what is already there. One train of thought leads to another, conjures up its own images, directs a sequence of actions, and this, perhaps, presents a new set of information for our visual inspection. At other times it is clear that the contents of our self-awareness are determined from elsewhere. An emergency may forcibly shift our attention to its source and fully occupy our self-awareness until it is resolved. This implies an evaluative process, within the representational systems underlying consciousness, which identifies some items for immediate re-representation into self-awareness (see Dixon, 1981, and Dixon and Henley, 1980, for excellent discussions of this selection process). Some emergencies, however, develop so quickly that we may react reflexively or through over-learned, habitual responses before self-awareness is appropriately engaged. In these cases we are left with the circumstances of the emergency and our reaction to it represented in self-awareness. We may then reflect on the appropriateness of that reaction and rehearse other solutions which might have been tried. It is also the case that actions, at least those which we are prepared to take responsibility for, are initiated via self-awareness, and this may give some clue as to its adaptive significance.

The animal body is a very limited output system and usually only one of its range of possible responses can be executed at a given time. Equally, of the vast array of stimulus inputs and central representations available, only some will be relevant to the solution of an immediate problem. It seems reasonable to suppose that originally some small part of the brain's overall capacity, perhaps within particular cortical systems, was held in permanent reserve to handle and rework relevant information from a variety of sources and to achieve a priority access to the effector systems. This area within which selected contents of consciousness systems could be re-represented forms the basis of self-awareness. When tackling an immediately pressing problem the self-awareness system is taken up completely with the relevant sensory data and representations upon which action is based. In less demanding conditions, when a physical response is not called for, however, the priority processing area remains available and can accept lower priority items, including items which are quite divorced from external events. The extreme of this last process in ourselves is a mental reverie or daydream, though there are normally sufficient numbers of external events earmarked for special attention and possible action to ensure that externally and internally derived events are mixed in self-awareness. It seems likely that the contents of self-awareness are preferentially passed back to representational systems for storage within biographical or 'episodic' memory (see Oakley, 1983; Oakley and Eames, chapter 8 of this volume), and for recall if necessary. If so, this would go some way to explaining the sense of continuity and unity which attends the stream of self-awareness. It is also worth reiterating that some representations within consciousness concern our own internal states and their identification as particular feelings or emotions. When they are re-represented in self-awareness a subjective emotional state is experienced which can influence action, whether or not its origin is known.

Self-awareness, then, is being presented here as derived from a priority decision making and action system, which re-represents information from representational systems elsewhere in the brain, particularly on the basis of relevance to the task in hand. As such it will contain only a selected subset of the contents of consciousness, and it is this subset which will be reportable by the individual as forming the immediate contents of his or her mind. The subjective aspects of all this are still hard to comprehend, and it must suffice to claim that subjective self-awareness *is* the operation of the self-awareness system. I would also claim that self-awareness has high biological adaptiveness and is present to some degree whenever representational systems have been developed. It serves to ensure rapid decision making and appropriate action, on the basis of immediate data and of stored representations of the real world. On this assumption it follows that all animals which display consciousness will also display self-awareness, the nature and contents of which will depend on the types of representation which exist as the substrate of consciousness itself. By the same token it would follow that a machine employing the same information processing strategies would share the subjective experience of self-awareness, though, as in animals, its existence would be difficult to detect. It is nevertheless worth considering the question of subjective experience a little further.

We are prepared to accept that some aspects of human behaviour are explicable only if subjective factors are taken into consideration. Particularly important among these subjective factors are those which we identify with different feelings or emotions. An account of the human activity of hang-gliding, for instance, would be curiously unsatisfactory if it omitted reference to feelings of pleasure, exhilaration and a sense of achievement in its participants. Indeed, the behaviour would be virtually inexplicable in other terms. What arrogance on our part, then, leads us to look for different explanations when we see birds soaring repeatedly on updraughts of air? Could it not be, as Griffin (1976) asks, at least in part for the sheer joy of the experience. Similarly, is it entirely foolish to say that a bird may sing because it is happy? Australian and New Guinean bower birds build particularly fine and elaborate bowers in a small clearing, which they keep tidy. They decorate the grass and twig structures with fruit and flowers, as well as human artefacts such as jewellery, coins and car keys. The males display their constructions to females and the bowers clearly play a part in mate selection, but there is a continuing debate as to whether they reveal in addition an aesthetic sense or whether the males enjoy creating their bowers. It is certainly the case that the birds select items which are beautiful to our eyes, and that they discard flowers when they wilt and feathers when they are past their best. The attribution of such feelings to animals and giving them a causal status will be seen by many as a retrograde step, and most of my readers will have felt uncomfortable as the above unfolded. Certainly I had to resist the temptation to litter what I wrote with apologetic quotation marks. We are curiously less reluctant to assume that a food-deprived animal feels something akin to hunger or that an injured animal feels pain. Perhaps we only wish to deny that animals can have pleasant emotions. The unpleasant ones we are more prepared to share.

Part of the problem in the examples I have given is that they all involve birds, and I am likely to have more success if I argue for subjective feelings as motivations in their own right in primates. Chimpanzees, for example, are renowned for an apparent sense of humour. They respond to certain situations with shrieks of appreciation and recreate similar situations whenever the opportunity arises. Chimpanzee humour tends to be somewhat earthy, involved as much of it is with the messier bodily functions, but at times it is much more subtle. Linden (1976) recounts that Lucy, one of the chimpanzees who had been taught Ameslan (American Sign Language), was much amused by a game in which her handler would turn his head to one side and then would slide a pair of sunglasses past his wide open mouth and along the far side of his face, giving the appearance from Lucy's position that he was swallowing them. Lucy would watch this act repeatedly with unfailing enthusiasm, finding its culmination hysterically funny. On one occasion when the game was finished Lucy took the glasses and her mirror and repeated the trick with evident delight, watching its effect in the mirror. Having passed the glasses along the concealed side of her face Lucy signed 'look swallow' to her human companion and went on to repeat the act twice more. I have recounted this story in the spirit in which it was originally told, quite deliberately retaining the attributions of subjective feelings to Lucy. The point is that without assuming amusement, delight and so forth, not only Lucy's willingness to watch the original demonstrations but also her repetition of them would be hard to account for, except by appealing to a pointless urge to imitate. Without some assumption of subjective self-awareness it would be difficult to understand why another chimpanzee, Washoe, in more traditional form, was moved to reward unfairly the opportunity of a shoulder ride from her trainer by urinating on him and then signing 'funny' in what Linden calls a 'self-congratulatory way'.

Should we continue to regard a cultivated disinterest in the possible explanatory value of subjective experience in animals as a mark of scientific respectability or is it, as Griffin (1976) suggests, an obsolete strait-jacket which limits our attempts fully to understand and explain animal behaviour? The arguments offered in this chapter, based on the biological continuity of mental capacities, would urge a greater willingness to search for appropriate evidence of subjective experience throughout the animal kingdom.

Self-image

One of the tasks of representational systems is to form an accurate model of the modeller himself. A representation, that is, of the self as an actor with a range of possible relationships with the environment and with other individuals. This model may be entered into self-awareness, generating as it does so an awareness of the self as an

initiator of actions, an entity in its own right with unique characteristics, with particular feelings, emotions and desires. For ourselves the
sense of identity, a sense of 'me-ness', is perhaps the most powerful
and influential part of the contents of self-awareness. Within self-
awareness we are able either to attend to the world around us or to
turn within, to contemplate ourselves as perceivers of the world, as
continuing beings with a past history, present and future goals, and
ultimately to contemplate an end, or possibly a new beginning, in
death. Self-awareness thus has a 'bidirectional' aspect (see also
Gallup, 1977; Suarez and Gallup, 1981). Once a self-representation
enters self-awareness it becomes a self-image, which is thus a reflection of a capacity to become the object of one's own attention.

Effective action in the world depends on representations which are
both predictive and consistent. This is equally true of self-representation in consciousness and its counterpart in self-awareness, the self-
image. We should expect to see a predisposition, therefore, towards
developing a functional self-image with both internal consistency and
constancy over time. We should also expect behaviour to be powerfully affected by the self-image and the need to retain its essential
features. These tendencies in ourselves are well documented in social
psychology, in theories which stress the importance of retaining consistency in our cognitions of ourselves, and of reducing dissonance
between beliefs and actions. Self-image and its effects on behaviour
are also reflected in the view that man is a scientist testing hypotheses
about himself and others, and behaves in response to such aspects of
personal theories as the perceived locus of control. A failure to
develop and maintain a consistent self-image would be expected to
result in behavioural pathology. Slobodkin (1978) has argued that the
tendency to form a self-image in humans is so strong as to warrant the
belief that it is biologically based. He notes that the behavioural
manifestations of the 'self' appear consistently around the age of 2 to 3
years, at which time the child can refer to himself or take on the roles
of others, suggesting that he sees himself as an entity with some sort of
separate existence. More important for Slobodkin, however, is that
though the formation of a self-image can be seen as the result of a biological imperative, the contents of the self-image are not biologically
predisposed but are determined by the individual's own experience
within his or her cultural group. Our behaviour as individuals is
determined in significant ways by whether we perceive ourselves, for
example, to be warriors or pacifists, and the conduct of whole societies

may reflect the self-image which they foster in their members. Slobod-kin offers this perspective as a counter to those who believe that humans are ordained by their biology to act aggressively, to fear their neighbours and so forth. The history of mankind, he proposes, is not determined by biology but by the contents of the self-image, and that is open to cultural influence.

The evidence for the existence of a self-image in humans comes from our own introspection and from sharing that introspection with others, by means of a common language. It is not clear how we would obtain acceptable evidence of a self-image in animals. One criterion of self-image, however, is the ability to become the focus of one's own attention, and one manifestation of such an ability may be self-recognition when confronted with a mirror. In pursuit of information on self-recognition in animals, a series of studies was conducted by Gallup (1977) on a group of wild-born pre-adolescent chimpanzees. Each animal was individually housed for the experiment and given access to a full-length mirror over a period of ten days. Initially the chimpanzees, like other animals, directed social responses towards the image in the mirror. They threatened it and vocalized towards it, as they would to another chimpanzee. Within two or three days, how-ever, these reactions were replaced by self-directed responses, and the animals were seen using their mirror image to groom themselves, remove particles of food from between their teeth and to inspect parts of their bodies which they could not otherwise see, as well as pulling faces and blowing bubbles at the mirror. On the eleventh day the chimpanzees were anaesthetized, the mirrors were removed and each animal was marked with a red, odourless, non-irritant dye above one eyebrow and on top of the opposite ear. Neither of these locations could be viewed by the chimpanzee without the use of a mirror. Once they had recovered the animals were observed closely and were seen to touch the marks very rarely. Once the mirrors were reintroduced, however, a twenty-five-fold increase in the number of touches to the marked places was seen – especially to the eyebrow. Interestingly, on a number of occasions the chimpanzees were seen touching the marked area and then looking at and licking their fingers, even though the dye was indelible. As a control, a group of chimpanzees who had no prior experience of mirrors was marked in a similar fashion. When they were introduced to a mirror for the first time they showed no particular interest in the marks on their faces. It would seem, therefore, that the first group of animals possessed an image of themselves which did not include red facial markings, and seemed at some pains thereafter to restore that image by removing their newly acquired blemishes.

The self-recognition experiment has been repeated with positive results with one other ape, the orang-utan, but, somewhat surprisingly, gorillas did not display evidence of self-recognition, though they readily groomed a marked area such as their wrist if it was visible without the mirror (Suarez and Gallup, 1981). This failure is particularly unexpected in view of the closeness of the gorilla's genetic relationship to ourselves and because on other measures their performance is equal to, or better than, that of the other great apes and human infants. One of Piaget's stages of sensorimotor development, that of object permanence, for instance, is reached via the same developmental sequence in gorilla and human infants (Redshaw, 1978). This is particularly relevant here as the achievement of object permanence has been claimed as a necessary step in achieving self-recognition (see Gallup, 1979). Attempts to demonstrate self-recognition have been unsuccessful in one other ape, the gibbon, and in a wide variety of monkeys (see Gallup, 1977). This was true even after 2400 hours of mirror experience in a wild-born crab-eating macaque, whereas as little as four days of mirror exposure has been found to be sufficient for chimpanzees to pass the marking test of self-recognition (Suarez and Gallup, 1981). By contrast monkeys are able to learn to use mirrors to help in manipulating objects and acquire the trick of turning away from a mirror to reach an object which they see reflected in it. Some human retardates have also been found to lack self-recognition in mirrors (e.g. Harris, 1977).

In connection with these failures in self-recognition, it should be noted that whilst the acquired skill of mirror recognition would seem to require the existence of a self-image, the self-image is not a product of the mirror experience, nor is failure of self-recognition a sure sign that a self-image is absent. It is quite possible that gibbons, gorillas and monkeys as well as non-primates possess a self-image, but are unable to use the subtle cues of simultaneous and parallel action from the mirror to make the connection between what they see there and their internal representation of themselves. The same point could be made in our own case. It seems clear that what we know of our physical appearance, and hence our capacity for self-recognition, is learned and derived from our obsession with our own reflection. Indeed, people who acquire sight in later life are said initially to treat their mirror image as another person (von Senden, 1960), and normally sighted children are also apt to respond to their mirror image in this way and show no signs of self-recognition below the age of two years. We would not, however, conclude that a self-image would be absent merely as a result of being deprived of mirrors during childhood or having been born blind.

If self-recognition is a means of revealing an existing self-image, conditions which prevent or impair the formation of a self-image should equally interfere with the acquisition of self-recognition, irrespective of the amount of practice with mirrors. An important source of information for forming a self-image is the observation of conspecifics and interaction with other individuals, providing data which can then be generalized to apply to the self. Depriving chimpanzees of this sort of information by rearing them in isolation has been found to prevent self-recognition. This may be because they have developed an inadequate self-representation, and hence self-image, upon which to make the connection between themselves and their reflection in a mirror. Similar failure of self-recognition, accompanied by prolonged mirror gazing, has also been reported for some human schizophrenics (see Gallup, 1977). If self-image is derived in part from observing other individuals of the observer's own species it is likely that the exclusive company of individuals of another species will affect the nature of an animal's self-image. Chimpanzees reared with humans have been reported to classify themselves as humans rather than apes, and this has been used to explain the generally poor sexual adjustment which these animals later show to other chimpanzees. In a similar vein the disparaging comments which Washoe made about other chimpanzees, signing them as 'black bugs', is widely quoted, as is the fact that another chimpanzee, Vicki, placed a picture of herself on a pile containing humans but committed her father's picture to the pile containing elephants and horses (see Linden, 1976).

The self-recognition studies with mirrors appear to show that an animal may become the object of its own attention and in this sense to display a self-image. The nature of subjective experience is such that I cannot conclude with any certainty that what a chimpanzee experiences when showing self-recognition is the same as a human being in the same situation. As noted many times before, however, the same can be said of my subjective experience as compared to yours. At the moment the self-recognition data is about the closest we have come to taking an introspective report from a chimpanzee, and the answer we

have received, if we choose to believe it, is consistent with the existence of a self-image and appropriate subjective accompaniments.
The species differences in self-recognition may reflect differences in
the underlying self-representations in the animals concerned, or they
may reflect the level of cognitive skill required to detect and understand the meaning of the concordance between one's own movements
and those of a reflection. In the future the problem of mapping
subjective experience in animals may be resolved by direct communication in a common language (see Griffin, 1976). At present the status
of sign-based language in chimpanzees is unsettled, with a healthy
scepticism prevailing (see Passingham, 1982; Terrace, Pettito,
Sanders and Bever, 1979). If the more optimstic claims prove justi-
fied, however, there is already evidence that these animals are able to
refer to themselves in a way which suggests self-image. Washoe and
others have used compound signs for 'me tickle you' and 'you tickle
me', for example, in appropriate contexts and with what some
observers have felt to be perfect understanding of their distinction (see
Linden, 1976). They may be a product of nothing more than rote
learning or may reflect underlying cognitive structures which relate to
the interaction between the self and others.

A note on terminology

As I indicated at the beginning of this chapter there are a large number
of conflicting usages of the terms 'awareness' and 'consciousness' and
my own proposals have added to that list. It would be a massive, and
probably unprofitable, exercise to try and relate many other
definitions to my own scheme, but a few comments on terminology as it
relates to authors within this volume, and to some of those whose work
has been cited in this chapter, may be useful. I have adopted the view
that consciousness can be defined, irrespective of its subjective
accompaniments, as synonymous with the use of mapping or representational strategies of information processing. This is very similar to
Jerison's view of consciousness as 'a simplifying device, a model of
possible reality' (Jerison, 1973 and this volume), and to Griffin's
equation of consciousness with 'the presence of mental images and
their use by an animal to regulate its behaviour' (Griffin, 1976). This
approach raises the problem that there are some contents of mind of
which we are immediately 'aware' in the sense that we can report them

to ourselves and to others. I have identified this subjectively experienced subset of mental events as constituting self-awareness, but for many this is true 'consciousness'. In common parlance we have ideas, percepts and so forth moving into, and out of, 'consciousness'. This is the sense in which O'Keefe uses the term 'consciousness' in chapter 4 of this volume, and is also what Gallup is referring to when he distinguishes outward looking 'consciousness' and inward looking 'self-consciousness' (or 'self-awareness'). Dixon labels what I have called self-awareness as 'consciousness' or 'conscious awareness', and identifies the areas of information processing which do not achieve 'conscious representation' as 'preconscious processing', mediating among other things 'perception without awareness' (Dixon, 1981; Dixon and Henley, 1980). He also identifies within the preconscious processing system (which is equivalent to consciousness in my scheme) a means of setting criteria for the entry of items into 'consciousness', on the basis of physical and semantic attributes of incoming stimuli as well as factors such as attention and set. The plethora of quotation marks which I have used to distinguish other people's labels from my own is a testimony to the difficulties which arise in trying to reconcile separately derived terminologies.

References

Baker, R. R. (1982) *Migration: Paths Through Time and Space*. London: Hodder & Stoughton.

Brattstrom, B. H. (1978) Learning studies in lizards. In N. Greenberg and P. D. MacLean (eds) *Behavior and Neurology of Lizards*, 173–81. Rockville, Md: National Institute of Mental Health.

Collett, T. S. and Cartwright, B. A. (1983) Eidetic images in insects: their role in navigation. *Trends in NeuroSciences 6*: 101–5.

Dixon, N. F. (1981) *Preconscious Processing*. Chichester: Wiley.

Dixon, N. F. and Henley, S. H. A. (1980) Without awareness. In M. A. Jeeves (ed.) *Psychology Survey 3*: London: George Allen & Unwin. 31–50.

Gallup, G. G. (1977) Self-recognition in primates: a comparative approach to the bi-directional properties of consciousness. *American Psychologist 32*: 329–38.

Gallup, G. G. (1979) Self-recognition in chimpanzees and man: a developmental and comparative perspective. In M. Lewis and L. A. Rosenblum (eds) *Genesis of Behavior*, vol. 2: *The Child and its Family*. New York: Plenum Press.

Griffin, D. R. (1976) *The Question of Animal Awareness: Evolutionary Continuity of Mental Experience*. New York: Rockefeller University Press.

150   Brain and Mind

Harris, L. P. (1977) Self-recognition among institutionalized, profoundly retarded males: a replication. *Bulletin of the Psychonomic Society 9*: 43–4.

Ince, L. P., Brucker, B. S. and Alba, A. (1978) Reflex conditioning in spinal man. *Journal of Comparative and Physiological Psychology 92*: 796–802.

Jerison, H. J. (1973) *Evolution of the Brain and Intelligence*. New York: Academic Press.

Jerison, H. J. (1976) Palaeoneurology and the evolution of mind. *Scientific American 234*: 90–101.

Karten, H. H. (1969) The organization of the avian telencephalon and some speculations on the phylogeny of the amniote telencephalon. *Annals of the New York Academy of Science 167*: 164–79.

Kolb, B., Sutherland, R. J. and Whishaw, I. Q. (1983) A comparison of the contributions of the frontal and parietal association cortex to spatial localization in rats. *Behavioral Neuroscience 97*: 13–27.

Linden, E. (1976) *Apes, Men and Language*. New York: Penguin.

Macphail, E. M. (1982) *Brain and Intelligence in Vertebrates*. Oxford: Clarendon Press.

Morgan, M. J. and Nicholas, D. J. (1979) Discrimination between reinforced action patterns in the rat. *Learning and Motivation 10*: 1–22.

Northcutt, R. G. (1978) Forebrain and midbrain organization in lizards and its phylogenetic significance. In N. Greenberg and P. D. MacLean (eds) *Behavior and Neurology of Lizards*, 11–64. Rockville, Md: National Institute of Mental Health.

Oakley, D. A. (1979a) Cerebral cortex and adaptive behaviour. In D. A. Oakley and H. C. Plotkin (eds) *Brain, Behaviour and Evolution*, 154–88. London: Methuen.

Oakley, D. A. (1979b) Learning with food reward and shock avoidance in neodecorticate rats. *Experimental Neurology 63*: 627–42.

Oakley, D. A. (1980) Improved instrumental learning in neodecorticate rats. *Physiology and Behavior 24*: 357–66.

Oakley, D. A. (1983) The varieties of memory: a phylogenetic approach. In A. Mayes (ed.) *Memory in Animals and Humans*. Wokingham: Van Nostrand Reinhold.

Oakley, D. A., Eames, L. C., Jacobs, J. L., Davey, G. C. L. and Cleland, G. C. (1981) Signal-centered action patterns in rats without neocortex in a Pavlovian conditioning situation. *Physiological Psychology 9*: 135–44.

Oakley, D. A. and Russell, I. S. (1977) Subcortical storage of Pavlovian conditioning in the rabbit. *Physiology and Behavior 18*: 931–7.

O'Keefe, J. and Nadel, L. (1978) *The Hippocampus as a Cognitive Map*. Oxford: Clarendon Press.

Passingham, R. E. (1982) *The Human Primate*. Oxford: W. H. Freeman.

Redshaw, M. (1978) Cognitive development in human and gorilla infants. *Journal of Human Evolution 7*: 133–41.

Sherman, B. S., Hoeler, F. K. and Buerger, A. A. (1982) Instrumental avoidance conditioning of increased leg lowering in the spinal rat. *Physiology and Behavior 25*: 123–8.

Slobodkin, L. B. (1978) Is history a consequence of evolution? In P. P. G. Bateson and P. H. Klopfer (eds) *Perspectives in Ethology*, vol. 3, 233–55. New York: Plenum Press.

Suarez, S. D. and Gallup, G. G. (1981) Self-recognition in chimpanzees and orangutans, but not gorillas. *Journal of Human Evolution 10*: 175–88.

Sutherland, R. J., Kolb, B. and Whishaw, I. Q. (1982) Spatial mapping: definitive disruption by hippocampal or medial frontal cortical damage in the rat. *Neuroscience Letters 31*: 271–6.

Terrace, H. S., Petitto, L. A., Sanders, R. J. and Bever, T. G. (1979) Can an ape create a sentence? *Science 206 (4421)*: 891–902.

von Senden, M. (1960) *Space and Sight: The Perception of Space and Shape in the Congenitally Blind Before and After Operation*. Glencoe, Ill.: Free Press.

Walker, S. (1983) *Animal Thought*. London: Routledge & Kegan Paul.

Yeo, A. G. and Oakley, D. A. (1983) Habituation of distraction to a tone in the absence of neocortex in rats. *Behavioural Brain Research 8*: 403–9.

6 Neuropsychology of consciousness: a review of human clinical evidence

Freda Newcombe

'wherefore I assert that the brain is the *interpreter of consciousness*' (Hippocrates)

'the first and foremost concrete fact which everyone will affirm to belong to his inner experience is the fact that consciousness of some sort goes on' (James, 1880)

'it is not the existence of consciousness but the nature of conscious experience that remains the open question' (Solomon, 1982)

'that of which I am conscious is that to which I have *access*, or (to put the emphasis where it belongs) that to which *I* have access' (Dennett, 1979)

Young (1951, p. 155–6) has suggested that 'the terminology of psychology consists of a series of occult qualities' interposed between the observer and that which he attempts to describe. As an illustration, he took the example of 'consciousness', and its disruption by concussion. Imprecise terminology leads to the fallacy that 'consciousness' is envisaged as '. . . a single thing, which could exist independently of the rest of ourselves'. The term 'consciousness' then becomes at best a metaphor that does not lend itself to scientific investigation.

The problem of defining consciousness is an occupational hazard not confined to philosophers and retired neurologists still determined to grapple with the body–mind problem. It emerges at a practical

clinical level in an intensive care unit, where estimates of 'level of consciousness' are made that have an important bearing on management
and prognosis. In this setting, experienced clinicians, who probably
do not use identical criteria, certainly do not make the same estimates
of level of consciousness. Thus, Jennett and Bond (1975) devised a
coma scale, measuring behavioural responses (eye movement, sensorimotor response to a painful stimulus and verbal response to the exam-
iner's spoken command) on a putative continuum from coma to the
conscious, responsive state. Not surprisingly, this scale has proved
remarkably consistent between examiners and across populations of
head-injured patients in three countries (Jennett, Snoek, Bond and
Brooks, 1981); and it assists in predicting – albeit in coarse categories
– patterns of recovery, in terms of physical independence and
residual psychological symptoms. Thus, one translation of the term
'consciousness' is that of the *wakeful and responsive state*.

In fact, neurologists have traditionally distinguished between a
state of wakefulness, described variously as 'vigilance' (Head, 1923:
'. . . this state of high-grade physiological efficiency') or 'crude consciousness' (Cazzullo and Mancia, 1964) and *the contents of conscious
experience* (see Frederiks, 1969, for a useful review). Some traumas,
such as severe closed head injury, may permanently or transiently
disturb the state; other neurological disorders – for example, partial
neglect of visual, tactual, auditory or somaesthesic stimuli – affect
and limit the contents. This distinction is instantiated in nervous
structure. Both approaches are necessary for the understanding of
man as an information processing creature. But the latter is undoubtedly a richer source of material for exploring both the variety of
highly modular organizations in the nervous system and the control
structures required for intercommunication between these independent modules (Allport and Funnell, 1981). In that case, we do not ask
'is the subject conscious?' but rather 'what is he conscious of?' We shall
not discuss the more arcane question – 'what is it like to be an "X"?'
Those interested in the intriguing biological and philosophical problems inherent in phylogeny will appreciate a lucid prelude by
Solomon (1982). As far as *the contents of consciousness* are concerned, a conceptual guideline is required. It cannot be definitive but
it may serve as a thread through the labyrinth of speculation and
uncoordinated data that confront the student of our topic. A
plausible schema is that of information processing. Accordingly, we
have to consider the treatment of information in terms of the routes

and representations and of the data-storage systems envisaged in our tentative sketches of the central nervous system. We need, therefore, to examine both the selectivity of input handled by the organism and the output modes. The former invokes the notion of attentional processes as instruments of access for information flowing from the environment or from internal sources. The latter is linked − to an appreciable extent − with the concepts of intention and voluntary control.

Consciousness is patently not dependent on language: the first generations of the congenitally deaf, who invented the initial frozen forms of their own idiosyncratic sign language, clearly had something to say before they had invented a symbolic system for communicating their conscious thoughts and feelings; and young children solve oddity problems before they can verbalize the solution (Lunzer, 1979; and see chapter 7 of this volume for another view on the relationship between language and consciousness). Nor are conscious processes synonymous with cognitive processes: incidental learning, priming, and the acquisition of motor skills are cognitive without being conscious (see also Davidson, 1981). Moreover, in physiological studies of learning, it is clear that much processing takes place at an unconscious level: unit responses occur earlier in the posterior thalamus than in the cortex (Disterhoft and Olds, 1972); and stimulation of the midbrain reticular formation improves retention and compensates for the amnesic effects of fluothane anaesthesia (Bloch, 1970).

The neuropsychologist studies disorders of consciousness for the light they shed on the processes of selective attention and intentional control of behaviour. Some cognitive psychologists have reservations about the extrapolation from pathological data to theories of 'normal' structure and functioning, but it is unreasonable to neglect such 'natural' fractionations of behaviour when designing research on normal populations (see Allport, 1979). They have proved valuable in studies of amnesia (Piercy, 1977; Shallice, 1979) and dyslexia (Marshall and Newcombe, 1973; Coltheart, Patterson and Marshall, 1980); and such 'natural' fractionations certainly occur within other domains of behaviour after brain damage.

In the section that follows we shall consider some pathological evidence with a bearing on the two approaches to a definition of consciousness: altered levels of activation of the central nervous system, and changes in the contents of conscious experience occurring in some of the cognitive disorders associated with brain damage.

Neuropsychological evidence

Alterations in activation

Since Moruzzi and Magoun's (1949) seminal publication, the 'wakeful state' has been associated with the reticular activating system: the structures of brainstem, hypothalamus and thalamus, and their projections to cerebral cortex. This system, receiving afferent input from both external and internal sources, exerts a widespread influence on both sensory and autonomic functions and on cortical activity. Anatomically, it has been subdivided into 'a grosser and more tonically operating component in the lower brainstem, subserving global alterations in excitability, as distinguished from a more cephalic, thalamic component with greater capacities for fractionated, shifting influences upon focal regions of the brain' (Magoun, 1958). In turn, the system is subject to cortical influence and 'this guarantees a kind of feedback relationship between the processing of specific information by the nervous system and the selection from this out of the total of the actual information which is always more than the information that is "used"' (Frederiks, 1969).

Given this widespread functional activity, it is hardly surprising that the search for the seat of consciousness has been unrewarding. Lashley's (1954) amusing but specious attack on the localization of consciousness, however, overstated the case: 'stopping the heart also produces unconsciousness, yet one does not therefore ascribe consciousness to the heart'. Penfield and Jasper's (1947) demonstration of the 'arrest' phenomenon provoked by intralaminar (thalamic) stimulation has to be accommodated; and Galton's earlier intuition — 'there seems to be a chamber in my mind where consciousness holds court' — implies that there are control centres to which evidence from various sources is brought for interpretation and decision. The study of patients at different stages of coma or concussion, produced by severe closed head injury, is informative. An experienced accident surgeon concluded: 'The reticular formation "drives" or "arouses" the cortex, which is responsible for the discriminative activities of the wakeful state. Neither alone suffices for full consciousness and the condition described as coma vigil is a striking and characteristic example of less than full function of the components of consciousness' (London, 1967). (In coma vigil the patient lies with eyes wide open, lips parted and may mutter incoherently, but cannot be roused even by strong external stimuli.) Indeed, if we consider a continuum of activation, then the inertia of coma and the hyperexcitability of an epileptic attack reflect the extremes.

Coma   In coma, automatic functions such as respiration are preserved, but responses to external stimuli such as speech, touch or pin prick are altered. A succession of uninterrupted generalized tonic-clonic seizures can produce coma and has to be treated vigorously in order to forestall anoxia and irreversible brain damage, if not death. Coma (see Jouvet, 1969 for a comprehensive review) has been described as 'a multiple disintegration of consciousness'. It is not produced by a disconnection of efference: tetanus patients under curare – unable to see, speak or move – are nevertheless aware of much that is happening in their immediate surroundings; and it is not synonymous with deep sleep: '. . . states of sleep are the result of an *active* process of inactivation of the waking system . . . prolonged loss of consciousness has never been induced experimentally in animals by stimulation of the sleep systems'. In man, the preservation of consciousness appears to depend on mesencephalon and diencephalon. Acceleration concussion with its widespread shearing of white matter and damage to brainstem structures (Strich, 1969) disrupts this functional system.

    The patient who has survived a long period of coma will inevitably show disturbances of memory that affect his ability both to recall events immediately preceding the accident (retrograde amnesia – RA) and to register and reproduce current information (post-traumatic amnesia – PTA). The period of time covered by RA varies from minutes to months, or even years in unusually severe closed head injury. Initially the amnesia is dense, but it shrinks as the patient recovers and the secondary complications of the injury, such as swelling and haemorrhage, resolve. Then a shorter but permanent RA is left, with a patchy period of recall immediately preceding it of which the patient cannot give a coherent account, though he may experience vivid 'flashbacks' (Williams and Zangwill, 1952). The galloping horse, transiently evoked by one of Russell's (1971) patients (who did not recall the context in which the horse figured as a contributory factor in his accident) is an example of these striking images. The loss of retrograde memories in such cases cannot, however, be ascribed to loss of consciousness *per se* when the events were experienced; the fact that the amnesia is partially reversible makes the point clear. Short periods of amnesia certainly occur without any obvious clouding of consciousness: the footballer may continue to play effectively after a brief concussion but with no subsequent recall of this post-traumatic period — the so-called 'ding' state (Yarnell and Lynch, 1973).

Epilepsy   Disturbances of consciousness, of which the duration may vary from seconds to hours, occur in the different forms of epilepsy. In his study of 'dissolution in post-epileptic conditions', Jackson (1881) referred to the three degrees of 'negative affection of consciousness' — mental confusion, insensibility and coma — as graded 'depths' of dissolution. He explicitly correlated these different stages with 'different degrees of severity of the epileptic discharge' and noted that all three stages might be observed in the same patient. He distinguished between the physical and psychical components and neatly finessed the predictable argument about their connection:

> How can you say that the neuromuscular phenomena spoken of as effecting adjustments of the organism to the environment constitute consciousness, or what is equivalent, that the loss of so many of the nervous arrangements which serve in effecting such adjustments is loss of consciousness? The reply is, that nothing of the kind was said; on the contrary, a very simple affirmation was and is made that consciousness *attends* activity of certain nervous arrangements, and ceases when those nervous arrangements are *hors de combat*.   (Jackson, 1881, reprinted in 1932, p. 16)

Consider now the repetitive, automatic behaviour patterns associated with psychomotor epilepsy, the 'partial complex seizures' of current terminology. During the seizure, the patients may initiate purposeless movements — e.g. lipsmacking, buttoning and unbuttoning a cardigan, displacing objects on the desk in front of them. They have no recollection of this behaviour, essentially aimless, after the seizure. Can they be said to have momentarily lost consciousness as these stereotyped motor programmes are released, or should we regard the phenomenon as yet another example of a selective disconnection (Geschwind, 1965) in which one aspect of behaviour has been triggered without conscious control? In one section of James's (1890, reprinted in 1950) acerbic demolition of the monist approach, he envisaged the possibility that consciousness of some actions may be '*split-off* from the rest of the consciousness of the hemispheres', or else rapidly forgotten after an epileptic attack or its analogue — hypnotic trance. But what of the positive phenomena occurring in epilepsy — the hallucinatory auras (sometimes involving visual or auditory experiences or sensations of taste and smell) and the dream-like feelings of depersonalization, or the *déjà vu* sensations so graphically described by some patients? These patients may appear to the external observer fully awake, even alert. They are undoubtedly conscious but responding to abnormal electrical discharges, probably subcortically driven, that trigger previous or new patterns of response, sometimes accompanied by feelings of strangeness, anxiety and fear.

The apparent loss of consciousness that is observed for seconds only in *petit mal* attacks is associated with the momentary appearance of generalized, bilaterally synchronous, three-per-second spike and wave rhythms on the EEG. This pattern can be produced experimentally by stimulation of the intralaminar nuclei of the thalamus (Penfield and Jasper, 1947). This is further evidence for the important role of the thalamic nuclei in the functional system subserving the alert and wakeful state.

Cognitive disorders

The wide range of these disorders creates a taxonomic problem. For the present purposes, we will consider first the confusional states and the *global* disorders of attention and memory. They have in common that they are often associated with a clouding of consciousness (whether permanent or temporary) or with an abnormal failure to maintain alert and responsive behaviour. We shall then turn to the more *selective* failures of perception, recognition, or response.

Confusional states and global disorders of attention   Attentional disorders are reported to be among the most common disturbances of the higher mental functions seen in neurological practice (Geschwind, 1982). They may occur in some epileptic conditions, and as a consequence of cerebral infarctions, cerebral tumours or CNS infections (such as meningitis, encephalitis or cerebral abscess). Consciousness is not lost but the patient can no longer be described as wakeful and alert. Speech and thinking are not coherent: patients are distractable, do not respond appropriately to cues from their immediate environment, and their behaviour may show a variety of disturbances including apathy, agitation and emotional lability.

Confusional states have not been comprehensively or experimentally explored, despite their frequent occurrence, but there have been attempts to study the pattern of attentional changes in schizophrenia. Conventional behavioural tests of attention are often ambiguous because, as Hink and Hillyard (1978) point out, 'one cannot ascertain whether the data reflect selective attention (i.e. a selective or *differential* allocation of processing capacity to the relevant stimuli in the environment) or general attentiveness (i.e. changes in the *overall* amount of processing capacity) or both'.

It is perhaps surprising that the evoked potential technique has not been used more frequently to study the attentional changes associated with diffuse damage to the central nervous system, as observed after severe closed head injury. Early investigations (Conkey, 1938; Ruesch, 1944) stressed the occurrence of attentional changes, and contemporary rehabilitation regimes (Wood and Eames, 1981) point to the need of retraining in this area. Systematic studies, however, are rare. Hence it is interesting that significant changes in evoked potential have recently been found in patients who incurred a *minor* head injury, for up to six months after the accident (Curry and Cummins, 1981). Conventional cognitive tests have been singularly unsuccessful in demonstrating impairment in this group but such tests rarely tap the patient's capacity to focus and shift attention.

The basic neural circuitry for attentional processes has traditionally included the brainstem reticular formation. But, as Mesulam and Geschwind (1978) emphasize, 'the efficient exercise of vigilance is a highly complex function which presupposes both recognition of what is irrelevant as well as elaborate processing of relevant information . . . it is likely that this process is highly dependent upon neocortical mechanisms'. They report on the acute onset of global inattention after strokes involving frontal, parietal or occipito-temporal areas of the right hemisphere and accordingly suggest that 'the association cortex in the right hemisphere of man may have a unique and essential role in integrating the neural processes which are necessary for the proper execution of selective attention'. This putative laterality effect and its role in unilateral-spatial neglect (to be discussed later) requires confirmation from systematic clinical studies. What can be more readily accommodated with the anatomical schema described earlier is the stress which Mesulam and Geschwind place on the importance of neural connections between neocortex and centres of motivation and emotion in the limbic brain. It is the limbic and paralimbic input, they suggest, that 'may be responsible for directing vigilance towards motivationally relevant events'. This is not a new hypothesis but it is being strengthened by neuropharmacological research, suggesting that dopaminergic and cholinergic synapses are both involved in limbic-cortical circuits, and by growing neuroanatomical evidence, tracking the efferent pathways from limbic system to cortex (Van Hoesen, Pandya and Butters, 1972; Van Hoesen, Rosene and Mesulam, 1979).

Global amnesia   Patients in post-traumatic amnesia may be conscious and able to answer questions of general knowledge despite their inability to remember what is happening around them from moment to moment. Is there any sense in which consciousness could be said to be diminished in severe amnesic disorders?

In the infrequent but interesting cases of transient global amnesia (Fisher and Adams, 1964), we find that patients usually show a transient clouding of consciousness and a mild degree of confusion at the sudden onset of this condition. Thereafter, during the amnesic episode, which lasts less than five hours and typically clears up completely, they appear to behave normally – walking, talking, playing games, even driving to an intended destination. But they generally can recall none of their activities during this period and have a short but permanent RA that is usually proportionate to the amnesia itself. The syndrome, observed in the sixth and seventh decades of life, is thought to be precipitated by transient ischaemia in temporal lobe structures supplied by the posterior cerebral arteries. In all probability most patients suffer from a variant of classical migraine (Caplan, Chedru, Lhermitte, and Mayman 1981). In some patients the condition may be due to focal epileptic discharges, an alternative explanation first suggested by Fisher and Adams (1964). In either case, the amnesia can be ascribed by a dysfunction of the hippocampal and parahippocampal structures subserving memory.

In the permanent amnesic states – the global amnesias associated with Korsakoff psychosis (Talland, 1965), herpes simplex encephalitis (Rose and Symonds, 1960), severe anoxia following status epilepticus (Delay, Brion, Lemperière and Lechevallier, 1965) or bilateral infarction or surgical ablation of the medial temporal lobes (Milner, 1970) – there is no apparent disturbance of consciousness after the acute stage of the illness. Nevertheless patients cannot recall what has happened to them minutes ago. On formal testing, despite a normal 'span of apprehension', measured by the conventional digit-span test, they cannot recall narrative material or remember pictures and faces presented an hour previously.

In some of these patients, the delicate relationship between consciousness and memory is brought into focus. One of the encephalitic patients studied by Rose and Symonds (1960) complained: 'I am in a dream. You don't know how awful it is, I get thousands of impressions and they don't mean anything'. Rose and Symonds described another patient as follows:

he was 'living thousands of different lives', and that this life (in which he was currently speaking) was only one of them . . . he did not know whether he himself was always the same, and could not say that he might not sometimes be himself at an earlier age, e.g. a boy.

A similar description of 'moment-to-moment consciousness' was given by H.M., the patient who sustained a permanent global amnesia after bilateral medial temporal-lobe resection for the relief of intractable epilepsy (Milner, 1966). In his own words:

you see, at this moment everything looks clear to me, but what happened just before? That's what worries me. It's like waking from a dream; I just don't remember.

These patients are therefore conscious of the here and now, in a curiously existential world, apparently deprived of conscious knowledge of the stream of events that led to the present moment. Chunks of information from the remote past are available, but the immediate past is not accessible in a coherent and lucid form. Some traces, a vague unease if some close family member is ill, for example, may remain.

Contemporary cognitive research emphasizes the importance of context in generating the sense of familiarity that leads to conscious recognition. A similar conceptual approach is plausible for the amnesias. In a theoretical analysis of disorders of face recognition, for example, it has been postulated that the role of limbic structures is to 'allow the consolidation of the template and provide it with the code for future activation of contextual information stored simultaneously in other cortices' (Damásio, Damásio and Van Hoesen, 1982).

In Talland's (1965) scholarly monograph on the amnesic syndrome, he drew attention to earlier work on the relation between cognitive and conative factors. Colella (cited by Talland, ibid.) stressed 'the importance of attention and volition as being the functions which, when regained, enable the patients to recover memories at will'. Bürger-Prinz and Büssow (cited by Talland, ibid.) 'affirmed that lack of initiative was the most pronounced defect in amnesic patients' and 'arguing from the absence of affective attitudes and the similarities between this syndrome and pathological sleep states, they advocated that it be regarded as an example of disturbed consciousness'. Talland observed that amnesic patients had been compared with dreamers or somnambulists, adding the gloss that

> even though the finding that the lesion in the amnesic syndrome is close to the centers that control wakefulness and consciousness does not explain anything, it does fit in rather nicely with the generally listless behaviour of the patients, and suggests that the source of their disturbance may be in conative function.

Two decades ago, Lewis (1961) sceptically concluded from a study of the literature on amnesia that 'little progress had been made since Descartes envisaged recall as a searching operation impelled by volition and mediated by the flexion of the pineal gland toward discrete traces in the brain'. Must we now accede that no advances have been made in the three hundred years that followed *Discourse on method*? Certainly not. Post-mortem studies of patients with Korsakoff psychosis (Adams, Collins and Victor, 1962) produced entirely fresh anatomical data, focusing attention on thalamic structures, specifically the dorsal medial nucleus. Neurosurgical and psychological studies of patients subjected to temporal lobectomies for the relief of temporal-lobe epilepsy emphasized the role of hippocampal structures in the functional systems subserving memory (Scoville and Milner, 1957; Milner, 1972). More recent research suggests that the basal forebrain structures are damaged in both Korsakoff's and Alzheimer's disease (Butters, in press). It is now clear that amnesia is not a unitary disorder and 'need not result from damage to a single functional system' (Squire, 1982; see also McEntee, Biber, Perl and Benson, 1976). Animal models have been inadequate and confusing in that human and infrahuman experimental paradigms were rarely comparable. But the recent demonstration (Mishkin, 1978) that

contrast with
Oakley's view

neither hippocampal nor thalamic lesions alone suffice to produce a severe memory impairment in monkeys on tasks more closely simulating those used in human studies, is a promising advance.

From both anatomical and practical, remedial points of view, the relative preservation of motor and 'procedural' learning in amnesic patients is of interest (Milner, 1970; Piercy, 1977; Cohen and Squire, 1980). Cohen and Squire drew on a neat distinction made by the philosopher Ryle between 'knowing how' and 'knowing that'. The 'knowing how' may be achieved without conscious knowledge of the period of acquisition: the patient with tuberculous meningitis who learned to type during the long period of retrograde amnesia retained the skill without remembering how and when he acquired it (Smith, cited by Symonds, 1966); the pianist with Korsakoff's psychosis who learned a new piece to accompany a singer at the hospital concert 'had no recollection of the episode the following morning' (Talland, 1969) and patients learn to read inverted text without remembering the practice sessions (Kolers, 1976). These data point to a separate functional system, presumably involving sensorimotor cortex and basal ganglia, that subserves the acquisition of motor skills.

Agnosias   These classical syndromes include disorders of recognition or identification, affecting a wide range of stimuli: words (auditory word imperception or pure word deafness: Gazzaniga, Glass, Sarno and Posner, 1973); sounds (auditory agnosia: Vignolo, 1982); colours (Oxbury, Oxbury and Humphrey, 1969); familiar faces (prosopagnosia: see Damásio, Damásio and Van Hoesen, 1982); and spatial relations (De Renzi, 1982). Some workers have ascribed agnosic disorders to generalized intellectual impairment and/or subtle alterations of sensation (Bender and Feldman, 1972). No doubt, the emphasis on detailed examination of sensory perceptual status in cases of agnosia is apposite: the clinical varieties of prosopagnosia, for example, suggest different patterns of functional deficit that can be ascribed to failures at different levels of processing, including a high-level integrative stage. There is unequivocal evidence that the agnosias cannot invariably be ascribed to sensory loss (Ratcliffe and Newcombe, 1982).

The relation between sensory processing and conscious identification has, in fact, been studied in more detail in the visual than in the auditory or haptic modality; and, within the visual modality, the identification of objects has perhaps attracted more research than the recognition of other stimuli. Hence we will take visual object agnosia (often loosely described in the literature as 'agnosia') as a paradigm case.

In these disorders (reviewed by Rubens, 1979), a traditional distinction was first put forward by Lissauer in 1890 between failures of 'apperception' (at the level of consciously perceiving a stimulus) and of 'association' (at the level of associating the stimulus with other concepts and properties, in order that its full meaning might be extracted). Patients with apperceptive loss are unable to copy stimuli (e.g. drawings, geometrical patterns) or to match such stimuli. In many respects they resemble patients with variants of the Balint syndrome, including visual disorientation or 'simultagnosia' (De Renzi, 1982). An important feature of Balint's syndrome is a reduction in the range of visual perception without a reduction in the visual field. This typically results in an inability to perceive more than one object at a time (i.e. simultaneous agnosia) irrespective of the size or location of the objects. Tracing or copying an outline becomes impossible because if the pencil point is perceived the line is lost and if the line is identified the pencil point can no longer be seen.

It is the patients with an 'associative' form of the disorder who are of particular interest in terms of the apparent 'disconnection' between sensory processing and 'conscious' identification of the meaning of sensory input — that is, knowledge of the properties and functions of the object. Note that identification does not depend on the retrieval of the object's name; word-finding difficulties are characteristic of aphasia and occur in other neurological conditions (Geschwind, 1967). But the aphasic patient or the mute observer can readily show by mime that he has identified the object. In contrast, patients with associative agnosia cannot identify — by name, mime, verbal descriptions or non-verbal matching task — a drawing of a familiar object (e.g. a bed, a piano or a glove) although they clearly see the object and may indeed be able to make a meticulous copy of it (Ratcliff and Newcombe, 1982). More surprisingly, they may be able to match by function two visually different representations of the same object, e.g. a furled and an open umbrella, rejecting the alternative match of two visually similar drawings — the furled umbrella and a stick — despite the fact that they cannot identify the drawings. The interpretation of this condition is still open to debate; explanatory concepts attribute the identification failure to 'disconnection' (Albert, Reches and Silverberg, 1975), inability to access semantic information (Warrington, 1975) and failure to generate a three-dimensional model of the object-stimuli (Ratcliff and Newcombe, 1982). Whatever the explanation, agnosic disorders of this type point to the complexity of the functional system underpinning our conscious appreciation of the external world, from the level of sensory analysis to the complex processes of identification that depend on access to rich stores of pictorial and semantic information.

The dissociation between conscious and unconscious awareness was well demonstrated by a patient (Damásio, McKee and Damásio, 1979) with agnosic and colour-naming problems, who was asked to colour object-drawings that she was not able to identify. Shown a drawing of a banana, that she did not recognize as such, she selected a yellow pencil but then hesitated, adding that the colour of the pencil looked right 'but really could not be used as it was "red" and that the object was not really red.' The split between conscious and unconscious awareness or detection has been even more dramatically illustrated in the study of commissurotomy patients, and also by the discovery of the phenomenon known as 'blindsight'.

The split-brain preparation: the two-consciousness hypothesis   Clinical examination of the first patients who had undergone surgical section of the corpus callosum suggested that 'no symptoms follow its division' (Dandy, 1936) or that effects on 'gnosis, praxis and language' were mininal (Akelaitis, 1944).

Later, section of the corpus callosum in cat and monkey led Sperry to claim that:

> under special training and testing conditions where the inflow of sensory information to the divided hemispheres can be separately restricted and controlled, one finds that each of the divided hemispheres now has its own independent mental sphere or cognitive system – that is, its own independent perceptual, learning, memory, and other mental processes . . . it is as if the animals had two separate brains.   (1961, p. 1749)

Subsequently, section of the forebrain commissures of patients suffering from intractable *grand mal* epilepsy (Bogen, Fisher and Vogel, 1965) and detailed neuropsychological examination of the sequelae of this radical operation led Sperry (1965) to make an analogous claim for man:

> Everything we have seen so far indicates that the surgery has left these people with two separate minds, that is, two separate spheres

of consciousness. What is experienced in the right hemisphere seems to lie entirely outside the realm of experience of the left hemisphere. This mental dimension has been demonstrated in regard to perception, cognition, volition, learning and memory.

Similar observations were reported eight years later: 'each left and right hemisphere has its own private chain of memories and learning experiences that are inaccessible to recall by the other hemisphere. In many respects each disconnected hemisphere appears to have a separate "mind of its own"' (Sperry, 1974). The experimental observations on which these conclusions were based have been widely published and need no summary here (see Sperry, Gazzaniga and Bogen, 1969; Sperry, 1974; Levy and Trevarthen, 1976; Gazzaniga, LeDoux and Wilson, 1977; Zaidel and Sperry, 1977; and chapters 7 and 8 of this volume). Sperry's claim patently rests on its definition of consciousness. Let us consider some of the evidence.

The restriction of visual input (Zaidel, 1975) to the right hemisphere in these patients provides a unique opportunity to test the cognitive and affective responses of this 'mute' half of the brain, without the support of verbal mediation or of the other processing skills of the left, language-based hemisphere. In these conditions, the right hemisphere can match a word with its object-associate selected from an array by the (right-hemisphere controlled) left hand (e.g. cigarette → ashtray); it can match pictures by appearance (e.g. cake → hat), in contrast to the left hemisphere which tends to match by function (e.g. cake → spoon and fork); chimeric figures (faces or objects) are matched with the object of which the left half was seen by the right hemisphere, instead of stimuli of which the right half was viewed by the left hemisphere; and there is the often-quoted example of the female patient who responded to the picture of a naked woman displayed in the left visual field with 'nothing, just a flash of light' but blushed and giggled as she said it (Sperry and Gazzaniga, 1967).

The novel contribution of the split-brain studies was its demonstration of the (albeit limited) language capacity of the right hemisphere. Using the Z lens, and a matching-to-sample paradigm (spoken word → picture selected from an array), Zaidel (1977, 1978) reported that the right hemisphere of a few patients with a history of early, severe epilepsy had a vocabulary comparable to that of a 10-year-old child, although grammatical comprehension, as measured by an adapted version of the Token test, was more like that of a 5-year-old: an interesting difference between lexical and grammatical knowledge analogous to that found in the twentieth-century feral child − Genie − as she was learning language in her teens. On the evidence of dichotic tests (Fromkin, Kraschen, Curtiss, Rigler and Rigler, 1974; Curtiss, 1977), Genie's right hemisphere was her language hemisphere although her 'right-hemisphere' skills − pattern recognition and visuo-spatial perception − were surprisingly good.

Within the small group of commissurotomy patients, individual differences (a long neglected domain in neuropsychology − see Marshall, 1973) are marked. The young man, P.S., studied in detail by Gazzaniga and his colleagues (Gazzaniga, LeDoux and Wilson, 1977; Gazzaniga and LeDoux, 1978), was singled out by them as 'one truly unique individual case' because of 'the psychological robustness of his right hemisphere . . . although only his left hemisphere can talk, other linguistic skills are extensively represented in both brains'. For example, to the question 'what (spoken) is tomorrow?' (exposed only to the left visual field − right hemisphere combination), P.S. was able to spell with scrabble letters the correct response 'Sunday'. An interesting difference between hemispheres emerged when he was asked what job he would choose. The left hemisphere frequently responded 'draughtsman', the right hemisphere 'automobile race'. Gazzaniga eventually concluded:

> The fact that this mute half-brain could generate personal answers to ambiguous and subjective questions demonstrated that in P.S. the right hemisphere has its own independent response priority determining mechanisms, which is to say its own volitional system. Thus it would appear that the right hemisphere, along with but independent of the left, *can* possess conscious properties following brain bisection. In other words, the mechanism of human consciousness *can* be split and doubled by split-brain surgery.
> (LeDoux, Wilson and Gazzaniga, 1979)

Are we in fact entitled to speak of two consciousnesses . . . two minds? Consider the conventional objection. It can legitimately be claimed that this small group of patients − brain-damaged from birth or in early life − is so atypical in brain development and organization as to prohibit any extrapolation to the normal population. In reply, the data from these studies accord well with contemporary notions of the functional specialization of the hemispheres, suggesting that such an extrapolation is of at least heuristic value. They should stimulate fresh theories of hemispheric function to improve on current, out-worn metaphors: the verbal, analytic, sequential left hemisphere, and the non-verbal, synthetic, holistic right hemisphere. But, even without this justification, the data *per se* require an explanation that cannot avoid the question of consciousness and intention. One interpretation is that 'cognitive processes within either hemisphere can gain access to whatever neural systems are concerned with volition and the latter need in no way be considered to be reduplicated' (Lishman, 1971). (See chapter 7 of this volume for a further discussion of the split-brain data.)

Unilateral neglect or 'inattention'   Failure to report or to respond spontaneously to events in the left visual field is traditionally associated with posterior lesions of the right hemisphere. Frequent clinical observations to this effect were amply confirmed in two of the rare studies of unselected neurological populations with posterior lesions (Hécaen, 1962). A comparable disability – neglect of the right visual field in patients with chronic left posterior lesions – is rare, but can be seen during the acute stage of left hemisphere disease. Recent physiological research, with a possible bearing on this asymmetry, implies that the preponderance of left-sided neglect may be associated with 'an asymmetry in the effect of eye movements after left and right parietal lesions'. On a detection task not involving eye movement, 'genuine contralateral sensory neglect was observed after lesions of either parietal lobe' (Latto, 1982; see also Ungerleider and Mishkin, 1982).

Marked neglect of the left-side of space has been illustrated on a variety of simple tasks: gross inaccuracy in bisecting lines and failure to complete the left side of drawings or to read and write material on the left-hand side of a page. It cannot be ascribed to visual sensory loss and may occur in the absence of a left homonymous hemianopia, although this field defect is a frequent concomitant of the lesions producing neglect. Nor is the defect modality-specific. Patients may neglect stimuli in the 'half-fields' of touch and audition (Heilman and Valenstein, 1972a). In the real world, severely impaired patients may fail to recognize their own left-sided limbs, fail to shave or make up their face on the left side or eat food on the left side of their plates (Denny-Brown and Banker, 1954). They may even deny the existence of hemiplegia or hemiparesis (anosognosia).

Milder manifestations of the neglect syndromes may be elicited when the patient is given stimuli in both half-fields simultaneously: those occurring in the space — visual, tactile or auditory — contralateral to the right hemisphere lesion are either not spontaneously reported or occasionally mislocated in ipsilateral space (allochiria or alloaesthesia). Critchley (1969) has noted the 'clinical resemblance between the unilateral neglect of parietal disease and the poverty of movement of unilateral pallidal affections' with the reservation that 'the other disorders of motility characterizing pallidal hypokinesia are not to be found'. He added: 'this subtle unilateral neglect is usually demonstrable at a stage when the patient's general sensorium is not very clouded. The defect lies outside the patient's awareness.'

The gross symptoms of neglect, a virtual denial of one half of the body, are usually found in association with a considerable degree of mental confusion and psychiatric disability. Critchley cites a number of telling instances: the distinguished scientist quoted by Lhermitte who denied his left hemiplegia and cast doubts on the sanity of his niece because she spoke of his paralysis; von Hagen and Lives' patient who described her left limbs as 'an old man who stays in bed'; and an interesting patient of Nielsen who replied, when shown that her 'neglected' left arm was attached to her body, 'but my eyes and my feelings don't agree, and I must believe my feelings. I know they look like mine, but I can feel that they're not, and I can't believe my eyes'. The last patient gives a clear picture of disconnection, free from the confabulation that often clouds the issue. Denial of blindness (Anton's syndrome) is perhaps the most dramatic example of such a disconnection.

In cases of neglect, therefore, we have to consider a cutting-off or a diminution of awareness, of a *selective* rather than a global nature. It is frequently but not invariably associated with right parietal lesions; thalamic disease has also been implicated as reported by Watson and Heilman (1979). They reported the symptoms of anosognosia, contralateral neglect, limb akinesia and visuo-spatial disorders in three patients with right thalamic lesions due to vascular disease. They suggest that unilateral neglect is 'an attention-arousal defect induced by lesions interrupting a cortico-limbic-reticular activating loop'. In support of this proposition, they point to the well-known physiological evidence that rapid stimulation of the mesencephalic reticular formation induces behavioral arousal with electrocortical desynchronization, the side ipsilateral to stimulation showing more arousal than the contralateral hemisphere (see also Weinburger, Velasco and Lindsley, 1965).

The frontal lobes are also involved in the complex circuitry mediating perception of the body and its external environment. Heilman and Valenstein (1972b) described six patients with lesions of the non-dominant frontal lobe – four attributable to infarction, one to a meningioma, and one to a metastatic tumour – observed during a two-year period. (Hence, as they point out, the association of neglect with frontal lesions is not that rare, even if less common than the co-occurrence of neglect and parietal lesions.) In considering the possible anatomical substrate, they note the physiological evidence of prominent corticocortical interconnections between the three regions implicated in the neglect syndrome in animals: the inferior parietal lobule, the dorsolateral frontal lobe and the cingulate gyrus; and the dense network of connections between these areas and the limbic system, hippocampus, hypothalamus and the diffuse ascending and descending reticular conduction systems.

Regarding the localization of the syndrome of unilateral visual neglect, five patients have recently been reported with lesions, charted from CT scan (Damásio, Damásio and Chui, 1980), in both mesial and dorsolateral aspects of the frontal lobe and in the basal ganglia (caudate nucleus, putamen, globus pallidus and amygdaloid complex). In fact, all but one of them had left hemisphere lesions, and in all cases the neglect seems to have cleared within a few weeks. It is therefore possible that routine clinical examination (which rarely, if ever, involves formal tasks such as line cancellation, the measure used here to elicit neglect for one half of the display) does not pick up this transient phenomenon. The preceding study supports Heilman's model of neglect, comprising sensory motor components and implicating neocortical, limbic and reticular mechanisms in attentional processes. To this circuitry the authors add the neostriatum, and suggest that disruption of any of these components can produce neglect, which will be lateralized or global depending on whether the lesion is unilateral or bilateral. (The basal ganglia excluding the amygdaloid complex comprise the striatum, which is composed of the neostriatum – caudate nucleus and putamen – and the palaeostriatum – globus pallidus.) Animal studies have produced analogous findings: unilateral damage of the striatum in rats produces unilateral neglect (Iversen, 1977) while bilateral damage leads to an akinetic state of global neglect (Ungerstedt, 1971). These authors also draw attention to the strong interconnections between the neocortical and limbic-cortical structures (damaged

in their patients) and area 7 (dorsal parietal cortex) in the parietal
lobe, which they describe as 'a high-level guidance system' (c.f. also
Mountcastle, Lynch and Georgopoulos, 1975; Yin and Mountcastle,
1977; Damásio and Benton, 1979). Of particular interest to our
theme is their reinterpretation of the functional status of area 7 (see
also Rolls, Thorpe, Maddison, Roper-Hall, Puerto and Perret, 1979;
Robinson, Goldberg and Stanton, 1978). They invoke a higher level
of executive decision coming from the sensorimotor area–anterior
cingulate complex, that receives input from both dorsolateral frontal
lobe and subcortical components of the limbic system. They conclude
that classical parietal neglect is principally related to damage to area
7, whereas the form of neglect observed in three of their five cases
results from damage in two sectors of the frontal lobe which constitute
a higher control for the so-called 'parietal command' device (its 'will',
as it were) and for other parietal lobe regions. This suggestion can be
considered in the light of Damásio's (1979) concept of the frontal
lobes as a comparator, capable of performing the environmentally
related 'gating' of diencephalic innate behaviours and able to handle
hypercomplex environmental contingencies.

Current theories of neglect are discussed in a study of Bisiach, Luzzatti and Perani (1979). They dismiss, somewhat peremptorily, explanations in terms of 'amorphosynthesis' (Denny-Brown, Meyer and
Horenstein, 1952) or a one-sided breakdown of mechanisms subserving
the 'orienting response' to incoming stimulations (Heilman and
Watson, 1977) as being unable to account for defective *tactual* 'search'
in the hemi-space contralateral to the lesion; and they invoke, as a test
case, 'the one-sided omission of details from verbal descriptions of
remembered scenes'. The latter symptom was described by Bisiach and
Luzzatti (1978) in two elderly patients with vascular disease who
neglected to describe *from memory* buildings to the left side of a view of
the Piazza del Duomo in Milan, even when the imagined perspectives
were changed. Accordingly, these authors suggested that

> the mechanisms underlying the mental representation of the en-
> vironment are topologically structured in the sense that the pro-
> cesses by which a visual image is conjured up by the mind may split
> between the two cerebral hemispheres, like the projection of a real
> scene onto the visual areas of the two sides of the brain.

In a later paper (Bisiach, Luzzatti and Perani, 1979), they explore
this hypothesis. Nineteen patients with right hemisphere lesions

(16 vascular cases and 3 patients with tumours) were required to make same/different judgements on pairs of patterns moving leftward or rightward behind a narrow vertical split. Differences occurring on the left side of the 'mentally reconstructed images' were less easily detected by both patients and controls, but effect of side was significant only in the patient group. Again, they concluded that 'a topological relationship . . . seems to link to the neural substrate the spatial schema where these percepts take shape' and that the spatial schema appears to be mapped across the brain. The data do show that the more abstractly coded internal representations are also subject to neglect, at least in the acute stages of disease. But the model does not explain why *persistent* neglect is so strongly associated with right rather than left hemisphere lesions, and it does not refute an attentional hypothesis. Moreover, it is difficult to reconcile with the fact that cases of hemispherectomy have complete images and representations of images.

Undoubtedly cases of unilateral neglect present a rich opportunity to study both functional mechanism and neuroanatomical substrate in patients who are often able to collaborate, without clouding of consciousness, in clinical and experimental studies (Heilman, Valenstein and Watson, in press). A similar opportunity was exploited to great effect in recent studies of 'blindsight' in patients with hemianopic visual field defects.

Blindsight and blindtouch   Patients with a homonymous hemianopia caused by postgeniculate lesions have been shown to possess residual vision in the allegedly blind field (for a synthesis of recent research see Weiskrantz, 1980). The particular interest of this phenomenon for our subject is the fact that the patient has information about stimuli in the 'blind' field that he can not *consciously* see or verbally report. The patient D.B., studied by Weiskrantz and his colleagues, initially denied any awareness of stimuli in the left hemianopic field, and was bewildered by the prospect of guessing where these invisible events occurred. In a forced choice situation, however, he proved able to localize stimuli and to differentiate between a cross and a circle, horizontal, diagonal and vertical lines, and a grating versus a homogenous grey field. Subsequent studies (Zihl, von Cramon and Pöppel, 1978; Weiskrantz, 1980) have confirmed these observations, and suggested that limited awareness of stimuli in the blind field may be achieved by systematic training.

These findings point to the contribution — for localization and visual detection — of extra-striate mechanisms: notably, the colliculus and the pulvinar. In the case of D.B., most of the calcarine cortex in the right hemisphere was removed, to excise an angiomatous malformation, probably of long-standing. This relatively restricted lesion spared most, if not all, of extra-striate cortex, thus leaving the possibility of processing via extra-striate and collicular pathways. 'Compensation by the homolateral superior colliculus' was, in fact, proposed by Damásio, Damásio, Ferro and Castro-Caldas (1974) as the explanation for the restoration of almost normal visual acuity in the right eye of their patient, aged 34, who had undergone a right hemispherectomy at the age of 20, as radical treatment of the sequelae (intractable epilepsy and behaviour disturbance) of a severe closed head injury sustained at the age of 5.

Collicular cells have both eye-movement and movement-receptive fields (see Goldberg and Robinson, 1978, for a detailed review), and therefore have been assigned a key role in both attentional (Wurtz and Goldberg, 1972a) and corollary discharge ('Teuber, 1974) hypotheses. Symptoms of neglect have been observed in a patient with a restricted right collicular lesion (Heywood and Ratcliff, 1975) and a patient with a lesion of the pulvinar (Zihl and von Cramon, 1979); and increased latencies of the saccades directed to contralateral visual targets are found in monkeys with collicular lesions (Wurtz and Goldberg, 1972b; Latto, 1978).

The question arises as to whether blindsight, or rather this phenomenon of knowing without knowing that you know (described by Aristotle) can be detected in other sensory modalities. There is now evidence of a similar finding in the haptic modality (Paillard, Michel and Stelmach, 1983). The observations were based on a patient, aged 57, who had a left occipital angioma, with subsequent obstruction of the left posterior cerebral artery. CT scan revealed softening of the left parietal lobe. The neurological signs included a right hemianopia, a right hemianacousia and right hemianaesthesia. This patient had a deafferented right upper limb but she was nevertheless able to locate a stimulus on the surface of this limb. She herself was greatly puzzled by the curious sensation: awareness of something happening that was too elusive, too fragile to be identified:

mais je ne comprends pas bien pour ça. Vous mettez quelque chose ici . . . je sens pas et pourtant j'y vais avec mon doigt . . . comment ça se fait? (but I don't understand that! You put something here. I don't feel anything and yet I go there with my finger . . . how does that happen?).

The authors of this study introduce the notion of localization without content. They consider the patient's resort to multimodal expressions to try to account for her response to tactual stimuli and the possible nature of the attentional cues that signalled the occurrence of stimulation at a given locus. Such results lend further support to the concept of multi-channelling of sensory information, already well established in the visual modality (Cowey, 1979). The concept itself can well accommodate the selective disruptions of conscious awareness that occur in pathology. Are similar disconnections found in the absence of disease of the central nervous system?

Normal and pathological data: some correspondences

It is not within the brief of this chapter to treat the huge corpus of data (from experiential sources or from experimental work with normal subjects) that has a bearing on the study of consciousness. This is extensively reviewed in contemporary publications (c.f. Underwood and Stevens, 1979, 1981; see also chapter 8 of this volume). But those data are of particular interest when they amplify and complement the neuropsychological evidence. We shall consider some of these correspondences.

Deep dyslexia and priming

The case for reciprocity in clinical and normal studies has been well argued by Marcel and Patterson (1978). They base their claim on parallel studies of patients with an acquired reading disorder, now labelled 'deep dyslexia', and of normal subjects in pattern-masking experiments. Germane to the present theme is the fact that the behaviour of both groups is influenced by stimuli of which they are not consciously aware. One of the salient features of deep dyslexia (Marshall and Newcombe, 1966, 1973; Coltheart, Patterson and Marshall, 1980) is the frequent occurrence of semantic errors in reading. Hence the patient may make the following errors: canary → parrot; craft → sculpture; sick → ill; XII → BC. These reading errors are not free-associations and may be presented confidently as a 'correct' response to the printed word. Consider now the phenomenon of 'priming'. It has been shown that normal subjects, who do not consciously perceive and report a pattern-masked word, are nevertheless influenced by it to the extent that latencies are reduced for the subsequent recognition of a stimulus drawn from the same semantic category. Thus, Marcel and Patterson (1978) conclude that 'pattern masking, rather than interfering with visual analysis, appears to be preventing access to consciousness', and they draw an analogy with the phenomenon of blindsight. Indeed their model of conscious and unconscious processes in reading allocates to consciousness only the 'synthesised percept' and the spoken response.

Conscious and unconscious processing

A similar view has been taken of memory and learning. Retention (Mayes, 1981) and memory search processes (Sternberg, 1966) are unconscious phenomena. 'Only the *products* of memory search (and for that matter thinking in general) are available to awareness' (Underwood, 1979). Indeed, more exhaustive searches of semantic memory and computation of data within that store – predominantly at an unconscious level – may account for the spontaneous emergence of original thoughts, intuitions and solutions. Experiential data (see Koestler, 1964) in this domain are abundant.

> The great discoveries are seldom fixed exactly in time. They are the result of a succession of intellectual events, of a protracted process of training the mind to deal with a single problem. They represent the intersection of the conscious and the unconscious, of purposeful observation and the errant dream. Only rarely is the solution achieved at one sudden stroke. (Ceram, 1960)

Absentmindedness and motor control

At a less distinguished level, the business of driving a car involves the same shifting between conscious and unconscious control. Motorists may drive along a short stretch of road with no subsequent recall of this brief episode. It is not known whether the unconscious pilot in these circumstances is capable of responding swiftly and effectively to sudden danger.

The drift away from conscious control is a feature of Reason's (1979) ingenious studies of absentmindedness. A behavioural goal requires a plan and a sequence of actions to carry out that plan. Reason concentrates on the executive stage and analyses the performance errors of normal, absentminded subjects. They produce errors of discrimination (shaving cream put on the toothbrush) and program assembly (e.g. putting a sweet in the wastepaper basket and the wrapping in the mouth), test failures (putting on pyjamas instead of evening clothes), subroutine failures (flicking on the light when leaving the room) and storage failures (e.g. the familiar problem of going into another room and then forgetting the errand). Most of the errors in normal subjects occurred at the level described as storage, and a similar pattern would be predicted of amnesic patients.

Of particular relevance to the present enquiry is Reason's discussion of motor control. 'Skilled performance involves continual switching between the closed loop and open loop control modes': the closed loop mode 'relies heavily on visual and proprioceptive feedback, and hence conscious attention, for the moment to moment control of motor output'; the open-loop or feed-forward mode involves motor programs or pre-arranged instruction sequences, that run off independently of feedback information, thus leaving the central processor free to concentrate upon future aspects of the task, or indeed to devote itself to matters quite unrelated to the current activity. Critical decision points occur when actions or situations are common to two or more motor programs. Errors tend to occur through a failure to select the closed loop mode of control at these critical points, usually during the running of automatic, highly practised activities; and these lapses tend to trigger another, 'strong' program — one frequently and recently used.

This instructive approach to human performance-errors has obvious clinical implications. Reason himself noted the disturbances of planning and sustained attention that have been associated with (at least a few) patients with large frontal-lobe lesions. His schema could, however, be applied more generally to the apraxias or disorders of motor control. The current taxonomy of apraxia is now being discussed in relation to the neurophysiology of motor control within the conceptual framework of information processing and computer science (Paillard, 1982). Briefly, the serial model of motor control considers three levels at which disorders may occur: motor apraxia, involving the selective destruction of kinetic formulae and associated with lesions of pre-Rolandic, motor cortex; ideomotor apraxia, associated with parietal lesions, and attributed to an inability to release *intentionally* motor programs that can nevertheless be envisaged and even mobilized in a familiar context – the patient who brushes his hair every morning in the bathroom but cannot mime this activity to command in the laboratory; and ideatory apraxia in which mental representations, including operational plans, are defective – the patient presented with a candle, a cigarette and a box of matches who cannot describe or carry out the appropriate sequence of operations.

Crucial to the analysis of the ideomotor disorders is the classical distinction between automatic and voluntary action, explicit in Jackson's studies of sensorimotor loss:

> The study of cases of hemiplegia shows that from disease of the corpus striatum those external parts suffer most which, psychologically speaking, are most under the command of will, and which, physiologically speaking, have the greater number of different movements at the greater number of different intervals. That parts suffer more as they serve in voluntary, and less as they serve in automatic operations, is, I believe, the law of destroying lesions of the central nervous centres.   (Jackson, 1875, reprinted 1932)

In a footnote, Jackson added the gloss: 'it is not to be implied that there are abrupt demarcations betwixt the two classes of movement; on the contrary, there are gradations from the most voluntary to the most automatic'.

Attention, detection and movement

A similar duality emerges from experimental studies of the human subject's ability to detect and locate, either visually or by reaching, stimuli in his external environment. Shiffrin and Schneider (1977) also distinguished different modes of automatic and controlled processing. Learned automatic sequences are in the repertory of long-term store; they do not demand attention but may, in appropriate circumstances, attract it. In contrast,

> controlled processing is a temporary activation of nodes in a sequence that is not yet learned. It is relatively easy to set up,

modify, and utilize in new situations. It requires attention, uses up short-term capacity, and is often serial in nature.

A more broadly based analysis of the 'willed and automatic control of behaviour' has been put forward by Norman and Shallice (1980). Action depends on memory schemata, organized in sequential or parallel patterns. Attention is required for the initiation or the termination of action. Here, clinical disorders are illustrative: the mutism of the cingulate syndrome (Cairns, Oldfield, Pennybacker and Whitteridge, 1941; Botez, 1962) and the perseverative responses of patients with frontal-lobe lesions (Luria, 1966). A critical feature of the model is the distinction between action initiated via the supervisory attentional mechanism (? consciously) and action triggered by 'contention scheduling', without the intervention of this mechanism. The authors define tasks or conditions that seem, on intuitive grounds, to require deliberate attentional resources. These include: planning or decision making; trouble-shooting; poorly learned or novel action sequences; dangerous or technically difficult actions; and the need to inhibit a strong, habitual response or to resist temptation (the last, an intriguing addition to the experimental psychologist's preoccupation with light and letter stimuli). Thus, it is hardly surprising that an analogy is sought with the phenomenology of frontal-lobe disorders. Indeed, clinical illustrations abound: the feckless behaviour of Phineas Gage after a crowbar had pierced his frontal lobes (Harlow, 1868); the perseverative errors of patients with dorsolateral frontal lesions on the Wisconsin card sorting task when arbitrary changes of 'correct' category are imposed (Milner, 1964); and the failure of patients with left frontal lesions to inhibit the familiar reading response in the Stroop task when they are required to name the incongruous colour of a colour name — that is, to respond 'red' when the word 'green' is printed in red ink (Perret, 1974).

Studies of the internal control mechanisms of attention and movement (see Posner and Cohen, 1980) may provide a sensitive tool for the analysis of syndromes such as apraxia and visual neglect. Regarding the control of saccadic eye movements, three complex functional systems have been postulated: eye movement to a peripheral target, under minimal central control, using retro-tectal pathways; conscious detection of a stimulus, involving striate and parietal cortices; and eye movement in the absence of an external target, under endogenous control and mediated by frontal and parietal lobes and other sources of stimulus control from higher centres. These systems can be experimentally dissociated by manipulating central expectancies and costs of stimulus detection. The authors point out the relevance — for the study of visual neglect — of their distinction between exogenously driven eye movements (controlled from the temporal field of the ipsilateral eye) and those under endogenous control. On the assumption that neglect is more closely associated with the endogenous control system, they ask whether it could be overcome in conditions maximizing exogenous control: presenting simultaneous stimuli to the *left* eye, thus exploiting 'a powerful peripheral tendency to move the eyes in the neglected (leftward) direction to capture the external stimuli'. They propose that similar studies of orienting by attention, in the eye-fixed condition, could clarify the relationship of covert orienting and pattern recognition: a potentially interesting approach to the study of perceptual disorders and the Balint syndrome.

Posner, Cohen and Rafal (1982) have already demonstrated the potential of this paradigm in their comparative study of patients with progressive supranuclear palsy and control patients with Parkinson's disease. The former group exhibit a loss of saccadic control (first vertical then horizontal), despite intact oculomotor reflexes. They are able to shift attention in response to light cues (but show longer delays in the direction of saccadic impairment). Hence, a midbrain pathway is implicated for the control of central attention, a hypothesis explicit in current explanations of cross-cueing in the split-brain preparation (Holtzman, Sidtis, Volpe, Wilson and Gazzaniga, 1981). However, whereas the midbrain lesions delay response, there are no failures of detection. In contrast, there are losses of information and detection failures in parietal lesions. These findings are consistent with the view that the parietal lobes are a critical component of complex attentional systems and, in the light of single-unit recording, 'may form a substrate for a complex interface between sensory and motor function under the control of attentional gating mechanisms, in which motivational states and past experience play a role' (Paillard, 1982; see also Lynch, 1980). Further advances in understanding attentional mechanisms may result from the interaction of behavioural studies, cognitive theory and neuroanatomical hypotheses (Treisman and Gelado, 1980; Crick, 1984).

Sensory deprivation, illusion and hallucination

The dependence of the human animal on environmental stimulation was dramatically illustrated by the perceptual isolation experiments in which healthy students participated (Hebb, 1966). In addition to the boredom and the intellectual decline that these subjects experienced, some of them saw such things as 'rows of little yellow men wearing black caps, squirrels marching with sacks over their shoulders, or prehistoric animals in a jungle'. These scenes were described as like animated cartoons. More fundamentally disturbing were somaesthesic hallucinations, when the subject perceived two bodies somaesthesically or felt as if his head were detached from his body; closely related to this was a feeling of bodily strangeness, for which the subject could give no more adequate description, and the report of several subjects that they felt that their minds were detached from their physical bodies (Hebb, 1966). Pilots flying at high altitude may experience this 'break-off phenomenon' — a feeling of disconnection from reality; and it is a frequently documented sequela of psychodelic drugs and opiates.

Lhermitte (1951) reminded us that 'for the founder of psychiatry, Esquirol, hallucination means a perception without an object' — a neat, if incomplete definition. The phantom self, facilitated by although not dependent on drowsiness, recurs in literature. Lhermitte cited many examples (including Dostoevsky's *The Double* and Guy de Maupassant's *Le Lorla*) and noted that the phenomenon is associated with, and indeed may alert the physician to, disease, including epilepsy, encephalitis, and other brain lesions. He suggested that we possess — 'at the boundary of our consciousness' — an image of our body that can vanish, undergo distortion, or even 'release itself partly from its material frame to become a hallucination — in other words, a perception without object'.

Jackson (1881) noted 'similar illusions in some peculiar healthy states', attributing the phenomenon to 'temporary relaxation of object consciousness'. But what input triggers these illusions? It is sometimes external: the 'cracks and marks in the burning coal', transiently 'seen' as faces, in what Jackson describes as reverie. Cortical stimulation, however, may also produce experiential hallucinations or interpretive illusions (Penfield and Roberts, 1959). In 1938, Penfield first published his serendipitous finding that electrical stimulation, only in the temporal lobe, evoked in some patients early memories with their original emotional colouring or feelings of depersonalization. Sometimes there was 'an altered interpretation of the present experience. Everything might seem suddenly familiar or farther away or nearer.' In contrast, 'when the motor convolution is stimulated, the patient may be astonished to discover that he is

moving his arm or leg. He may be surprised to hear himself vocaliz-
ing, but he never has the impression that he has willed himself to do
those things.'

Thus, normal subjects and patients alike are 'conscious', in certain
conditions, of sensations and images that are not triggered by an
external event. These illusory phenomena may result from abnormalities of nervous functioning – whether neurophysiological, as in
the case of epilepsy, or neuropharmacological; or they may be due to
a faulty hypothesis about external stimuli that are ambiguous or
glimpsed in conditions of fatigue, sensory deprivation or fasting.

In a useful review of perceptual isolation experiments, Reed (1979)
draws attention to the inconsistency of the data, and notes that
reports of hallucinatory phenomena decreased markedly when
explicit criteria were used to analyse subject reports. Nevertheless,
most subjects did find it increasingly difficult to concentrate and
focus attention, and they did experience an increase of 'unwilled
imagery'. In isolation, subjects are forced to rely on their internal
schemata, without the continual feedback that corrects our translation of events in the busy external world. The regulatory role of the
reticular formation is thus disturbed. 'If one deprives the reticular
system of its sensory input, it meets an unfamiliar situation, and only
within limits can it adjust to this change' (Lindsley, 1961). However,
the quotation, out of context, probably underestimates the potential
of the nervous system for adaptation. There are remarkable individual differences in response to isolation. Compare the qualitative and
physiological differences in the response of two scientists to thirty-two
days of isolation in a cave (Blakemore, 1977) and the disparate effects
on different hostages or prisoners-of-war of long periods of solitary
confinement.

Coda

In a critical analysis of the contribution and the limitations of 'a
thoroughgoing behaviouristic mode of thinking', Hebb (1960) diagnosed 'a disinclination, at the least, to come to grips with problems of
the higher processes – mind or consciousness'. He took a clear stand
on the issue:

  should we not teach undergraduate and graduate alike that the
  whole domain of behavior comes within the scope of objective

psychology; that 'mind', 'consciousness', and so on are references to crudely conceived intervening variables – no more, no less – about which we do not know nearly as much as we might be expected to, after 50 years of behaviorism and the proscription of animistic notions?

He identified a particular weakness: 'the failure of experimental psychology to deal with the "I" or "ego" is a cause of its continued inadequacy with regard to clinical matters'. He goes on to concede that the self may be construed as

a mental construct or set of mediating processes arising out of experience, in part consisting of the so-called body image, in part what seems to be a pure fantasy of an immaterial self which in certain circumstances separates itself from the body. This is fantasy, but a *real* fantasy, with effects on behavior.

In an earlier paper, Hebb (1954) had made explicit the two senses in which the term 'consciousness' is habitually used: descriptions of wakefulness, and 'something inside which is thought of as a causal agent'. The latter is an inference from behaviour, more specifically from behaviour involving thought, decision and planning. Hence Lloyd Morgan's conclusion that 'the primary aim, object and purpose of consciousness is control'. This objective requires a dynamic system capable of foresight, 'forever busy with the organization of the present' (Penfield and Roberts, 1959) against the background of past experience and in the light of predictions about the future.

Attentional processes have a dual capacity: selective attention or a sharp focus on the current target with appropriate filtering of relevant input; and a readiness to respond to peripheral stimuli when and if they become urgent, important or even dangerous to the organism. This classical notion of focus and fringe was cogently developed by James (1890).

My experience is what I agree to attend to. Only those items which *I notice* shape my mind – without selective interest, experience is utter chaos. Interest alone gives accent and emphasis, light and shade, background and foreground – intelligible perspective, in a word. . . . Everyone knows what attention is. It is the taking possession by the mind, in clear and vivid form, of one of what seem several simultaneously possible objects or trains of thought. Focalization, concentration, of consciousness are of its essence.

Valéry's (1960) less dichotomous approach gives more latitude to the creative artist:

> L'esprit va, dans son travail, de *son* désordre, à *son* ordre. Il importe qu'il se conserve jusqu'à la fin, des resources de *désordre*, et que l'ordre qu'il a commencé de se donner ne se lie pas si complète-ment, ne lui soit pas un si rigide maître, qu'il ne puisse le changer et user de sa liberté initiale. (The mind at work moves from *its* dis-order to *its* order. It is essential that it retains the resources of dis-order, and that the order that it begins to impose upon itself does not bind it so completely, is not such a rigid master, that it cannot change it and use its initial freedom).

In the same spirit, Polanyi's alternative and more flexible concept of focal and subsidiary awareness (see Pollio, 1979) seems a useful exten-sion of James's concept, and would accommodate a gamut of behaviour from the creative arts to the interesting but neglected phenomenon of incidental learning. (See chapter 3 of this volume for a further dis-cussion of foreground and background in consciousness.)

The putative neural substrate of conscious activity is dependent on our operational definition. The function of wakefulness is dependent on structures that include mammillary bodies or the neighbouring posterior hypothalamus and anterior mesencephalon, and the intra-laminar and midline nuclei of the thalamus. But our major interest is in a wider definition of consciousness, embracing the concept of selective attention and volitional control. Attentional processes depend on the septo-hippocampal system exerting an inhibitory influ-ence on both ascending reticular formation and sensory input. Within this context, an increasingly important role is being assigned to the basal ganglia, not only in the selective release of learned motor plans (Marsden, 1980) but more generally in cognitive behaviour (Öberg and Divac, 1979). In animals, striatal damage appears to change the priorities accorded to 'self-generated and external constraints on the selection of new behaviour patterns' (Cools, 1980); their defects in the planning of the order and sequence of movements are reminiscent of those shown by patients with Parkinson's disease.

When we consider the volitional control of behaviour, however, a more extensive nervous apparatus has to be envisaged, in which the highly specialized areas of association cortex are vital components. While rejecting Lashley's principle of equipotentiality, we must assume that an extensive network of corticocortical and corticothalamic pathways are involved in conscious, sentient behaviour. Day-to-day human problem solving is seldom, if ever, confined to one modality. Take the straightforward problem of crossing a busy road. The decisions will be influenced by limbic information; and the selection of important perceptual and spatial cues will depend on the activity of neurones in the parietal lobe. Calculations of cost and risk will involve the frontal lobes.

The frontal lobes – formerly dismissed as 'silent areas' or accorded a vague role in social adaptability – are now envisaged as the 'comparator' of cerebral activity (Damásio, 1979). The activation of these areas in man, prior to the initiation of a voluntary movement, has been mapped (Kornhuber and Deecke, 1965) in terms of a slow negative wave that expands to the parietal areas; and similar data have emerged from cerebral blood flow studies, showing a high level of activation in the supplementary motor area when subjects are told to 'imagine' a complex sequence of finger movements (Roland, Larsen, Larsen and Skinhoj, 1980). Physiological studies of the unanaesthetized animal suggest that prefrontal cortex is associated with a sensorial attention mechanism for visual stimului, promoting reward of a correct behavioural choice (Kubota, Tonoike and Mikami, 1980). This interpretation is in accordance with Teuber's (1974) hypothesis that such structures are sources of 'corollary discharges' whereby the organism presets its sensory systems for the anticipated consequences of its own action.

Consciousness may be but the culmination of a complex continuum of operations in which orientation, detection, recognition and choice interact and trigger the behavioural end-product, whether awareness of sensation, the taking of an intellectual decision, or a motor act. The extent to which this behavioural end-product is 'conscious' and 'voluntary' may depend on the attentional demand it makes on an executive decision-maker that has limited resources, and whose interest it is to relegate as much activity as possible to unconscious or automatic control-systems (see Posner and Cohen, 1980). That there is a price to pay for automatization is also shown by Reason's (1976) study of aircraft disasters. Voluntary action, however, is expensive in terms of effort and processing capacity and it can be selectively impaired in disorders of praxis. It is usually required to initiate or end activity, and may play a special role in adapting our finite repertoire of information processing capabilities to new situations voluntarily rather than waiting for evolution to do the job for us. (See an informative review by Carr, 1979).

The gaunt outline of man as an information processing machine has not contented all scientists engaged in the mind—body problem. Compare Eddington and Sherrington. Eddington (1939) cautiously suggested the limitations of the epistemological approach:

> I have little excuse for extending my survey beyond the limits indicated by the term 'knowledge'. But I would not like to leave an impression that the description of the human spirit as 'something which knows' can be the whole truth about its nature. . . . Consciousness has other functions besides those of a rather inefficient measuring machine; and knowledge may attain to other truths besides those which correlate sensory impressions.

Sherrington (1942) briskly concluded that 'the individual becomes part of a probability system. In that system the biological advantage which mind seems to confer on the concrete individual is improvement and control of the motor act.' The reader must take his choice.

The theme of consciousness, as Hebb (1954) trenchantly observed, is a well-known booby trap. That being so, the writer claims a conventional last wish: the space to record a caveat. The reductionist approach has explanatory force. It lends itself well to the subject matter of neuropsychology where, strategically, it must be the conceptual tool of choice. And, after all, the ghost in the machine may still turn out to be a higher level of neuronal patterning. Nevertheless, it seems a far cry from the laboratory observer of stimuli, on whom cognitive theory is based, to Renaissance man or even his paler twentieth-century counterpart. There is an alternative view that seeks to interpret consciousness as 'a process of self-reflection . . . that region of being which is the instrument of relational life; the means whereby a man confronts his world, constructs for himself a here-and-now, and through it, his personality' (Evans, 1972). This more abstract version, if not relegated to the domain of epiphenomena, may yet prove accessible to systems theory: a complex, higher-order system instantiated in a biological machine. If, as Popper has suggested, consciousness is evolution's greatest achievement, it is hardly surprising that it eludes our conceptual grasp and that the 'agent' in charge of the neuronal machine 'has escaped detection even by the most delicate physical instruments' (Eccles, 1953). Thus, Hippocrates must — for the time being — have the last word.

Acknowledgements

I should like to record my grateful thanks to colleagues who gave advice or information during the preparation of this chapter. They include Dr G. Buchtel, Dr J. Davidoff, Dr J. Marshall and Dr G. Ratcliff; and I am much indebted to Dr A. Damásio and Dr J. Paillard for detailed and invaluable criticism of the penultimate draft.

References

Adams, R. D., Collins, G. H. and Victor, M. (1962) Troubles de la Mémoire et de l'Apprentissage Chez l'Homme: Leurs Relations avec des Lésions des Lobes Temporaux et du Diencéphale. In *Physiologie de l'Hippocampe*, 273–96. Paris: CNRS.

Akelaitis, A. J. (1944) A study of gnosis, praxis, and language following section of the corpus callosum and anterior commissure. *Journal of Neurosurgery 1*: 94–102.

Albert, M. L., Reches, A. and Silverberg, R. (1975) Associative visual agnosia without alexia. *Neurology 25*: 322–6.

Allport, D. A. (1979) Conscious and unconscious cognition: a computational metaphor for the mechanism of attention and integration. In L-G. Nilsson (ed.) *Perspectives on Memory Research*. Hillsdale, NJ: Erlbaum.

Allport, D. A. and Funnell, E. (1981) Components of the mental lexicon. *Philosophical Transactions of the Royal Society (London), Series B, 295*: 397–410.

Bender, M. B. and Feldman, M. (1972) The so-called 'visual agnosias'. *Brain 95:* 173–86.

Bisiach, E. and Luzzatti, C. (1978) Unilateral neglect of representational space. *Cortex 14*: 129–33.

Bisiach, E., Luzzatti, C. and Perani, D. (1979) Unilateral neglect, representational schema and consciousness. *Brain 102*: 609–18.

Blakemore, C. (1977) *Mechanics of the Mind*. Cambridge: Cambridge University Press.

Bloch, V. (1970) Facts and hypotheses concerning memory consolidation. *Brain Research 24*: 561–75.

Bogen, J. E., Fisher, E. D. and Vogel, P. J. (1965) Cerebral commissurotomy: a second case report. *Journal of the American Medical Association 194*: 1328–9.

Botez, M. I. (1962) The starting mechanism of speech. Paper read at the VIIIth Congress of the Hungarian Neurologists and Psychiatrists, Budapest, October.

Butters, N. (in press) Alcoholic Korsakoff's syndrome: some unresolved issues concerning etiology, neuropathology and cognitive deficits. *Journal of Clinical and Experimental Neuropsychology 7*.

Cairns, H., Oldfield, R. C., Pennybacker, J. B. and Whitteridge, D. (1941) Akinetic mutism with an epidermoid cyst of the 3rd ventricle. *Brain 64*: 273–90.

Caplan, L., Chedru, F., Lhermitte, F. and Mayman, C. (1981) Transient global amnesia and migraine. *Neurology 31*: 1167–70.

Carr, T. H. (1979) Consciousness in models of human information processing: primary memory, executive control and input regulation. In G. Underwood and R. Stevens (eds) *Aspects of Consciousness*, vol. 1: *Psychological Issues*, 123–53. London: Academic Press.

Cazzullo, C. L. and Mancia, M. (1964) Psychopathological aspects of the relation between vigilance and consciousness. *Acta neurochirurgica (Wien) 12*: 366–78.

Ceram, C. W. (1941) *Gods, Graves and Scholars. The Story of Archaeology*. London: Gollancz.

Cohen, N. J. and Squire, L. R. (1980) Preserved learning and retention of pattern analyzing skill in amnesia. Dissociation of knowing how and knowing that. *Science 210*: 207–9.

Coltheart, M., Patterson, K. E. and Marshall, J. C. (eds) (1980) *Deep Dyslexia*. London: Routledge & Kegan Paul.

Conkey, R. C. (1938) Psychological changes associated with head injuries. In R. S. Woodworth (ed.) *Archives of Psychology* (New York), *232*: 5–62.

Cools, A. R. (1980) Physiological significance of the striatal system: new light on an old concept. In J. Szentágothai, J. Hámori and M. Palkavits (eds) *Regulatory Functions of the CNS Subsystems*, Adv. Physiol. Sc. vol. 2, 227–30. Budapest: Akadémiai Kiadó.

Cowey, A. (1979) Cortical maps and visual perception. *Quarterly Journal of Experimental Psychology 31*: 1–47.

Crick, F. (1984) Function of the thalamic reticular complex: the searchlight hypothesis. *Proceedings of the National Academy of Sciences (USA) 81*, 4586–90.

Critchley, M. (1969) *The Parietal Lobes*. New York: Hafner Publishing Co. Inc.

Curry, H. and Cummins, B. H. (1981) Electrophysiological changes after head injury. Paper given at the Seventh International Congress of Neurological Surgery, Munich, July.

Curtiss, S. (1977) *Genie: A Psycholinguistic Study of a Modern-day 'wild child'*. New York: Academic Press.

Damásio, A. R. (1979) The frontal lobes. In K. M. Heilman and E. Valenstein (eds) *Clinical Neuropsychology*, 360–412. New York: Academic Press.

Damásio, A. R. and Benton, A. L. (1979) Impairment of hand movements under visual guidance. *Neurology 29*: 170–8.

Damásio, A. R., Damásio, H. and Chui, H. C. (1980) Neglect following damage to frontal lobe or basal ganglia. *Neuropsychologia 18*: 123–31.

Damásio, A. R., Damásio, H. and Van Hoesen, G. W. (1982) Prosopagnosia: anatomical basis and behavioral mechanisms. *Neurology 32*: 331–41.

Damásio, A. R., McKee, J. and Damásio, H. (1979) Determinants of performance in color anomia. *Brain and Language 7*: 74–85.

Damásio, A. R., Damásio, H., Ferro, J. M. and Castro-Caldas, A. (1974) Recovering from hemianopia in man: evidence for collicular vision? *The Lancet*, 13 July: 110.

Dandy, W. E. (1936) Operative experience in cases of pineal tumour. *Archives of Surgery 33*: 19–46.

Davidson, R. J. (1981) Cognitive processing is not equivalent to conscious processing. Open peer commentary. *The Behavioral and Brain Sciences 4*: 104–5.

Delay, J., Brion, S., Lemperière, T. and Lechevallier, B. (1965) Cas anatomo-clinique de syndrome de Korsakoff post-comitial après corticothérapie pour asthme subintrant. *Revue Neurologique 113*: 583–94.

Dennett, D. C. (1979) *Brainstorms: Philosophical Essays on Mind and Psychology*. Hassocks: Harvester Press.

Denny-Brown, D. and Banker, B. Q. (1954) Amorphosynthesis from left parietal lesions. *Archives of Neurology and Psychiatry 71*: 302–13.

Denny-Brown, D., Meyer, J. S. and Horenstein, S. (1952) The significance of perceptual rivalry resulting from parietal lesions. *Brain 75*: 433–71.

De Renzi, E. (1982) *Disorders of Space Exploration and Cognition*. New York: John Wiley & Sons.

Disterhoft, J. F. and Olds, J. (1972) Differential development of conditioned unit changes in thalamus and cortex of rat. *Journal of Neurophysiology 35*: 665–79.

Eccles, J. C. (1953) *The Neurophysiological Basis of Mind: The Principles of Neurophysiology*. Oxford: Clarendon Press.

Eddington, A. (1939) *The Philosophy of Physical Science*. Cambridge: Cambridge University Press.

Evans, P. (1972) Henri Ey's concepts of the organization of consciousness and its disorganization: an extension of Jacksonian theory. *Brain 95*: 413–40.

Fisher, C. M. and Adams, R. D. (1964) Transient global amnesia. *Acta Neurologica Scandinavica 40*: Suppl. 9. Copenhagen: Munksgaard.

Frederiks, J. A. M. (1969) Consciousness. In P. J. Vinken and G. W. Bruyn (eds) *Handbook of Clinical Neurology*, 48–61. Amsterdam: North Holland Publishing Co.

Fromkin, V., Kraschen, S., Curtiss, S., Rigler, D. and Rigler, M. (1974) The development of language in Genie: a case of language acquisition beyond the critical period. *Brain and Language 1*: 81–107.

Gazzaniga, M. S. and LeDoux, J. E. (1978) *The Integrated Mind*. New York: Plenum Press.

Gazzaniga, M. S., LeDoux, J. E. and Wilson, D. H. (1977) Language, praxis, and the right hemisphere: clues to some mechanisms of consciousness. *Neurology 27*: 1144–7.

Gazzaniga, M. S., Glass, A. V., Sarno, M. T. and Posner, J. B. (1973) Pure word deafness and hemispheric dynamics: a case history. *Cortex 9*: 136–43.

Geschwind, N. (1965) Disconnexion syndromes in animals and man. *Brain 88*: 585–644.

Geschwind, N. (1967) The varieties of naming errors. *Cortex 3*: 97–112.

Geschwind, N. (1982) Disorders of attention: a frontier in neuropsychology. *Philosophical Transactions of the Royal Society of London B298:* 173–85.

Gloning, I., Gloning, K. and Hoff, H. (1968) *Neuropsychological Symptoms and Syndromes in Lesions of the Occipital Lobe and the Adjacent Areas.* Paris: Gauthier-Villars.

Goldberg, M. E. and Robinson, D. L. (1978) Visual system: superior colliculus. In R. B. Masterson (ed.) *Handbook of Behavioral Neurobiology*, vol. 1: *Sensory Integration.* New York: Plenum Press.

Harlow, J. M. (1868) Recovery from the passage of an iron bar through the head. *Massachusetts Medical Society Publication 2*: 327–47.

Head, H. (1923) The concept of nervous and mental energy. Vigilance: a physiological state of the nervous system. *British Journal of Psychology 14*: 126–47.

Hebb, D. O. (1954) The problem of consciousness and introspection. In J. F. Delafresnaye (ed.) *Brain Mechanisms and Consciousness*, 402–17. Oxford: Blackwell.

Hebb, D. O. (1960) The American revolution. *American Psychologist 15*: 735–45.

Hebb, D. O. (1966) *A Textbook of Psychology.* Philadelphia: Sanders.

Hécaen, H. (1962) Clinical symptomatology in right and left hemisphere lesions. In V. B. Mountcastle (ed.) *Interhemispheric Relations and Cerebral Dominance.* Baltimore: Johns Hopkins Press.

Heilman, K. M. and Valenstein, E. (1972a) Auditory neglect in man. *Archives of Neurology 26*: 31–5.

Heilman, K. M. and Valenstein, E. (1972b) Frontal lobe neglect in man. *Neurology 22*: 660–4.

Heilman, K. M. and Watson, R. T. (1977) The neglect syndrome – a unilateral defect of the orienting response. In S. Harnad, R. W. Doty, L. Goldstein, J. Jaynes and G. Krauthamer (eds) *Lateralization in the Nervous System*, 285–302. New York: Academic Press.

Heilman, K. M., Valenstein, E. and Watson, R. T. (in press) Attentional disorders induced by hemispheric lesions. In D. E. Sheer (ed.) *Attention: Theory, Brain Function and Clinical Applications.* New York: Academic Press.

Heywood, S. and Ratcliff, G. (1975) Long-term oculomotor consequences of unilateral colliculectomy in man. In G. Lennerstrand and P. Bach-y-Rita

190   Brain and Mind

(eds) *Basic Mechanisms of Ocular Motility and their Clinical Implications*, 561–4. Oxford: Pergamon Press.

Hink, R. F. and Hillyard, S. A. (1978) Electrophysiological measures of attentional processes in man as related to the study of schizophrenia. *Psychiatry Research 14*: 155–65.

Holtzman, J. D., Sidtis, J. J., Volpe, B. T., Wilson, D. H. and Gazzaniga, M. S. (1981) Dissociation of spatial information for stimulus localization and the control of attention. *Brain 104*: 861–72.

Iversen, S. D. (1977) Striatal function and stereotyped behaviour. In A. R. Cools, A. H. M. Lohman and J. H. L. van den Bercken (eds) *Psychobiology of the Striatum*, 99–118. New York: Elsevier/North-Holland Publishing Co.

Jackson, J. H. (1875) On the anatomical and physiological localisation of movements in the brain. Reprinted in J. Taylor (ed.) *Selected Writings of John Hughlings Jackson*, vol. 1, 37–76. London: Hodder & Stoughton, 1932.

Jackson, J. H. (1881) Remarks on dissolution of the nervous system as exemplified by certain post-epileptic conditions. *Medical Press and Circular 1*: 329. Reprinted in J. Taylor (ed.) *Selected Writings of John Hughlings Jackson*, vol. 2, 3–28. London: Hodder & Stoughton, 1932.

James, W. (1890) Reprinted in *The Principles of Psychology*. London: Constable, 1950.

Jennett, B. and Bond, M. R. (1975) Assessment of outcome after severe brain damage. *Lancet*, 1 March: 480.

Jennett, B., Snoek, J., Bond, M. R. and Brooks, N. (1981) Disability after severe head injury: observations on the use of the Glasgow Outcome Scale. *Journal of Neurology, Neurosurgery, and Psychiatry 44*: 285–93.

Jouvet, M. (1969) Coma and other disorders of consciousness. In P. J. Vinken and G. W. Bruyn (eds) *Handbook of Clinical Neurology*, 62–79. Amsterdam: North Holland Publishing Co.

Koestler, A. (1964) *The Act of Creation*. London: Pan.

Kolers, P. (1976) Reading a year later. *Journal of Experimental Psychology: Human Learning and Memory 2*: 554–65.

Kornhuber, H. H. and Deecke, L. (1965) Hirnpotentialänderungen bei willkürbewegungen und passiven Bewegungen des Menschen: Bereitschaftspotentiale und reafferente Potentiale. *Pflügers Archiv 284*: 1–17.

Kubota, K., Tonoike, M. and Mikami, A. (1980) Neuronal activity in the monkey dorsolateral prefrontal cortex during a discrimination task with delay. *Brain Research 183*: 29–42.

Lashley, K. S. (1954) Dynamic processes in perception. In J. F. Delafresnaye (ed.) *Brain Mechanisms and Consciousness*, 422–43. Oxford: Blackwell.

Latto, R. (1978) The effects of bilateral frontal eye-field, posterior parietal or superior collicular lesions on visual search in the rhesus monkey. *Brain Research (Amsterdam) 146*: 35–50.

Neuropsychology of consciousness   191

Latto, R. (1982) A comparison of the roles of parietal and frontal cortex in spatial vision in the monkey. *Behavioural Brain Research 5*: 106–7.

LeDoux, J. E., Wilson, D. H. and Gazzaniga, M. S. (1979) Beyond commissurotomy: clues to consciousness. In M. S. Gazzaniga (ed.) *Handbook of Behavioral Neurobiology*, vol. 2, 543–54. New York: Plenum Press.

Levy, J. and Trevarthen, C. (1976) Metacontrol of hemispheric function in human split-brain patients. *Journal of Experimental Psychology: Human Perception and Performance 3*: 299–311.

Lewis, A. (1961) Amnesic syndromes. *Proceedings of The Royal Society of Medicine 54*: 955–61.

Lhermitte, J. (1951) Visual hallucination of the self. *British Medical Journal 1*: 431–4.

Lindsley, D. B. (1961) Common factors in sensory deprivation, sensory distortion, and sensory overload. In P. Solomon, P. E. Kubzansky, P. H. Leiderman, J. H. Mendelson, R. Trumbull and D. Wexler (eds) *Sensory Deprivation*, 174–94. Cambridge, Mass.: Harvard University Press.

Lishman, W. A. (1971) Emotion, consciousness and will after brain bisection in man. *Cortex 7*: 181–92.

London, P. S. (1967) Some observations on the course of events after severe injury of the head. *Annals of the Royal College of Surgeons 41*: 460–79.

Lunzer, E. A. (1979) The development of consciousness. In G. Underwood and R. Stevens (eds) *Aspects of Consciousness*, vol. 1: *Psychological Issues*, 1–19. London: Academic Press.

Luria, A. R. (1966) *Human Brain and Psychological Processes*. New York: Harper & Row.

Lynch, J. C. (1980) The functional organization of posterior parietal association cortex. *The Behavioral and Brain Sciences 3*: 485–534.

McEntee, W. J., Biber, M. P., Perl, D. P. and Benson, D. F. (1976) Diencephalic amnesia: a reappraisal. *Journal of Neurology, Neurosurgery, and Psychiatry 39*: 436–41.

Magoun, H. W. (1958) *The Waking Brain*. Springfield, Ill.: Thomas.

Marcel, A. J. and Patterson, K. E. (1978) Word recognition and production: reciprocity in clinical and normal studies. In J. Requin (ed.) *Attention and Performance*, vol. VII, 209–26. Hillsdale, NJ: Erlbaum.

Marsden, C. D. (1980) The enigma of the basal ganglia and movement. *Trends in Neurosciences 3*: 284–7.

Marshall, J. C. (1973) Some problems and paradoxes associated with recent accounts of hemispheric specialization. *Neuropsychologia 11*: 463–70.

Marshall, J. C. and Newcombe, F. (1966) Syntactic and semantic errors in paralexia. *Neuropsychologia 4*: 169–76.

Marshall, J. C. and Newcombe, F. (1973) Patterns of paralexia: a psycholinguistic approach. *Journal of Psycholinguistic Research 2*: 175–99.

Mayes, A. (1981) The physiology of memory. In G. Underwood and R. Stevens (eds) *Aspects of Consciousness*, vol. 2: *Structural Issues*, 1–38. London: Academic Press.

Mesulam, M-M. and Geschwind, N. (1978) On the possible role of neocortex and its limbic connections in the process of attention and schizophrenia: clinical cases of inattention in man and experimental anatomy in monkey. *Journal of Psychiatric Research 14*: 249–59.

Milner, B. (1964) Some effects of frontal lobectomy in man. In J. M. Warren and J. Akert (eds) *The Frontal Granular Cortex and Behavior*, 313–34. New York; McGraw-Hill.

Milner, B. (1966) Amnesia following operation on the temporal lobes. In C. W. M. Whitty and O. L. Zangwill (eds) *Amnesia*, 109–33. London: Butterworths.

Milner, B. (1970) Memory and the medial temporal regions of the brain. In K. H. Pribram and D. E. Broadbent (eds) *Biology of Memory*, 29–50. New York: Academic Press.

Milner, B. (1972) Disorders of learning and memory after temporal lobe lesions in man. *Clinical Neurosurgery 19*: 421–46.

Mishkin, M. (1978) Memory in monkeys severely impaired by combined but not by separate removal of amygdala and hippocampus. *Nature* (London) *273*: 297–8.

Moruzzi, G. and Magoun, H. W. (1949) Brainstem reticular formation and activation of the EEG. *Electroencephalography and Clinical Neurophysiology 1*: 455–73.

Mountcastle, V. B., Lynch, J. C. and Georgopoulos, A. (1975) Posterior parietal association cortex of the monkey: command functions for operations within extrapersonal space. *Journal of Neurophysiology 38*: 871–908.

Norman, D. A. and Shallice, T. (1980) Attention to action: willed and automatic control of behavior. Report No. 8006, Center for Human Information Processing. San Diego: University of California.

Öberg, R. G. E. and Divac, I. (1979) 'Cognitive' functions of the neostriatum. In I. Divac and R. G. E. Öberg (eds) *The Neostriatum*, 291–313. Oxford: Pergamon Press.

Oxbury, J. M. Oxbury, S. M. and Humphrey, N. K. (1969) Varieties of colour anomia. *Brain 92*: 847–60.

Paillard, J. (1984) Apraxia and the neurophysiology of motor control. *Philosophical Transactions of the Royal Society of London B298*: 111–34.

Paillard, J., Michel, F. and Stelmach C. E. (1983) Localization without content: a tactile analogue of 'blind sight'. *Archives of Neurology 40*: 548–51.

Penfield, W. and Jasper, H. (1947) Highest level seizures. *Research Publications of the Association for Research in Nervous and Mental Disease (New York) 26*: 252–71.

Penfield, W. and Roberts, L. (1959) *Speech and Brain-Mechanisms*. Princeton, NJ: Princeton University Press.

Perenin, M. T. and Jeannerod, M. (1975) Residual function in cortically blind hemifields. *Neuropsychologia 13*: 1–7.

Perret, E. (1974) The left frontal lobe of man and the suppression of habitual responses in verbal categorical behaviour. *Neuropsychologia 12*: 323–30.

Piercy, M. F. (1977) Experimental studies of the organic amnesic syndrome. In C. W. M. Whitty and O. L. Zangwill (eds) *Amnesia*, 2nd edn, 1–51. London: Butterworths.

Pollio, H. R. (1979) Intuitive thinking. In G. Underwood and R. Stevens (eds) *Aspects of Consciousness*, vol. 1: *Psychological Issues*, 21–43. London: Academic Press.

Posner, M. I. and Cohen, Y. (1980) Attention and the control of movement. In G. E. Stelmach and J. Requin (eds) *Tutorials in Motor Behavior*. Amsterdam: North Holland Publishing Co.

Posner, M. I., Cohen, Y. and Rafal, R. D. (1982) Neural systems control of spatial orienting. *Philosophical Transactions of the Royal Society of London B298*: 187–98.

Ratcliff, G. and Newcombe, F. (1982) Object recognition: some deductions from the clinical evidence. In A. W. Ellis (ed.) *Normality and Pathology in Cognitive Functions*, 147–71. London: Academic Press.

Reason, J. (1976) Absent minds. *New Society*, 4 November.

Reason, J. (1979) Actions not as planned: the price of automatization. In G. Underwood and R. Stevens (eds) *Aspects of Consciousness*, vol. 1: *Psychological Issues*, 67–89. London: Academic Press.

Reed, G. F. (1979) Sensory deprivation. In G. Underwood and R. Stevens (eds) *Aspects of Consciousness*, vol. 1: *Psychological Issues*, 155–78. London: Academic Press.

Robinson, D. L., Goldberg, M. E. and Stanton, G. B. (1978) Parietal association cortex in the primate: sensory mechanisms and behavioral modulations. *Journal of Neurophysiology 41*: 910–32.

Roland, P. E., Larsen, B., Larsen, N. A. and Skinhoj, R. (1980) Supplementary motor area and other cortical areas in the organization of voluntary movements in man. *Journal of Neurophysiology 43*: 118–36.

Rolls, E. T., Thorpe, S. J., Maddison, S., Roper-Hall, A., Puerto, A. and Perret, D. (1979) Activity of neurones in the neostriatum and related structures in the alert animal. In I. Divac and R. G. E. Öberg (eds) *The Neostriatum*, 163–82. Oxford: Pergamon Press.

Rose, F. C. and Symonds, C. P. (1960) Persistent memory defect following encephalitis. *Brain 83*: 195–212.

Rubens, A. B. (1979) Agnosia. In K. M. Heilman and E. Valenstein (eds) *Clinical Neuropsychology*. New York: Oxford University Press.

Ruesch, J. (1944) Intellectual impairment in head injuries. *American Journal of Psychiatry 100*: 480–96.

Russell, W. R. (1971) *The Traumatic Amnesias*. London: Oxford University Press.

Scoville, W. B. and Milner, B. (1957) Loss of recent memory after bilateral hippocampal lesions. *Journal of Neurology, Neurosurgery and Psychiatry* 20: 11–21.

Shallice, T. (1979) Neuropsychological research and the fractionation of memory systems. In L-G. Nilsson (ed.) *Perspectives in Memory Research*, 257–77. Hillsdale, NJ: Erlbaum.

Sherrington, C. (1942) *Man on his Nature*. Cambridge: Cambridge University Press.

Shiffrin, R. M. and Schneider, W. (1977) Controlled and automatic human information processing: II. Perceptual learning, automatic attending, and a general theory. *Psychological Review 84*: 127–89.

Solomon, R. C. (1982) Has not an animal organs, dimensions, senses, affections, passions? *Psychology Today*, March: 36–45.

Sperry, R. W. (1961) Cerebral organization and behavior. *Science 133*: 1749–57.

Sperry, R. W. (1965) Brain bisection and mechanisms of consciousness. *Pontificiae Academiae Scientiarum Scripta Varia 30* (Semaine d'étude 'cerveau et expérience consciente'): 441–68.

Sperry, R. W. (1974) Lateral specialization in the surgically separated hemispheres. In F. O. Schmitt and F. G. Worden (eds) *The Neurosciences Third Study Program*. Cambridge, Mass.: MIT Press.

Sperry, R. W. and Gazzaniga, M. S. (1967) Language following surgical disconnection of the hemispheres. In F. L. Darley (ed.) *Brain Mechanisms Underlying Speech and Language*. New York: Grune & Stratton.

Sperry, R. W., Gazzaniga, M. S. and Bogen, J. E. (1969) Interhemispheric relationships: the neocortical commissures; symdromes of hemisphere disconnection. *Handbook of Clinical Neurology 4*: 273–90.

Squire, L. R. (1982) The neuropsychology of human memory. *Annual Review of Neuroscience 5*: 241–73.

Sternberg, S. (1966) Memory scanning: new findings and current controversies. *Quarterly Journal of Experimental Psychology 27*: 1–32.

Strich, S. J. (1969) The pathology of brain damage due to blunt head injuries. In A. E. Walker, W. F. Caveness and M. Critchley (eds) *The Late Effects of Head Injury*, 501–26. Springfield, Ill.: Thomas.

Symonds, Sir Charles (1966) Disorders of memory. *Brain 89*: 625–44.

Talland, G. A. (1965) *Deranged Memory: A Psychonomic Study of the Amnesic Syndrome*. New York: Academic Press.

Talland, G. (1969) Interaction between clinical and laboratory research on memory. In G. A. Talland and N. C. Waugh (eds) *The Pathology of Memory*, 273–9. London and New York: Academic Press.

Teuber, H. L. (1974) Key problems in the programming of movements. In J. Paillard and J. Massion (eds) *Motor Aspects of Behavior and Programmed Nervous Activities*. *Brain Research 71*: 535–68.

Treisman, A. M. and Gelade, G. (1980) A feature-integration theory of attention. *Cognitive Psychology 12*: 97–136.

Underwood, G. (1979) Memory systems and conscious processes. In G. Underwood and R. Stevens (eds) *Aspects of Consciousness*, vol. 1: *Psychological Issues*, 91–121. London and New York: Academic Press.

Underwood, G. and Stevens, R. (eds) (1979) *Aspects of Consciousness*, vol. 1: *Psychological Issues*. London and New York: Academic Press.

Underwood, G. and Stevens, R. (eds) (1981) *Aspects of Consciousness*, vol. 2: *Structural Issues*. London and New York: Academic Press.

Ungerleider, L. G. and Mishkin, M. (1981) Two cortical visual systems. In D. J. Ingle, R. J. W. Mansfield and M. A. Goodale (eds) *The Analysis of Visual Behavior*. Cambridge, Mass.: MIT Press.

Ungerstedt, U. (1971) Striatal dopamine release after aphetamine or nerve degeneration revealed by rotational behavior. *Acta Physiologica Scandinavica Suppl. 367*: 49–68.

Valéry, P. (1960) *Oeuvres*, vol. II, ed. J. Hytier, p. 714. Coll. Pleiade. Paris: Gallimard.

Van Hoesen, G. W., Pandya, D. N. and Butters, N. (1972) Cortical afferents to the entorhinal cortex of the rhesus monkey. *Science 175*: 1471–3.

Van Hoesen, G. W., Rosene, D. L. and Mesulam, M-M. (1979) Subicular input from temporal cortex in the rhesus monkey. *Science 205*: 608–10.

Vignolo, L. A. (1982) Auditory agnosia. *Philosophical Transactions of the Royal Society of London B298*: 49–57.

Warrington, E. K. (1975) The selective impairment of semantic memory. *Quarterly Journal of Experimental Psychology 27*: 635–58.

Watson, R. T. and Heilman, K. M. (1979) Thalamic neglect. *Neurology 29*: 690–4.

Weinburger, N. M., Velasco, M. and Lindsley, D. B. (1965) Effects of lesions upon thalamically induced electrocortical desynchronization and recruiting. *Electroencephalography and Clinical Neurophysiology 18*: 369–77.

Weiskrantz, L. (1980) Varieties of residual experience. *Quarterly Journal of Experimental Psychology 32*: 365–86.

Williams, M. and Zangwill, O. L. (1952) Memory defects after head injury. *Journal of Neurology, Neurosurgery and Psychiatry 15*: 54–8.

Wood, R. I. and Eames, P. (1981) Application of behaviour modification in the rehabilitation of traumatically brain-injured patients. In G. Davey (ed.) *Applications of Conditioning Theory*, 81–101. London: Methuen.

Wurtz, R. H. and Goldberg, M. E. (1972a) The primate superior colliculus and the shift of visual attention. *Investigative Opthalmology 11 (6)*: 441–50.

Wurtz, R. H. and Goldberg, M. E. (1972b) Activity of superior colliculus in behaving monkey. IV. Effects of lesions on eye movements. *Journal of Neurophysiology 35*: 587–96.

Yarnell, P. R. and Lynch, S. (1973) The 'ding': amnetic states in football trauma. *Neurology 23*: 196–7.

Yin, T. C. T. and Mountcastle, V. B. (1978) Mechanisms of neural integration in the parietal lobe for visual attention. *Federation Proceedings of the American Physiological Society 37*: 2251–7.

Young, J. Z. (1951) *Doubt and Certainty in Science*. Oxford: Clarendon Press.

Zaidel, E. (1975) A technique for presenting lateralized visual input with prolonged exposure. *Vision Research 15*: 283–9.

Zaidel, E. (1977) Unilateral auditory language comprehension on the Token Test following cerebral commissurotomy and hemispherectomy. *Neuropsychologia 15*: 1–18.

Zaidel, E. (1978) Auditory language comprehension in the right hemisphere following cerebral commissurotomy and hemispherectomy: a comparison with child language and aphasia. In A. Caramazza and E. Zurif (eds) *Language Acquisition and Language Breakdown*. Baltimore: Johns Hopkins University Press.

Zaidel, D. and Sperry, R. W. (1977) Some long-term motor effects of cerebral commissurotomy in man. *Neuropsychologia 15*: 193–204.

Zihl, J. and von Cramon, D. (1979) The contribution of the 'second' visual system to directed visual attention in man. *Brain 102*: 835–56.

Zihl, J., von Cramon, D. and Pöppel, E. (1978) Sensorische Rehabilitation bei Patienten mit postchiasmatischen Sehstörungen. *Nervenarzt 49*: 101–11.

7 Brain, mind and language

Joseph E. LeDoux

Questions concerning the nature of and causative forces underlying mental states are sticky ones, to say the least. Hardly anyone today doubts that such states are mediated by brain mechanisms, but passionate debate ensues over whether brain biology strictly determines subjective experience, whether subjective experiences can themselves determine neuronal events, and over a host of related issues concerning the manner in which mind and brain interact (see Ryle, 1949; Hook, 1960; Eccles, 1966; Armstrong, 1968; Sperry, 1969; Putnam, 1975; Fodor, 1975; Popper and Eccles, 1977; Rorty, 1979). These are long-standing, perhaps eternal, issues but the quest goes on because the solution to the problem of mental causality will be a fundamental piece in the puzzle of life.

Two assumptions have been at least implicit in most contemporary treatments of mental causality:
(1) consciousness is the primary avenue through which the mind is externally affected and through which mental events regulate behavior;
(2) the mind is an integrated, unitary system.
There are, however, good reasons for questioning both of these assumptions, and much of this chapter is concerned with these reasons and their implications for our understanding of the relation between brain and mind.

The discussion to follow admittedly appears headed down a

philosophical if not a metaphysical path. However, the points to be made have emerged not out of metaphysics but out of experimental analyses of neurological patients. The objective throughout has been to stick as close to the data as possible, but in any discussion of this type, speculation is bound to play a key role.

Some of the ideas to be discussed were borrowed from, developed in conjunction with, or inspired by Michael Gazzaniga during our collaboration several years ago. However, I take full responsibility for the present representation of the concepts and their implications for models of brain and mind.

The main thesis is this: natural language plays a crucial role in human consciousness. It allows for the common coding of divergent experiences and for the construction of a continuous, unified sense of self and reality. Natural language and consciousness, however, are evolutionarily recent facets of brain function, and they coexist with other systems which are more a part of our biological heritage as vertebrates. These relatively primitive systems, which are also capable of registering experiences and regulating purposeful behaviors, operate largely outside of conscious awareness. The conscious self thus only comes to know and understand these hidden mental dimensions when they are expressed in behavior. Once expressed, however, the behavioral output of these systems becomes subject to conscious interpretation and incorporation into the subjective experience of self.

Mental consequences of physical insult to the brain

Brain damage can lead to a variety of types of disturbance in mental function (see Geschwind, 1965; Gazzaniga, 1978, 1984). Injury to select cell populations in the human brain can cause rather specific deficits in perception, memory, attention and language, to mention but a few examples. To some, observations of this type are proof enough that mental events are one and the same with, or at least reducible to, brain states. Others, however, are not moved. They argue that while such observations may show that the brain is necessary for the expression of mental events, the possibility remains that the causal forces underlying mental events exist outside of brain function.

These positions represent a philosophic polarity which may or may not be useful in a scientific approach to understanding the relationship between brain and mind. Brain scientists are particularly interested in this relation rather than in the philosophical argument itself. Nevertheless, there is some rather compelling evidence that favors the view that neural mechanisms underlie, and in some (theoretically) determinable way, account for mental experience. Much of this evidence comes from split-brain studies conducted over the past thirty years.

Where is your mind when your brain is split?

In the early 1950s, Myers and Sperry (1953), in the process of tracing the flow of visual information from eye to brain, found that when cats were surgically prepared so that each eye only projected to one hemisphere, visual information presented to one eye alone was available for use by the other eye. The implication of this observation was that integration took place inside the brain. In later experiments, they demonstrated that section of the neural pathways connecting the two hemispheres prevented the necessary integration (see Sperry, 1958; Myers, 1965). In fact, in these 'split-brain' cats, each hemisphere was capable of attending to, learning, and remembering information outside of the awareness of the other hemisphere. The two half-brains could even simultaneously acquire conflicting information. Each hemisphere of the split-brain cat was a complete mental system.

The importance of the observation, that following brain bisection the mental experiences of the two hemispheres were not shared, was that it seemed to leave little room for any conclusion other than that mental experiences are directly tied to neural tissue. The mind could, it seemed, be neatly compartmentalized by a physical act.

The drama of these observations was greatly amplified when in the 1960s splitting the brain re-emerged as a way of treating intractable epilepsy (Bogen and Vogel, 1962). All of the animal observations proved applicable to man, but with the added complication that certain differences existed in the representation of cognitive processes in the two hemispheres. While the human studies (see Gazzaniga, 1970; Sperry, 1974) in some sense provided an even more compelling case that splitting the brain split the mind, they also resulted in a good deal of opposition to such notions.

Practically no one doubted that certain mental functions like perception could be surgically separated. The controversy was really about whether the self was divided in split-brain man. In other words, when the brain is split, is each hemisphere a self-conscious entity? John Eccles (1965) argued that consciousness was a property of the language dominant hemisphere, with the capacities of the other half-brain being automatic or stimulus-bound. This sort of reasoning was certainly consistent with most of the data at the time. While the conscious properties of the left hemisphere were apparent from its verbal behavior, the right hemisphere seemed capable of responding only at a much lower level, perhaps more like a smart chimpanzee rather than a fully developed human. Donald MacKay (1965) took another tack. His point was that unless it could be shown that each half-brain had its own independent system for assigning values and setting goals, a split brain could not be viewed as a split mind.

And there things stood for some years. No one could figure out whether the attribution of an inferior status to the right hemisphere of split-brain humans was a fair judgment or whether the mental properties of the right hemisphere were just less accessible to linguistically biased humans. The next chapter, however, provided a new twist to the story.

Language and consciousness in split-brain man

In the early 1970s, the effort to manage intractable epilepsy by split-brain surgery was revitalized by Donald Wilson of the Dartmouth Medical School (Wilson, Reeves, Gazzaniga and Culver, 1977). This series of patients provided the opportunity to reassess some of the old findings as well as pursue some new possibilities (Gazzaniga and LeDoux, 1978).

It was obvious from the start that case P.S. of the Wilson series was no ordinary split-brain patient. His right hemisphere responded with unusual readiness when probed in the typical way. At first, the tests were mainly non-verbal. A picture would be flashed into the left visual field and the left hand would be required to reach into a box and retrieve the object from several choices. While any split-brain patient can do this, usually the right hemisphere requires some training or coaxing, probably because it cannot understand verbal commands. And when the tests of P.S. were extended to an assessment of linguistic abilities, it was discovered that language was represented in his right hemisphere as well as his left (Gazzaniga, LeDoux and Wilson, 1978). While only the left could speak, both could understand speech. (Some time later, P.S. did develop right hemisphere speech

(Gazzaniga *et al.*, 1979), but all of the tests described here took place prior to any evidence of right hemisphere speech.)

In subsequent tests of P.S. an effort was made to determine whether his right hemisphere could express itself linguistically, albeit without speech. Letters were provided and he was instructed to spell his response to various probes. Object pictures were presented to the left visual field and in most instances he was able to spell the object name.

This ability to spell object names using letters raised the interesting possibility that this speechless right hemisphere might also be able to spell answers to personal and subjective questions. In other words, here was a case where human interaction with the right hemisphere was not limited by the usual absence of linguistic competence in the right hemisphere. Case P.S. thus seemed to be a potential test case concerning whether the right hemisphere, along with the left, could possess conscious properties following brain bisection.

A series of tests were designed to assess various features of self-consciousness (LeDoux, Wilson and Gazzaniga, 1977). With little precedent in the matter, we chose somewhat unsystematically, but not arbitrarily, the following properties of self-consciousness: a sense of self; a sense of the relation between self and others; an understanding of the relation of self to past, current and projected time frames; an ability to characterize present mood states; and an ability to construct goals and aspirations for the future. To assess these properties, questions were asked of P.S.'s right hemisphere. For example, a sense of self was assessed by asking him through the left visual field, 'Who are you?' The left hand reached into the pile of letters and spelt his name. On other trials designed to assess the other properties, he spelt the name of his girlfriend and his favorite person, he described his mood and indicated the month, day and year, and stated his choice for a preferred professional career. These were amazing responses coming from a silent part of this boy's brain.

While these data from P.S. seem clearly to indicate that the right hemisphere of a split-brain patient can be a conscious entity along with the left, the question naturally arises as to whether these two selves are simply duplicated, or instead, truly represent double consciousness (Puchetti, 1980). The data on this clearly suggest double consciousness in P.S. (LeDoux and Gazzaniga, 1980).

In tests examining the attitudes of the two hemispheres, quite different results were sometimes obtained (LeDoux *et al.*, 1977). A word was presented to one visual field or the other and he was required to select (by pointing) a rating varying from 'like very much' to 'dislike very much', which characterized his feeling for the item. The two hemispheres had very different attitudes concerning many of the items. In another set of probes, an even more dramatic dissociation was observed. The left hemisphere described its occupational choice as 'draftsman', while the right aspired to be a 'race car driver'.

These observations, it would seem, argue quite convincingly that the self *can be split* and doubled following brain bisection. The questions raised by MacKay, Eccles, and others seem answered by P.S., whose right hemisphere clearly has its own volitional control system capable of setting its own response priorities.

If we could identify the factor that distinguishes the right hemisphere in P.S. from the right hemisphere in other split-brain patients, we might have a clue to the underlying nature of human consciousness. That factor is undoubtedly the extensive linguistic representation seen in the right hemisphere of P.S. These findings, and others that have come since (see Gazzaniga, 1983), support the view that natural language plays an important role in human consciousness.

Hemisphere dominance, language and consciousness

The observation that language and consciousness are closely associated in split-brain man obviously raises the question of whether in the normal brain, where language is usually only present in the left hemisphere, the left hemisphere is conscious and the right hemisphere is unconscious. This sort of question, however, has a misplaced focus. In the split brain, it is appropriate to speak of hemispheres as conscious or not because the brain has been physically partitioned. But in the absence of such a partition, the attribution of consciousness to one hemisphere or the other is inappropriate. While language is usually tied to the left hemisphere, linguistic processing is not one and the same with left hemisphere processing. Much of the left hemisphere is engaged in non-linguistic processing. It is thus not the left hemisphere which is conscious. Instead, there are mechanisms associated with the linguistic system (which is often in restricted parts of the left hemisphere) that play an important role in the type of conscious awareness we experience as human beings.

Animal consciousness

The suggestion that consciousness is closely tied to linguistic mechanisms in man seems to leave little room for consciousness in non-human organisms. Perhaps more to the point, however, is the suggestion that consciousness, as we humans experience it, is closely tied to our capacity for natural language. This view allows for human consciousness to be unique and at the same time leaves open the possibility that non-human organisms are aware and perhaps even self aware, only not in the ways made possible by natural language.

Natural language is a species-typical characteristic of humans. It is thus not surprising that human consciousness is embedded in this infinitely flexible system of thought and communication. While other species may be found to be capable of self-reflection, their conscious capacities will no doubt not mirror those made possible by human natural language.

In the same sense, it should not be surprising that the isolated, language-deprived right hemisphere of a split-brain patient has a limited capacity for conscious agency, as described earlier. Conscious awareness has been attributed to such right hemispheres on occasion (Sperry et al., 1979), but similar observations have been made for higher primates (Gallup, 1977). All things considered, the cognitive status of a language-deficient isolated right hemisphere is, as noted before, more like that of a chimpanzee than a human being.

An important, though largely overlooked potential contribution of split-brain studies concerns this primitive status of the right hemisphere. Elsewhere, I have argued that the human right hemisphere represents a quantitative elaboration of the non-human primate brain (LeDoux, 1982; 1984b; 1984c) and, in this sense, when it is artificially disconnected from the linguistic mechanisms of the left hemisphere, it becomes a missing neurological link. That is, the isolated right hemisphere may be useful as a model of the human brain arrested at an earlier, prelinguistic cognitive stage. Studies of the isolated right hemisphere might thus be able to tell us something about a lost aspect of cognitive evolution much too subtle to be present in the fossil record.

In the normal human brain, the dissociation between linguistic and non-linguistic ways of knowing is of course not so clear. Nevertheless, both are there. Our capacity for language does not exclude our pre-linguistic, evolutionarily ancient ways of knowing ourselves and our world. These are present and part of the integrated function of both hemispheres. And though non-linguistic processing is often over-shadowed in consciousness by linguistic coding, its underlying role in mental life is, as we shall see, crucial.

Non-conscious processing in man

In cognitive psychology, consciousness is for the most part equated with attention (see Posner, 1975; Neisser, 1967). We are consciously aware of those things to which we attend. This is a relatively impoverished view of consciousness, but is useful as a starting point for discussing non-conscious processing.

If conscious processing is equated with attention, then non-conscious processing must be reduced to inattention. This is only so, however, if we narrowly define attention as the pathway to consciousness rather than as the pathway to perception, for there are ample examples of perception, which presumably requires attention, in the absence of conscious awareness of the perceived information. Consider first a study we conducted involving patients with damage to the right parieto-occipital cortex (Volpe *et al.*, 1979).

Damage to this region produces a variety of disturbances, but the particular disorder of interest here is referred to as extinction. If a stimulus is presented to the patient's left visual field, it can be named. Similarly, stimuli presented to the right visual field are readily named. If, however, two stimuli are simultaneously presented to the left and right visual field, the left field stimulus goes unnoticed by the patient. In other words, the patient treats the trial as though only the right field stimulus was present. The patient has no awareness of the left field stimulus. What then is the fate of the left field stimulus? Was it not processed or was it processed but not available to the conscious speaking person? To answer this question the task can be changed slightly. Instead of requiring that the patient name the left field items, this task is one of determining whether the items in the two visual fields are the same or are different. In this situation, although the patient is still unable to identify the left field items, the level of accuracy in comparing the stimuli is high. Thus, the patients were able to make decisions on the basis of stimuli they obviously attended to and perceived, though they were not consciously aware of having done so.

The implication of this observation is that behavior can be influenced by information of which the conscious person is ignorant. This situation is hardly attributable to abnormalities arising from the brain injury, for numerous studies of normal, healthy individuals have shown the same thing (Lazarus and McCleary, 1951; Erikson, 1960). While the earlier studies on normals have been criticized on methodological grounds and neatly dismissed, more recent studies (e.g. Marcel, 1981; Zajonc, 1980) are not so readily put aside.

For example, Zajonc (1980) and his colleagues, making use of the fact that exposure to nonsense shapes leads to the development of preferences for these items over previously unseen shapes, have shown that rapid presentation of stimuli, whilst too fast for subsequent recognition, nevertheless leads to the development of item preferences. They concluded that such reactions must be based not only on properties of the stimuli themselves but on the subject's internal states. Such states, it must be noted, developed in the absence of conscious awareness of stimulus content.

Returning to the split-brain literature for another example we find results analogous to those just described. In this case the test again involved the case P.S., in whom the anterior commissure was left intact during the surgery. Test after test revealed that, unlike many similar patients (Risse *et al.*, 1977), the anterior commissure did not mediate the interhemispheric transfer of visual information in P.S. Thus he was unable to name visual stimuli presented to his left visual field and right hemisphere because the information did not cross between the hemispheres. But the anterior commissure has fibers which interconnect areas in the limbic system (the emotional brain) in the two hemispheres, in addition to interconnecting the visual areas of the temporal lobe. We thus attempted to demonstrate whether emotional information might be transferred between the two hemispheres (LeDoux, 1978; Gazzaniga and LeDoux, 1978b).

We made use of the fact that P.S.'s right hemisphere could read. We presented words (taken from his speech) separately to each visual field and required that he verbally rate the word on a five-point scale ranging from 'like very much' to 'dislike very much'. In other words, the speech system was required to produce a rating of words presented to each hemisphere. While the speech system had direct access to the left hemisphere words, it had no access to the right hemisphere presentations. If the ratings were similar, it could only mean that the emotional tone of the word had crossed the midline. As it turned out, the ratings were almost identical. The emotional tone of an external stimulus was thus dissociated from the conscious content of the stimulus. Although the conscious person did not know what the stimulus was, he was able to access how he felt about the stimulus.

As a final example of non-conscious processing consider an experiment conducted by Risse and Gazzaniga (1978). They used a procedure where, for medical purposes, one hemisphere of a callosum intact brain could be selectively anesthetized by injection of a barbiturate, sodium amytal, into one carotid artery, the main vascular supply to the brain. While the left hemisphere was anesthetized, the subject palpated an object with his left hand. When both hemispheres were again awake the patient was asked to name the object. In such situations the patients were unable to provide the name with any accuracy but were able to select the object among several choices by pointing.

The patients, thus, on request, could not generate the response. They repeatedly said they did not know. Though the conscious self did not know, the information had obviously been registered, though not in verbal codes. Information coded in the absence of language proved to be inaccessible to consciousness, though it was readily accessible through behavior. Linguistic codes, it would seem, are the codes of human consciousness.

These studies clearly demonstrate that lasting and significant effects on behavior and thought processes can be produced by activities that go unnoticed by the conscious person. Consciousness, in other words, is only one avenue through which the brain accepts inputs and produces behavior. When input is registered by non-conscious systems, that input is not available to the conscious self. It is coded in a way that cannot be decoded by the verbally dominant conscious mechanisms. Yet, it is as much a part of the store of information that directs our moods and behavior as input which is initially processed in consciousness.

Conscious–non-conscious dynamics

What happens when behavior is produced by systems operating non-consciously? What, in other words, is the reaction of the conscious person to behaviors of non-conscious origin? It turns out that the split-brain patient is ideally suited for studying such a question. From the point of view of the left hemisphere, behaviors produced by the right are produced by a non-conscious mental system. Thus, inducing behaviors through the right hemisphere and examining how the left hemisphere deals with the behavior provides an experimental model of conscious–unconscious dynamics.

In tests again involving case P.S., verbal commands were presented to his left visual field (Gazzaniga, LeDoux and Wilson, 1977).

Following the command, he produced the response requested. Subsequently, he was asked 'Why did you do that?' In trial after trial his left hemisphere responses were consistent with the information available from his behavior. When the command was 'rub' he said 'itch', and when it was 'laugh' he said we (the experimenters) were funny. These were not said as guesses or jokes, however, but as facts as to why he behaved the way he did.

In another test, two pictures were simultaneously presented, one in each visual field, and the required response was to select from eight choices the one that went with the picture (Gazzaniga, LeDoux and Wilson, 1977; LeDoux, Wilson and Gazzaniga, 1978). Each hemisphere, in this situation, selected a choice. When the left field item was a snow scene, the left hand pointed to a shovel, while the right hand pointed to a chicken to match the chicken claw presented to the right visual field. When asked why he chose those items, he said that he saw a chicken claw so he picked the chicken and you have to have a shovel to clean the chicken shed. As before, this was not said in jest, but as a statement of fact as to the origin of the overt response of pointing to the shovel. The speaking left hemisphere in these situations thus witnessed its body performing behavioral responses and it immediately incorporated these responses into its perspective on the situation.

These observations of course are only relevant to the extent that it can be shown that in our daily lives the conscious self is confronted with behaviors produced by non-conscious systems. As we have seen, however, this is a reasonable suggestion if not a demonstrable fact.

It is through overt behavior that the conscious self comes to know fully the passions and prejudices that rule below. It is on the basis of observing our own behavior and moods that we come to construct a true understanding of ourselves. The activity of non-conscious mental systems is often not decodable internally in the brain by the conscious self, and can only be known and incorporated into our verbally constructed sense of self when exposed through behavior.

Summary

(1) Physical partitioning of the human brain through split-brain surgery can, but does not necessarily, lead to a splitting and doubling of consciousness.

(2) The limiting condition on whether the right hemisphere, along with the left, can be conscious following split-brain surgery appears to involve the presence of linguistic mechanisms in the right hemisphere.

(3) In the absence of extensive linguistic representation, the cognitive capacities of the right hemisphere are more like those of a chimpanzee than like those of a fully developed human.

(4) Consciousness reflects the activity of select neuronal populations, not hemispheres, and in the absence of surgical bisection of the brain, it is inappropriate to speak of hemispheres as conscious or not.

(5) Consciousness, as we experience it, is a species-specific characteristic of humans and is directly related to our capacity for natural language and its infinite flexibility as a system of thought and communication.

(6) While non-human organisms may be aware and even self-aware, they are not aware in the unique ways made possible by natural language.

(7) In spite of the importance of consciousness to human nature, we retain many of the prelinguistic ways of knowing ourself and our world; these mechanisms, which operate largely though not exclusively outside of conscious awareness, play a crucial role in regulating moods and behavioral responses.

(8) Since prelinguistic systems encode information in a way that is not decipherable by the verbal system, which dominates consciousness, the conscious self can only come to know and understand these hidden mental dimensions when they are expressed through behavior.

(9) When the conscious self observes behaviors produced by non-conscious systems, it is often compelled to interpret the activity subjectively.

(10) Through the interpretation of experience the conscious self subjectively constructs reality.

Discussion

In the introduction, it was noted that most treatments of mental causality have assumed that the human mind is unitary and that consciousness is the mechanism through which the human mind is externally influenced. The preceding discussion, however, has, through examples drawn from studies of neurological patients, developed a view of the human mind that is in direct opposition to both these assumptions (also, see chapter 8 of this volume, on plurality of consciousness and behavioral control). In the following, this view will be pursued. While it is at this point that efforts to stick to the data stop, the relation of the following speculative discourse to the experiments described before is direct and, I hope, obvious.

As a starting point, consider a situation that is familiar to many persons who have driven a car over a long distance. At certain points, the driver can suddenly be surprised to realize that he has no recollection of the miles just past, for his conscious mind was occupied by thoughts that had nothing to do with the driving experience. But in spite of this lapse of conscious focus on driving, the car did not stray out of the lane or off the road, and the curves were somehow navigated. And when the conscious self again grabbed the wheel, the reaction was, of course, one of startle, confusion and fear. Even the most attentive driving is life-threatening and the thought of having gone, for who knows how long, without paying attention is frightening.

The next stage in the sequence is an effort to account for what happened and explain how the navigation took place: 'Well, it probably was a short distance on a straight road', or 'Now, I think I actually remember a bridge, so I must have been attending all along', or 'I guess I've been driving for so many years I can do it with my eyes closed', and so on. Such thoughts are the result of the conscious self having been confronted with the fact that purposeful activities have been carried out without its sanction or assistance. The conscious self thus attempts to weave a tale that it can live with.

I use the example of driving because so many people have had this experience. However, the condition is far more general, and is commonplace in daily activities. We are not consciously aware of all the information our mind processes or of the causes of all the behaviors we produce, or of the origin of all the feelings we experience. But the conscious self uses these as data points to construct and maintain a coherent story, our personal story, our subjective sense of self.

But our personal story is not nourished in a vacuum. It is maintained in the context of our attitudes and beliefs about how the external world operates. From earliest childhood we are, through our interactions with our physical and social environments, developing attitudes towards the elements of these environments and their function. These environmental attitudes and beliefs are modified and consolidated with further experience until they become so firmly established that even the greatest amount of conflicting experience is often insufficient to change our minds. These beliefs and attitudes about our social and physical worlds, though, are, in the final analysis, simply tales woven by the conscious self through interaction with a particular cultural milieu. When such tales, through verbal communication, become the shared experience of many, they become societal beliefs and take on the appearance of truth. But even scientific truths are subject to modification and abandonment. Though the physical world may be real, our experience of it, like our experience of our conscious self, is ultimately subjective.

Weaving such tales about the self and its world is a prime function of consciousness. The reality we experience is a personal one, a subjective construction of the conscious self and its arsenal of verbal skills. Each individual, on the basis of his past experiences, present situation and future plans, and through the use of natural language and its flexibility in analyzing and codifying experiences and interrelating experiences systematically, constructs a subjective view of the world and his place in it.

The central focus from which subjective reality emanates, then, is the conscious self – that collection of matter and energy that constitutes what the individual believes he is and can be. And the conscious self, like the subjective reality it experiences, is largely the creation of the individual's verbal system or, in the case of deaf and dumb individuals, presumably of closely related symbol systems. Proper names and personal pronouns serve as reference points that are anchored in subjective reality and, through linguistic differentiation and association, are given meaning. The conscious self, in this way, is provided with its salient features, its self-concept.

Language, in this view, is at the core of human subjective reality. It provides a universal code through which divergent subjective experiences can be commonly registered and thus woven into a coherent life story. Events that are consciously processed can (within the limits of memory) be readily related to one another and to the conscious self in space and time, even if they initially occurred as spatially or temporally distinct events. Linguistic encoding provides a sense of experiential continuity and thus allows human conscious experience, in spite of its dynamic ever-changing content, to be more like a movie than like series of snapshots.

If forced to describe the conscious life of organisms such as advanced primates, with rather sophisticated cognitive repertories but without linguistic skills, I would in fact use the snapshot analogy. Such creatures may have glimpses of self-consciousness, but without the tools of linguistic encoding I doubt that they can generate the sense of experiential continuity that we so readily construct.

But drop down the evolutionary tree a few branches and consider the nature of reality experienced by creatures whose existence is largely dictated by species-specific response patterns elicited by largely invariant environmental stimuli. Such stimuli are the critical reality of the organism. In contrast, consider the nature of existence of animals whose environmental interactions are partly controlled by innate, species-specific tendencies and partly by experience. The reality of such creatures takes on a personal air. To the extent that the behavior of one species member in a particular situation is influenced by an event that another member did not experience, then the two animals may be said to have different constructions of reality.

The implication of this analysis is that the greater the role of experience in an organism's existence, the more personal is the reality experienced. The behavior of all primates, including man, is minimally dictated by invarient stimuli outside the organism; man, however, possessing nature's most sophisticated mechanism (natural language) for coding, storing, analyzing and retrieving past experience, individually constructs a subjective reality to an extent unmatched by other creatures.

But just as language giveth, language taketh away the self, or such is the attempt of the language of science. Prior to the Copernican Revolution, man considered himself in the center of the universe. In effect, such a view reflected the collective subjective reality of human consciousness, as represented in the shared linguistically encoded belief structure of the day. The rise of modern science was an effort to create a collective objective reality by using languages (mathematics, physics, chemistry, etc.) with little or no room for subjective interpretation. What this means is that the so-called objective languages of the sciences attempt to bypass the user's subjective reality by constructing reality impersonally. The limiting condition in such an approach is of course the fact that, even in the most objective circumstance, the subjective self is the ultimate arbitrator of reality.

Though the conscious self is the keeper of who we believe we are, there is, as we have noted, more to ourselves than meets our mind's eye.

Operating outside of conscious awareness are neural systems capable of comprehending external events and regulating organized inter-actions with the world. Unlike the conscious self, however, the non-conscious systems are not integrated into a unified non-conscious self. Individual non-conscious systems can, nevertheless, come to be significant forces in controlling behavior and can, in fact, take on the status of selves that dominate behavior.

As selves or as simpler constructions, non-conscious systems may work in concert with, or in opposition to, the conscious self. When behaviors or moods produced by the non-conscious systems are consistent with the attitudes, beliefs, and/or situational perspective of the conscious self, the behavior or mood is readily incorporated into the conscious self's subjective appraisal of the situation. When, how-ever, there is inconsistency, the conscious self is forced to re-evaluate what has transpired. An analysis of this sort is supported by the continued survival of dissonance and balance theories in social psy-chology.

These non-conscious systems are direct descendants of comparable systems of our evolutionary ancestors. These, more so than the mechanisms of language and consciousness, reflect our biological heritage as vertebrates. And one way of characterizing an important subset of these systems is as emotional systems — systems capable of registering the significance of events and capable of regulating affec-tively charged behavioral responses and feelings (internal affective responses). (See LeDoux, in press; LeDoux *et al.*, 1984.)

It was suggested by philosophers many centuries ago that what distinguishes man from other creatures is reason, or the ability to override our passions and willfully and prudently direct our behavior. An important corollary to this notion is the fact that it is much easier to control our emotional behavior than our emotions. It is, for example, easier to hold back a punch than it is to eliminate the feel-ings that make us want to fight. Feelings must, in most instances, run their course.

This dissociation between control over feelings and behavior suggests some rather specific predictions about the organization and interconnectivity of the brain systems underlying consciousness and emotion (LeDoux, 1984a). Conscious mechanisms in man, based on linguistic encoding, have limited connectivity with emotional systems. The conscious self, thus, cannot readily enter into the causal chain of events which initiate and maintain emotional arousal. However, the conscious self can regulate behavior and thus is capable of entering into the causal chain through which emotional behavior is expressed.

Though the neural pathways between the mechanisms of consciousness and emotion are limited, the conscious self is not an expression of 'pure reason'. The conscious self obviously has its passions and prejudices and makes decisions on the basis of these. However, the question is, how well does the conscious self understand its passions and prejudices? Do these affective responses reflect an apprehension of the underlying causal factors that gave rise to the emotion, or do they reflect a conscious interpretation upon being faced with an emotional response?

If the initiating circumstances of an emotional reaction were consciously encoded, the conscious self has a chance of understanding later emotional responses in similar situations. Even then the possibility for interpretive error arises. In this case, the conscious self is left to its own devices to figure out the affective significance of an event. In doing so, finding a socially or personally acceptable interpretation often takes precedence over a correct interpretation.

Conscious interpretation of emotional life is a crucial aspect of mental health and mental illness. As it presently stands, the conscious self can, on its own, only regulate the most primitive emotional responses – survival responses. That is, through its stories it can rationalize or deny its bodily experiences when they are the work of non-conscious systems. It is as if these stories are protective responses evolved by the verbal system to defend the dignity and unity of the subjective self it creates.

Some day in a more advanced human form, the conscious self may be freed from the task of having to deal with emotional systems through bodily experiences – through moods and behavior. This freedom, of course, would depend on the development of neural connectivity between the mechanisms of consciousness and emotion. The question of whether the conscious self could enter the causal chain of emotion would then be moot. The conscious self would be a crucial participant in the emotional experience.

If these speculations are correct, we as humans are moving toward a state of psychic synthesis. Concerns over an impersonal, dispassionate future may be accurate but short-sighted. If mankind makes it through this awkward phase of conscious–emotional separation, the way may be paved for the emergence of a new kind of man, one who consciously apprehends his emotional life and thus fully understands his self in the fullest meaning of the word.

214   Brain and Mind

References

Armstrong, D. M. (1968) *A Materialist Theory of Mind*. London: Routledge & Kegan Paul.

Bogen, J. E. and Vogel, P. J. (1962) Cerebral commissurotomy: a case report. *Bulletin of the Los Angeles Neurological Society 27*: 169.

Eccles, J. C. (1965) *The Brain and Unity of Conscious Experience. The 19th Arthur Stanley Eddington Memorial Lecture*. Cambridge: Cambridge University Press.

Eccles, J. C. (1966) *Brain and Conscious Experience*. Heidelberg: Springer-Verlag.

Eriksen, C. W. (1960) Discrimination learning without awareness. *Psychological Review 67*: 279–300.

Fodor, J. A. (1975) *The Language of Thought*. Cambridge, Mass.: Harvard University Press.

Gallup, G. G. Jr (1977) Self recognition in primates. *American Psychologist 32*: 329–38.

Gazzaniga, M. S. (1970) *The Bisected Brain*. New York: Appleton-Century-Crofts.

Gazzaniga, M. S. (1978) *Handbook of Neuropsychology*. New York: Plenum Press.

Gazzaniga, M. S. (1983) Right hemisphere language: a twenty year perspective. *American Psychologist 38*: 525–37.

Gazzaniga, M. S. (1984) *Handbook of Cognitive Neuroscience*. New York: Plenum Press.

Gazzaniga, M. S. and LeDoux, J. E. (1978) *The Integrated Mind*. New York: Plenum Press.

Gazzaniga, M. S., LeDoux, J. E. and Wilson, D. H. (1977) Language, praxis, and the right hemisphere: Clues to some mechanisms of consciousness. *Neurology 24*: 1144–7.

Gazzaniga, M. S., LeDoux, J. E., Smylie, C. S. and Volpe, B. T. (1979) Plasticity in speech organization following commissurotomy. *Brain 102*: 805–15.

Geschwind, N. (1965) The disconnexion syndromes in animals and man. *Brain 88*: 237–94; 585–644.

Hook, S. (1960) *Dimensions of Mind*. New York: Collier.

Lazarus, R. S. and McCleary, R. A. (1951) Autonomic discrimination without awareness. *Psychological Review 56*: 113–22.

LeDoux, J. E. (1978) The neurology of emotion: clues from the split brain. In F. Angeli (ed.) *Bisocial Aspects of Development*. Milan: Casa Editrice.

LeDoux, J. E. (1982) Neuro-evolutionary mechanisms of cerebral asymmetry in man. *Brain, Behavior and Evolution 20*: 196–212.

LeDoux, J. E. (1984a) Cerebral asymmetry and the integrated function of the brain. In A. Young (ed.) *Functions of the Right Hemisphere* 203–16. London: Academic Press.

LeDoux, J. E. (1984b) Cognition and emotion: processing functions and brain systems. In M. S. Gazzaniga (ed.) *Handbook of Cognitive Neuroscience.* New York: Plenum Press.

LeDoux, J. E. (1984c) Cognitive evolution: clues from brain asymmetry. In A. Ardilla and F. Ostrovsky (eds) *The Right Hemisphere* 51–60. New York: Gordon & Breach.

LeDoux, J. E. (in press) Neurobiology and emotion. In J. E. LeDoux and W. Hirst (eds) *Mind and Brain: Dialogues in Cognitive Neuroscience.* New York: Cambridge University Press.

LeDoux, J. E. and Gazzaniga, M. S. (1981) A duel with duality as a model of mind. *Behavioral and Brain Sciences 4*: 109–10.

LeDoux, J. E., Sakaguchi, A. and Reis, D. J. (1984) Subcortical efferent projections of the medial geniculate nucleus mediate emotional responses conditioned to acoustic stimuli. *Journal of Neuroscience 4*: 683–98.

LeDoux, J. E., Wilson, D. H. and Gazzaniga, M. S. (1977). A divided mind: observations on the conscious properties of the separated hemispheres. *Annals of Neurology 2*: 417–21.

LeDoux, J. E., Wilson, D. H. and Gazzaniga, M. S. (1979) Beyond commissurotomy: clues to consciousness. In M. S. Gazzaniga (ed.) *Handbook of Behavioral Neurobiology*, vol. 2, 543–54. New York: Plenum Press.

MacKay, D. (1972) Personal communication cited in M. S. Gazzaniga, One brain – two minds? *American Scientist 60*: 311–17.

Myers, R. E. and Sperry, R. W. (1953) Interocular transfer of a visual form discrimination habit in cats after section of the optic chiasm and corpus callosum. *Anatomical Record 175*: 351–2.

Neisser, U. (1967) *Cognitive Psychology.* New York: Appleton-Century-Crofts.

Popper, K. and Eccles, J. C. (1977) *The Self and its Brain.* Heidelberg: Springer-Verlag.

Posner, M. I. (1975) Psychobiology of attention. In M. S. Gazzaniga and C. Blakemore, *Handbook of Psychobiology.* New York: Academic Press.

Puchetti, R. (1981) The case for mental duality. *The Behavioral and Brain Sciences 4*: 93–9.

Putnam, H. (1975) *Mind, Language, and Reality.* Cambridge: Cambridge University Press.

Risse, G. L. and Gazzaniga, M. S. (1978) Well kept secrets of the right hemisphere: a sodium amytal study. *Neurology 28*: 950–93.

Risse, G. L., LeDoux, J. E., Springer, S. P., Wilson, D. H. and Gazzaniga, M. S. (1977) The anterior commissure in man: functional variation in a multisensory system. *Neuropsychology 16*: 23–31.

Rorty, R. (1979) *Philosophy and the Mirror of Nature.* Princeton, NJ: Princeton University Press.

Ryle, G. (1949) *The Concept of Mind.* London: Hutchinson.

Sperry, R. W. (1958) The corpus callosum and interhemispheric transfer in the monkey. *Anatomical Record 131*: 297.

Sperry, R. W. (1969) A modified concept of consciousness. *Psychological Review* 76: 532–6.

Sperry, R. W. (1974) In F. O. Schmitt and F. G. Worden (eds) *Neuroscience Third Study Program*. Cambridge, Mass.: MIT Press.

Sperry, R. W., Zaidel, E. and Zaidel, D. (1979) Self recognition and social awareness in the disconnected minor hemisphere. *Neuropsychology 17 (2)*: 153–66.

Volpe, B. T., LeDoux, J. E. and Gazzaniga, M. S. (1979) Information processing of visual stimuli in an extinguished field. *Nature 282*: 722.

Wilson, D. H., Reeves, A. G., Gazzaniga, M. S. and Culver, C. (1977) Cerebral commissurotomy for the control of intractable seizures. *Neurology* 27: 708–15.

Zajonc, R. B. (1980) Feeling and thinking. *American Psychologist 35*: 151–75.

8 The plurality of consciousness

David A. Oakley and Lesley C. Eames

Introduction

One of the most persuasive aspects of what we intuitively label as 'consciousness' or 'conscious awareness' is its unity, both in the immediate sense that the self-perceiver always appears to be the same person ('me') and also over time. Despite interruptions for sleep, during concussion or drug-induced insensibility the flow of consciousness continues as the same subjective stream of experience. The purpose of this chapter is to review evidence which suggests that the unity of consciousness is illusory. At least two and sometimes many more domains of consciousness may co-exist within the human brain. First, however, it is necessary to turn to the thorny question of definition, and we propose to tackle that problem via a model of human awareness (see also chapter 5 of this volume).

A model of human awareness

The model we wish to offer is shown as Figure 8.1. Awareness serves the overall function of allowing us to produce appropriate actions in the real world, and for this we need adequate sensory and motor systems. These are depicted at the bottom of the figure and have both cortical and subcortical components. 'Cortical' here refers to derivatives of the medial, dorsal and lateral covering (i.e. 'cortex') of the

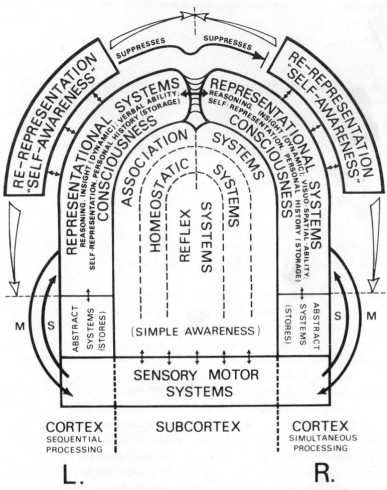

Fig. 8.1 A quasi-anatomical model of awareness in the human brain. This model is an elaboration of that developed in chapter 5 of this volume.

vertebrate forebrain, and in particular to neocortex and hippocampus (see chapter 5). At the core of the figure are shown subcortical systems mediating reflex actions, homeostatic mechanisms and association learning (habituation, Pavlovian conditioning and instrumental learning). These processes constitute *simple awareness* and provide for immediate adaptive responses to environmental stimuli.

Surrounding the subcortical core are cortical systems devoted to forming inner representations of the real world. A neurological map or model retains the essential features of the external world and the relationships which exist between the parts of that world (see chapters 1–4 of this volume). Representational systems form the basis for perception, as opposed to sensation, and have a dynamic aspect in the sense that internal models or maps can be used to construct novel realities and derive possible outcomes. That is, they form the basis for internal experimentation, for thinking about problems and for testing a variety of possible solutions against what is known of the real world. They are the substrates of reasoning and insight. There is a further aspect to representational systems which reflects their use as a basis for storing information from experience as a biographical record. This personal history, or episodic memory, retains events in spatially and temporally coded form.

Representational systems provide a way of 'knowing' about the world and for this reason we would suggest that the processing which takes place within these systems is conscious processing and the types of behaviours which depend on representational systems are reflections of *consciousness* (see chapter 5). Consciousness is defined in this way by Griffin (1976) and by Jerison (1973, 1976). We have shown for completeness (though we will have little to say about them here) cortical stores for information abstracted from the ongoing stream of representational processing. These stores consist of 'meanings', rules and items of general knowledge, which are accessible without reference to their original spatial or temporal contexts and so constitute abstract, or semantic, memory (for a discussion of representational and abstract memory systems see Oakley, 1981, 1983a). In recognition of the fact that the human brain has two cerebral hemispheres and hence two sets of cortical systems, the cortical section is divided at the top of the figure and linked by a band of fibres, the most important of which are those of the corpus callosum. The modal dispositions of the left and right hemispheres are summarized as specializations for sequential and simultaneous processing respectively (see, for example, Davidoff, 1982; Dimond, 1979; Springer and Deutsch, 1981).

This description omits one important aspect of awareness, however, and that is that we are often subjectively aware of a subset of the contents of consciousness. We are aware of ourselves as perceivers, thinkers and actors. We can introspect and can share some at least of the products of that introspection with others, by using a common language. It would appear that representations can be selected from the general pool of consciousness for re-representation within a system of priority processing. This system has a superior command over actions and is coextensive with the realm of subjective experience (see chapters 3 and 5). This capacity for re-representation constitutes *self-awareness*, the awareness of being aware, and is shown in Figure 8.1 as a separate cortical system superimposed on the cortical representational systems of each hemisphere. Self-awareness has a double aspect, in that it can be outwardly directed as an awareness of our perception of the outside world (which includes our own bodies), or inwards as an awareness of our own thoughts, our own internal dialogues and our feelings or emotions. Within representational systems are developed models of the self as an actor in the world, with particular characteristics and related to a particular past history. Re-representation of this self-model allows awareness of a self-image and the possibility of contemplating our own lives, ultimate death or even the nature of our own consciousness. Self-awareness is coextensive with the moment to moment subjective content of mind. It is composed of those events about which we can speak to ourselves or to others, about which in effect we can provide an introspective report. For many people what we are calling self-awareness is 'consciousness' (e.g. O'Keefe in this volume; Dixon, 1981) or 'conscious awareness' (Dixon and Henley, 1980). The difference in preferred terminology depends on whether one considers 'consciousness' as equivalent to subjective awareness or equivalent to the capacity to process information on the basis of central representations. The two are not at all the same thing. We have chosen the latter to define consciousness, and so need a new term ('self-awareness') for the limited capacity system which is coextensive with subjective experience.

Into and out of consciousness

Before considering plurality *within* consciousness it is necessary to consider a little further the types of processing which do not depend on representational systems, and so by our definition never form part of consciousness. We will also look at some constraints which seem to operate in determining which events in consciousness either cannot or do not enter self-awareness.

What does not enter consciousness and so cannot enter self-awareness?

Our model excludes simple reflex systems, homeostatic systems and association learning systems from consciousness, on the grounds that they do not depend on truly flexible representational processes and are not based on cortical substrates. Animals can be deprived of their neocortex and still carry out the type of information processing fundamental to these behavioural systems. The evidence for this, especially in relation to association learning, has been extensively reviewed elsewhere (see Oakley, 1979, 1981, 1983a; Russell, 1980). Whilst it is not a definitive indication of the contents of consciousness it is also true that we do not become directly self-aware of blood sugar levels, our own body weight set point, changes in pupil size under different levels of illumination or arousal, or of the course of association learning. Nevertheless, if we have an internal representational system we can monitor the operation of these subcortical systems quite independently, entering the stimulus events and our own responses, if we can detect them in some way, into representations, and then introspect on the basis of those. In the case of instrumental learning there is evidence of this parallel processing, in that a capacity for handling the relevant information via cognitive representational systems interferes with the simpler association processes in favour of hypothesis-based performance. Increasing cognitive abilities, in other words, compete with concurrent association mechanisms and make performance on association learning tasks more variable (see Goldstein and Oakley, 1985; Oakley, 1983b).

In a Pavlovian eye-blink conditioning situation we are normally aware of the antecedent conditional stimuli (a light or a tone for example) and the subsequent unconditional stimulus (such as an air puff to the cornea) as well as our own reaction to it, and eventually to the conditional stimulus alone. We may well then go on to rationalize our own behaviour, try to inhibit the learned response or to enhance its effectiveness with voluntary blinks; but this is all in addition to the non-conscious association process, which automatically provides a precisely timed blink to the conditional stimulus once the pairing of conditional stimulus and unconditional stimulus has been repeated a number of times. Some evidence of this dissociation comes from human amnesics who, though the dynamic processing within representational systems appears to be intact, do not transfer information into representational stores of episodic memory. In one particular study by Weiskrantz and Warrington (1979) two human amnesics were trained in an eye-blink conditioning paradigm, and were found to acquire conditional responses to a combined light/tone stimulus and to retain them over a twenty-four-hour interval. When questioned at the end of 260 conditioning trials, however, neither of the subjects could recall having seen the apparatus before or what it was for. One of them suggested that he was 'telling where the position of certain things were in relation to others' and that he was required to give an answer 'in the form of, I think, some Eastern language'. Our interpretation of this is that the subjects were fully able to use their association systems to acquire and store the appropriate conditional responses, but were not able to enter any information about the conditioning procedure into self-awareness because the appropriate representations had been lost from consciousness. In the more dramatic case of a human being completely deprived of cortex we would expect that association learning would progress readily in the absence of any representational capacity and consequently without self-awareness.

What enters consciousness but cannot enter self-awareness?

One important factor which determines whether or not an external event will be re-represented in self-awareness is the amplitude (or more precisely the signal-to-noise ratio) of the stimuli involved. It is well documented that stimuli presented below the threshold of subjective awareness, because they are either too brief or too low in amplitude, may nevertheless be processed by the human brain to the level at which their meaning is extracted, and that these stimuli can affect concurrent percepts, verbal behaviour and emotional responses without ever being available to subjective experience (see Dixon, 1981; Dixon and Henley, 1980). The entry of material into conscious processing and storage systems despite its exclusion from self-awareness is evident in the effect which the subliminal presentation of the words 'happy' and 'sad' has on the perception of a neutral face. Similarly, in the Poetzl effect, those aspects of a stimulus display (a colour slide of temple ruins at Thebes in one study) which are not subjectively perceived may later appear, frequently in symbolic transformation, in dream reports.

It also seems that the re-representations of self-awareness depend on a particular form of processing in cortical systems. Humans with damage to their primary visual cortex, for instance, are still able to use vision based on subcortical sites and other cortical projections, but do not become subjectively aware of their visual capacity (see chapter 6 in this volume; Weiskrantz, 1977, 1980; Zihl and Von Cramon, 1980). With a good deal of encouragement and practice these 'blind' patients can point accurately to the location of spots of light and distinguish a circle from a cross whilst still professing to see nothing and claiming that they are simply guessing. Presumably in these cases visual information is either not entering representational systems at all or is entering in a form which is inaccessible to self-awareness. The phenomenon is known as 'blindsight' and the patient's reluctance to use his residual visual capacity is presumably because he has no record of its existence in self-awareness, and so he remains blind to the fact that he can see. The last point is discussed by Humphrey (1980) in relation to a monkey deprived of visual cortex. In an analogous way we may suppose that some stimuli do not enter self-awareness even in intact brains because they have no anatomical counterpart to primary visual cortex, and we, like the blindsight patients, would be expected to deny vigorously their existence. Some aspects of spatial mapping and in particular the recently described, and much disputed, human magnetic sense (Baker, 1981) are strong contenders. So is the reputed influence of olfactory stimuli (pheromones) on human behaviour, including our appraisal of others (see Keverne, 1983, for a critical review of human pheromones).

A further way in which material may be denied entry into self-awareness is by the use of general anaesthetics to a depth at which surgery is possible. This level of anaesthesia does not, however, appear to prevent the entry of information into consciousness, or its storage. There is evidence that anaesthetized patients hear and understand much of what goes on in the operating theatre, especially things which are said which relate to themselves or their condition. The following two examples are based on Cheek and LeCron (1968). In the first a female patient is reported to have refused to go back to her surgeon for reasons which she could not understand and despite the fact that she had liked him prior to her operation. Under hypnosis the woman was later able to quote the surgeon as saying while she was anaesthetized 'Well, that will take care of this old bag'. In a second case a woman undergoing plastic surgery on her face, after an automobile accident, was found to have a lump on her lip, whereupon the surgeon commented 'My gracious, this is not a cyst. It could be cancer.' The lump in fact turned out to be benign, but though this fact was communicated to the patient she became more and more depressed after surgery. Some three months after her operation the woman was hypnotized and was able to recall the remark made by the surgeon at the time but changed the word 'cancer' to 'malignant'.

These and other anecdotes prompted a more formal test carried out by Levinson (1965, cited in Cheek and LeCron, 1968). Ten un-informed patients who were undergoing routine surgery were selected, and when EEG and other measures indicated that a surgical plane of anaesthesia had been obtained, the anaesthetist by prior agreement told the surgeon to wait, as the patient looked as if he needed more oxygen. A brief period of rebreathing followed, and the anaesthetist closed the experimental episode by announcing that the patient now looked all right and the surgeon could continue. Despite the customary claim of total amnesia for the period of the operation, four of the patients were later able under hypnosis to repeat the conversation exactly as it had occurred and showed alarm as they relived the experience. Apart from its importance for views of consciousness and self-awareness, this type of observation is significant in indicating not only that the patient's perception of the surgeon, but also the course of recovery, may be affected by what the patient hears whilst anaesthetized. Similar conscious monitoring should perhaps be assumed in all individuals who appear to be 'unconscious', for whatever reason.

What enters consciousness but does not enter self-awareness?

Self-awareness is a limited capacity system of re-representations, specifically designed to facilitate priority processing of information which is to form the basis for immediate action. It is clear, however, that many actions are sufficiently routine or familiar not to require priority processing and, provided there is no conflict on the output side, they can be carried out solely within consciousness. The stan-dard example of this is driving a car and holding a conversation (see for example chapters 3, 6 and 7 in this volume). When the demands of driving are low, quite an elaborate conversation can be sustained and the actions of driving remain outside self-awareness. If a change in road conditions occurs, or an emergency presents itself, self-awareness is flooded with the process of driving and conversation on other topics must temporarily cease. It would be possible to elaborate the car-driving example a little further by suggesting that prior to the car journey our driver had been pondering the nature of consciousness or, more likely perhaps, what to cook for the children's dinner. Processing of this issue could well continue outside self-awareness, with the result that at the journey's end a decision had been reached, to emerge into self-awareness at the appropriate moment. This type of thinking and problem solving outside self-awareness is accepted in the popular belief that 'sleeping on a problem' has some efficacy, and is more formally attested by evidence that covert thought processes contribute to flashes of creative insight (Valentine, 1978).

The sustained behaviours carried out outside self-awareness in driving a car constitute simply one example of a whole range of familiar or habitual routines which underlie professional or sporting skills as well as everyday acts. We become aware of these automatic subroutines when they are misapplied at times of absentmindedness to result in 'actions-not-as-planned' (Howe, 1980; Reason, 1979; see also chapter 6 in this volume). Whilst I was preparing this chapter a colleague from another department came to present one of our weekly seminars and, as a prelude to his talk, recounted the following, which illustrates the point quite well. On the previous week he had come along to my seminar in the same series, and as he entered the lift on the ground floor, intending to travel to level five, had pressed the button for the fourth floor 'out of habit' (his own room is on the fourth floor). This week, whilst waiting for the lift he had remembered his previous error and reminded himself that he must press button 5 and not 4 this time. On entering the lift, however, and much to his own irritation, he watched as his finger stabbed the fourth-floor button once more.

In the previous section it was noted that stimuli of low intensity may fail to enter self-awareness, yet be processed within conscious systems. It has also been shown that some stimuli, of intensities which would normally allow their entry into self-awareness, are prevented from doing so by a censor within conscious processing systems. Obscene or threatening words, for example, in many subjects require longer or more intense exposure than neutral words in a tachistoscope before they are verbally recognized. In other subjects or with other stimulus words the reverse is true, and the more emotive words are more readily recognized than accompanying neutral material. Suppression of input to self-awareness in this type of situation is the phenomenon of perceptual defence, and recent work indicates that the censor in conscious systems operates by suppressing sensitivity within the appropriate sensory system, rather than affecting willingness or ability to respond (see Dixon, 1981; Dixon and Henley, 1980). Apparently similar phenomena to perceptual defence are hysterical or hypnotically induced blindness, deafness, analgesia, etc., in which the subject appears to be consciously processing and reacting to stimuli of which he remains introspectively unaware (see for example Hilgard, 1977; Sackeim, Nordlie and Gur, 1979). We shall return to this topic later, but it is worth noting here that the suppression of input to self-awareness in cases of hysterical or hypnotically induced sensory loss is more than a simple blockade of the particular sensory input to re-representational systems. It has the appearance of a naïve conspiracy on the part of elements within consciousness to deceive both the individual himself and outside observers.

Multiplicity of consciousness revealed through self-awareness systems

The most direct way we have at present of assessing the contents of consciousness systems is to take introspective reports from the individual concerned via re-representations within self-awareness. We are assuming that in this way a representative sample of items within consciousness can be obtained. It is important to note that the individual providing the introspection will always regard his 'consciousness' as unitary, and only the observer will be in a position to decide if the evidence is consistent with a pluralistic view. We are thus viewing self-awareness as a sampling device, though as noted earlier the sampling is not random but has constraints set within consciousness. The open arrows at either side of the self-awareness systems in Figure 8.1 are intended to signify that, though these systems can sample only a subset of the contents of consciousness at any one time, they are at least potentially capable of sampling from a wide range of representations within consciousness. The following examples, we believe, show that consciousness systems themselves are not organized in a unitary fashion, but that at the point of read-out by self-awareness systems an illusion of mental unity is created. This illusion may be seen as a reflection of the role of self-awareness in achieving unified and decisive action from what is essentially a single executive apparatus.

illusion of consciousness unity - aided by
1) self awareness
2) corpus callosum

Two hemispheres

Figure 8.1 reflects the anatomical fact that the human brain has two cerebral hemispheres and hence two separate representational systems. We have also shown two independent self-awareness systems capable of reading out the contents of consciousness from their own hemisphere. A dual system of this sort has a number of potential advantages (see Dimond, 1979). The two systems can specialize in different information processing strategies, and so increase the possibility of achieving a rapid solution to a greater variety of problems; processing can occur in parallel; independent control of limbs is possible; and so forth. There are, however, serious disadvantages also. The dual information processing system is housed within a single body, which for the most part can pursue only a limited number of actions, achieve one set of goals and has a limited capacity for gaining new information. This problem is especially marked where unpaired, midline motor systems are concerned, and in humans the vital function of speech is not only executed via a single system but depends on an ability to sustain precisely timed motor sequences. Behaviour, if it is to be speedy, consistent and effective, requires a single originator. This could be achieved in Figure 8.1 either by allowing only one hemisphere access to output systems or by allowing executive functions to alternate between the two hemispheres. The solution suggested in Figure 8.1 is that one hemisphere has an overall, though perhaps not total, dominance, and that it suppresses the executive functions of its partner (see also Galin, 1974; Nottebohm, 1979). The importance of speech for human behaviour suggests further that the dominant hemisphere is likely to be the one more specialized for language, and for most people this is the left hemisphere. In line with our previous comments, we have shown the achievement of executive control by one hemisphere in Figure 8.1 as a suppression of the self-awareness system in the other hemisphere. (In our example the suppressed, or non-dominant, hemisphere is the right hemisphere.) The corpus callosum is the avenue by which the advantages and disadvantages of cerebral duality are reconciled. It mediates the suppression of executive action by one hemisphere over the other, and it preserves the advantage of having two specialized hemispheres by making the products of representational processing in the second hemisphere available to the executive hemisphere.

If the corpus callosum is cut in human beings, as a way of alleviating severe epilepsy, the patient shows a number of interesting side-effects, which become less noticeable as he acquires techniques for coping with them (e.g. Gazzaniga, 1978). These so-called 'split-brain' data, and the fact that independent processing of information is possible in the two separated hemispheres, have been extensively reviewed elsewhere and we shall select only those points which seem relevant to our present discussion (see Dimond, 1979; chapters 6 and 7 in this volume; Sperry, Zaidel and Zaidel, 1979). Also, for convenience we shall base our description on the most common condition, in which the left hemisphere is the dominant, linguistically specialized hemisphere with more direct access to and control over speech, and over sensory and motor events on the right side of the body. We realize that other patterns of dominance exist, and apologize to our left-handed readers (see Herron, 1980). One effect we would expect from what we have said is release of left hemisphere dominance over executive action once the corpus callosum has been severed. This is indeed seen, particularly soon after the split-brain operation, and in these patients the left hand, under right hemisphere control, has been found to put down objects picked up by the right hand, to turn too many pages in a book held by the right hand, and even to slap the patient's face to waken her in the morning (see Dimond, 1979). The case histories also illustrate the fact that means of dominance other than via the corpus callosum can be developed, and as one patient noted, in relation to conflicts between the left and right hands, 'the more I use them, the less fight they give me' (Dimond, 1978 personal communication).

A second and closely related point is that the patient regards actions carried out by his right hand (under left hemisphere control) in these conflict situations as being his own actions, carried out by 'me'. The actions of the left hand (under right hemisphere control) are seen as products of alien volition. As one patient notes 'Sometimes I go to get something with my right hand, the left hand grabs it and stops it — it seems to have a mind of its own' (Dimond, 1979). These observations are consistent with the view that the dominant, linguistic hemisphere is the repository of subjectively experienced self in these patients. It would also seem that this may be the case in intact brains also, and that the right hemisphere self-awareness system does not normally contribute to subjective self-awareness. Neither sectioning the corpus callosum or removing the right hemisphere entirely has been reported to result in any changes in the subjectively experienced self. What is missing after such surgical interventions is the ability of the left, speaking hemisphere to directly access representations within consciousness systems in the right hemisphere. As a consequence, the speech of split-brain patients is said to become flatter and less responsive to the emotional aspects of experience, and dreams are less frequently reported. Both emotional reponsiveness and dreaming have been claimed as predominantly right hemisphere processes (see Dimond, 1979; Hoppe, 1977). Similarly the distinctive visuo-spatial skills of the right hemisphere are lost to the patient 'himself' and to his left hemisphere/right hand executive system. The right hand has been found to become less adept at drawing in three dimensions and in block sorting tasks following split-brain surgery, though the left hand is still capable of reaching over and speedily demonstrating the correct solution, if it chooses (see for example Gazzaniga, 1967; Springer and Deutsch, 1981).

If sectioning the corpus callosum releases the right hemisphere and its self-awareness system from suppression, we should be able to go a little further in analysing the contents of its conscious processing systems. We should be able to take introspective reports from the right hemisphere. The problem here is that we normally use speech both to give and to receive information when communicating with split-brain patients, and consequently we are taking introspections from the left hemisphere by virtue of its greater linguistic specialization. Despite the release of the right hemisphere, the left hemisphere seems able to retain its priority of access to speech mechanisms. Occasionally, however, it would appear that the right hemisphere in the split-brain patient can mobilize its more limited linguistic skills and briefly gain control of speech. This is particularly the case when visual information is sent directly to the right hemisphere by presenting stimuli in the left visual field, effectively giving the right hemisphere a momentary time advantage in which to respond, before the left hemisphere realizes that a response is called for and again takes over speech output. One example based on a report by Sperry, Zaidel and Zaidel (1979) will give an idea of this process in action. On one trial, in a routine picture recognition series, a split-brain subject's right hemisphere was unexpectedly shown an array of four different photographs of herself in different poses. After some seven seconds of inspection she suddenly said loudly 'Oh no! . . . Where'd you g . . . . . . What are they?', then, again loudly but now laughing, 'Oh God!' This was followed after a three-second pause by a hesitant 'Dr Sperry . . . You sure there's people there?' Further questioning by the experimenters as to the nature of the stimulus elicited from the patient the belief that it was 'Something nice whatever it was . . . something I wouldn't mind having probably.' The interpretation offered by Sperry and his colleagues, on the basis of these and similar observations, is that the exclamations 'Oh no!' and 'Oh God!' were generated by the right hemisphere as it recognized photographs of the patient herself, whilst the rest of the typically more muted comments were generated by the ignorant left hemisphere, reasserting its control over speech and struggling to account for the patient's behaviour.

The above example also reveals evidence of self-recognition by the right hemisphere, implying a self-representation within its consciousness system. In fact further probing using non-verbal responses generated by the right hemisphere, such as hand gestures (pointing or thumbs up/thumbs down) or allowing the left hand under right hemisphere control to use plastic letters to spell out words, has revealed not only self-recognition but a well established personal history and store of general information in the right hemisphere (see LeDoux, Wilson and Gazzaniga, 1979; Sperry, Zaidel and Zaidel, 1979; and chapters 6 and 7 in this volume). The right hemisphere in split-brain subjects not only knows what day of the week it is but can identify, for example, flags of different nations, as well as American presidents and other historical figures, much of which information must have been acquired prior to surgery. The right hemisphere is also able to offer social evaluations, using the thumbs up/thumbs down gesture, which coincide with ratings offered for the same pictures by the left hemisphere, though revealing overall that the right hemisphere was more socially conforming than the left. A certain wry humour was also evident in one test, in which the right hemisphere gave a picture of the subject himself a 'thumbs down', accompanied by a knowing grin.

If we accept these data and the interpretation offered above, the right hemisphere in the split-brain individual (and, we would argue, in the normal as well) has a well established self-representation and a complete set of life history data and general information which corresponds closely to that contained in the left hemisphere. This is not surprising in view of the fact that both hemispheres have shared the same body and hence the same life experiences, though it would seem that their aspirations for the future can differ. The split-brain patient P.S. claimed via his left hemisphere that 'he' wanted to be a draughtsman, whereas his right hemisphere responded in plastic letters to the same question with 'automobile race' (LeDoux, Wilson and Gazzaniga, 1979). Emotions and even cognitive sets ('historical', 'geographical', 'entertainment', 'personal') generated within the right hemisphere are identified accurately by the left hemisphere, even though the nature of the stimulus giving rise to them remains unknown to it. The left hemisphere acts as 'spokesman' for the split-brain individual, and provides as plausible an account as possible for the individual's behaviour (see chapter 7 in this volume for a full discussion of this view). There seems to us no reason to suppose that the same should not be true of intact brains, and that many of the indecisions, inspirations and 'unaccountable' mood changes about which our left hemispheres rationalize are consequences of conscious processes within our right hemispheres. Clearly, if the reactions of two connected hemispheres to similar situations are too divergent, mental pathology may result. It is perhaps no coincidence that the majority of psychosomatic symptoms appear on the left side of the body, possibly as the right hemisphere, denied a verbal outlet, finds its own means of communicating its distress (see Galin, 1974, and Hoppe, 1977, for further discussion of these possibilities).

We are assuming that introspections taken from the right hemisphere in split-brain patients are mediated via its own self-awareness system. The existence of a right hemisphere self-awareness system, albeit under suppression, in intact brains is further indicated by the fact that surgical removal of the dominant hemisphere, even in adults, produces remarkably little intellectual impairment. Although it may be accompanied by personality changes, it leaves the patient still able to give introspective reports of his everyday experiences and past history, as well as being able to comprehend language. The ability to produce speech, however, is limited (see Dimond, 1972; Sperry, Zaidel and Zaidel, 1979; Zaidel, 1976). The transfer of the individual from one self-awareness system to the other may be very rapid. Dimond (1972) has noted that when dominant hemispherectomy is carried out under local anaesthesia there is no loss of 'consciousness' (which we assume means subjective self-awareness in our terminology) on the part of the patient, and the remaining hemisphere is just as capable of 'operating in the alert state'.

Multiple personality

We assume that the dominant self-awareness system is capable of reading the self-related data in its own hemisphere, and in so doing normally generates the same personality, the same 'me', with a consistent and continuous past history, the same styles of behaviour, preferences, and so forth. There are instances, however, where self-awareness systems seem to discover within consciousness systems a different set of self-representations, which when they are re-represented become another 'me'. The simplest of such situations is the fugue — literally a 'flight' — in which, it is implied, the individual escapes his current problems by seeking a new environment and starting afresh. The person, usually having transported himself to a new place, will commence a new lifestyle, often with a new personality and with complete and genuine amnesia for his previous name and his former existence. The fugue state is of variable duration and when it is over the events of the fugue are lost to memory, and the person reverts to his former life and personality exactly where he left off. A typical case is that of the Reverend Ansel Bourne who, on 17 January 1887, suddenly quit his life as an itinerant preacher and became a shop-keeper calling himself A. J. Brown (see Hilgard, 1977, for a full account of this case). One night, some two months after the start of his new career, he awoke in fright as Ansel Bourne, to find himself in a strange bed with no recollection of how he came to be where he was. Bourne was later hypnotized by William James and was able to go straight back to the Brown personality, and was able to fill in many details of his experiences during the lost two months. As Brown he was not able to recall anything about Bourne, he did not recognize Bourne's wife and he reported feeling 'hedged in' by the inability to recall anything before or after the shopkeeping episode. James was unable to fuse the two sets of memories during hypnosis, as he had hoped to do, and on cessation of the trance Bourne was still unable to recall the Brown episode.

The fugue in many cases is never repeated, but in others the subjects return to the dissociated state many times. If the same personality is adopted on each occasion this second persona develops to the stage where it must be considered as an entity in its own right, with its own lifestyle and personal history. As in the fugue state described above, these two personalities may be mutually amnesic, leading their own separate lives in alternation, with no knowledge of their other selves. Rarely, the two may be quite aware of each other and share many memories, holding back just a few, as good friends might do. The most common situation, however, is that of unilateral amnesia in which one personality, usually the natal one, has its own memories but is unaware of the other. The second personality, on the other hand, knows all about the first and will often talk in disparaging terms of its weaknesses. Indeed, by most criteria it is the second personality which is usually the happier, better adjusted of the two. In terms of our model in Figure 8.1 an obvious explanation for both the fugue state and for dual personality would be that they represent an alternation in executive control between the two self-awareness systems housed in the two hemispheres. But this is not an acceptable explanation. First, as we shall see below, multiple personality states do not stop at two. Secondly, we have already argued that the personal history and self-representation in the hemisphere with a suppressed self-awareness system are very similar to those of the dominant hemisphere. An alternation between these two systems would result in two rather similar personalities with a common life history, though perhaps different skills, goals and aspirations. It may be speculated that individuals who are particularly gifted in both arts and science are able to achieve this alternation, but we must look elsewhere for an explanation of multiple personality.

In some cases the process of forming novel personalities is repeated several times during development, and three or more personalities may coexist. In fact there seems to be no limit to the number of personalities which can be formed in a single lifetime. The recently reported case of 'Sybil Dorsett' documents sixteen, two of whom were male and did the carpentry and other odd jobs whilst Sybil was 'away' (see Schreiber, 1973, for an excellent, dramatic account). It is particularly clear from the story of Sybil's early life that each new personality emerged in response to a particular crisis or change in circumstances, and this relationship is common to many such cases. Equally clear is the distress caused to Sybil herself at finding wardrobes full of clothes she could not remember buying and did not even like, bank balances depleted inexplicably as a result, and medicines running out before they should because the others would insist on taking their own doses independently. Sybil's other selves were not always inconsiderate, and one of them, Vanessa, took a job in a launderette, whilst another, Marcia, submitted a pop song to a publisher, in order to help with the financial situation. Both did so without Sybil's knowledge.

Perhaps the most extensive psychological and physiological study of a multiple personality in recent years is that of 'Jonah', a 27-year-old with three additional personalities. The personalities were independently tested as they repeatedly emerged, at first spontaneously, and later as they were called out using hypnosis (Ludwig, Brandsma, Wilbur, Bendfeldt and Jameson, 1972). Jonah himself was a shy, retiring conventional person (dubbed 'The Square') who was often frightened and confused during clinical interviews. He was unaware of the other three personalities, and their behaviour during the 'lost' periods of his life often led him into trouble, both with his family and with the law. The worst offender in this regard was Usoffa Abdulla, Son of Omega ('The Warrior'), who had originally emerged when Jonah was 9 or 10 years old and was being beaten by a gang of other boys. Jonah was dismissed from self-awareness and Usoffa fought viciously, claiming later to have almost killed two of the boys. Usoffa was cruel, sarcastic and immune to pain. The researchers found him a formidable and scary person to interview. Usoffa said he knew Jonah well and was his protector. The other two personalities were quite different to Usoffa. Sammy ('The Mediator') emerged first when Jonah was 6 years old, on the occasion of a fight during which his mother stabbed his stepfather. Sammy re-emerged later to intervene between them, and to urge them not to fight in front of the children. Sammy also knew Jonah well and, with his love of words, took over whenever Jonah needed legal advice, or to talk himself out of a difficult situation. The fourth personality was King Young ('The Lover'), who also first appeared when Jonah was 6 or 7, a time when Jonah was confused about his sexual identity, partly as a consequence of his mother's habit of dressing him in girls' clothes. King Young put Jonah straight and took control of Jonah's sexual activities thereafter. King Young was well aware of Jonah, was charming and never took 'no' for an answer. He took control whenever Jonah could not find the right words in the company of a woman. The three subsidiary personalities themselves were only peripherally aware of each other, though one of them, Sammy, was able to tell the interviewers of a new personality who was brewing inside Jonah. Sammy described this personality as 'scattered but gathering' and he predicted it would be 'five times worse than Usoffa'. To the researchers relief this fifth character never emerged as a separate entity.

Personality tests administered to the four personalities showed predictable differences between them, though no differences were found on either verbal or performance IQ tests, and all four scored low on the normal range. This suggests that abstract memory systems were not divided in this case, though interestingly one of Sybil's personalities kept the mathematical knowledge which she had gained in the fourth grade to herself. In a word associates test, in which each personality had to learn a different ten-pairs list, Jonah remembered only half of the associate words on a retest. The other three personalities could also remember the list which Jonah had learned, and did about as well as him on the later test. On their own lists, however, each of the three subsidiary personalities produced almost perfect retention scores, whilst neither Jonah nor the other two personalities were able to score above chance. This suggests that, for the three subsidiary personalities at least, memory for the originally learned list remained isolated, and accessible only to the one who had learned it. A similar isolation was shown for emotional reactivity, in other tests using GSR measures. In these tests each of the four personalities was asked for two words which were of particular emotional significance. These were then mixed with twelve neutral words to give a list of twenty words, which was then presented to each personality in turn. All four personalities responded with marked GSR changes to Jonah's words, but each of the three subsidiary personalities reacted strongly only to their own emotional words. Interestingly, Pavlovian conditioning, using leg shock as the unconditional stimulus and a different conditional stimulus for each personality, showed no such compartmentalization and the response to each of the conditional stimuli tended to generalize to the others. If, as we have argued, association learning takes place outside cortical representational systems we would expect generalization of this sort, despite subdivisions within cortically based systems.

We would like to offer the following as a tentative account of multiple personality in relation to the model shown in Figure 8.1. In normal development we adopt new roles, new subpersonalities which are normally integrated and are read into self-awareness as facets of one self-representation with a common background. It is possible that some events, particularly during childhood, force so dramatic a role shift that the dominant self-awareness system is able to read either the original self-representation or the newly dissociated one as an entity in its own right. From the time that the new self-representation is entered focally into self-awareness a new set of personal memories is generated, creating a unique life history which cannot be accessed during the time that the primary, natal self-representation is occupying self-awareness. In some cases the blockade in memory between personalities or self-representations is mutual, and this is the easier condition to explain. More often, however, the secondary or subsequent personality is able to incorporate information from the current life experiences of the primary personality and some, if not all, of any other subsidiary personalities which may coexist. It also seems clear from the multiple personality cases considered above that each self-representational system is capable of reasoning, generating its own thoughts and planning actions, even when it is outside self-awareness. The apparent capacity, reported by Schreiber (1973) and others, for several of the mutually cognizant personalities to confer outside self-awareness suggests information transfer between the dynamic components of the self-representations. This reinforces the idea that all subpersonalities are concurrently active and that behaviour and subjective experience of the individual is determined by whichever of these systems is read into the self-awareness system. Again, it would seem that the contents of self-awareness can be selected either from within itself or externally from the consciousness system which contains the multiple self-representations.

We do not wish to speculate further concerning the location of the self-representations underlying multiple personality, other than to reassert that they are cortical, within representational systems. To what extent the two hemispheres are mutually or separately involved is not clear – a split-brain operation, if one were necessary, on a multiple personality case might be revealing. It is also not clear whether we should regard the different personalities as separately located within representational systems or as corresponding to a state change in the system as a whole. Our comments on simultaneous activity within several self-representational systems would seem to demand an anatomical rather than a purely functional distinction between them, though again diffuse but distinct autonomous systems are not excluded. There is some evidence that the brain is different in its operation depending on which of the personalities occupies self-awareness at the time of measurement, and though they tell us little about location of multiple representations some of the relevant data are worth mentioning here. In the Jonah study discussed earlier, for instance, there were clear differences in overall EEG patterns, and flash evoked cortical responses were different in amplitude when the different personalities were in control. Similarly, alpha blocking was seen in the EEG record in response to eye opening in Jonah and Sammy, but not in King Young or Usoffa. The majority of neurological tests revealed no differences between personalities though Usoffa, in keeping with his character, had very much reduced two-point touch and pain sensitivity, and had unusual difficulty in distinguish-ing salt from sugar (Ludwig *et al.*, 1972). A more recent study, however, has claimed EEG differences in a normal control subject simulating different personalities, and has raised the possibility that some of the effects may be due to changes in concentration, mood and muscle tension as the various personalities are evoked, rather than brain state changes as such (Coons, Milstein and Marley, 1982).

It seems likely that the multiple parallel streams of conscious activity, which are implied by the multiple personality data, are no different from those which are present in normal individuals, and which we referred to earlier as covert thought processes. The differ-ence in the multiple personality case is that these processes can be attached to different self-representations, and so when re-represented are revealed as the thoughts of different individuals. When only one self-representation is available to self-awareness all conscious process-ing, covert or otherwise, is attributed to a single 'me'. It was an important part of our account of multiple personality that each self-representation developed its own set of episodic memories, and that these gave each personality its stability and substance. The absence of an episodic memory apparently produces a curious feeling of imper-manence. The amnesic patient may feel that he lives many different lives and be unsure whether he is always the same person (see chapter 6 in this volume). To others, however, the amnesic, with presumably a single self-representation available to self-awareness, is seen as a single personality. In many ways this is the converse of the multiple personality state.

Hypnosis and the hidden observer

The evidence of multiple personality implies that subdivisions or dis-sociations may be created in consciousness and that items from these subdivided areas may be selectively entered into self-awareness. Where the subdivisions have high internal consistency and behave in a relatively autonomous fashion the effect is equivalent to the existence of separate consciousness systems, giving rise to subjectively different personalities when the relevant representations are re-represented. It is also evident from accounts of clinical interventions in such cases that hypnosis provides a means of calling dissociated areas of con-sciousness into self-awareness. Specifically, secondary personalities can be called forth at will when the primary personality is hypnotized.

In view of this it is perhaps less surprising to discover that hypnosis can be used in normal subjects to create similar dissociations within consciousness, and one reviewer has claimed that multiple personality itself results from an 'unrecognised abuse of self-hypnosis' (Bliss, 1980). The most direct example of hypnotically induced dissociation in normal individuals is found in the so-called 'hidden observer' procedure. According to Hilgard (1977), a hidden observer in hypnosis was discovered by chance during a classroom demonstration of hypnotic deafness. The hypnotized subject had been told that at the count of three he would become deaf, but that his hearing would be restored by the hypnotist's hand being placed on his shoulder. During the hypnotic deafness the subject duly proved to be unresponsive to questioning, and unexpected loud noises behind his back evoked no reaction. A student then asked if it was possible that 'some part' of the subject could know what was going on. The experimenter quietly explained to the subject that, just as our automatic biological processes proceed without our being aware of them, more intellectual processing might occur in the same way. He then asked the subject (still deaf) to raise his right index finger if that was the case and that some part of him was listening to what was going on. To the hypnotist's surprise the finger rose and the subject immediately asked for his hearing to be restored. He had just felt his finger move of its own accord and he wanted an explanation! With his hearing back to normal the subject was clearly unable to recount anything which had transpired between the count of three and the mysterious raising of the finger. In fact, he said he had been so bored during this period that he had passed the time by working on a statistics problem which had been bothering him. He again asked for an explanation of the finger movement. The hypnotist asked to be allowed to defer the answer and, with the subject still hypnotized, suggested that if he placed his hand on the subject's arm, the part of the subject which had listened whilst the subject himself was deaf would be able to speak and answer questions. Once the signal was given the subject, after a brief reluctance, recounted all that had been said during his period of deafness, including the significant question from a member of the class which had resulted, after the hypnotist's comments, in the finger raising in response. With the hypnotist's hand removed from the subject's arm it was clear that the subject had no idea what had transpired between the time that the hand was placed until it was removed. The subject now insisted on an explanation of the two

Hypnosis + model

missing episodes. He was duly brought out of hypnosis with the suggestion of total recall, whereupon he was able to remember all that had happened during hypnosis, everything which he had said and everything which had been said to him, both as himself and via the omniscient hidden observer.

It would appear that appropriate suggestions during hypnosis can prevent information which is being processed normally in consciousness systems from entering self-awareness. This situation is of course very close to that which is presumed to obtain with subliminal stimuli and perceptual defence. In the example above it was auditory information which was blocked, and the 'deafness' which resulted was as subjectively real according to our model as the blindness of the clinical blindsight patient. With further appropriate suggestions the barred information, which is fully processed, understood and stored within conscious systems, can be released upon a signal into self-awareness as a memory for the episodes in question. These items remain dissociated from the rest of episodic memory, however, in that once the 'hidden observer' signal is removed they are no longer available to self-awareness, unless a further suggestion of integration is given or the hidden observer is reinstated. It seems clear that in the terms of our model the hypnotist's remarks are processed by consciousness systems, and then only material which is consistent with these suggestions is allowed into self-awareness. From the individual's point of view, subjective reality consists of what is in self-awareness.

Thus the consciousness system, or part of it, is the 'hidden observer'. This view allows an account to be given, not only of negative hallucinations in hypnosis, in which a whole sensory modality or certain perceptual configurations are excluded from self-awareness, but also of positive hallucinations. The deeply hypnotized subject who reports seeing a familiar (but absent) dog, feels its fur against her fingertips as she strokes it and wriggles to one side as it licks her ear, does so because this is the material which is passed on as current experience by conscious systems, drawing presumably on episodic memory stores (example based on unpublished observations by the authors). The hidden observer is now used routinely by 'explaining' to the subject prior to a standard hypnotic induction that during hypnosis 'part of the mind' is continuously monitoring what goes on, even those things of which the subject herself is unaware. A physical signal such as that described above or, as in our own investigations, the device of calling the hidden observer 'B' and then asking to speak to 'B' during hypnosis, can be pre-arranged with the subject to allow the hypnotist to bring selected items from consciousness into self-awareness. 'B' frequently speaks and acts in a manner more like that of a non-hypnotized subject, and the similarity to calling out other personalities in multiple personality cases is obvious.

Two reports may thus be taken from a hypnotized subject. In hypnotic analgesia for instance it is possible for a subject to smile benignly and, despite physiological evidence to the contrary, to fail to experience pain in a hand which is plunged into icy water. The hidden observer, however, when called upon leaves the experimenter in no doubt as to the severity of the pain in the affected hand and will give a pain rating, either verbally or in the form of 'automatic writing' with the non-immersed hand, which matches that given in the waking state under the same conditions (Gibson, 1982; Hilgard, 1977). The absence of pain is none the less real to the hypnotized subject. Transfer of a similar dissociation to the waking state is possible in some types of chronic pain, and therapies which aim to relegate pain to the hidden observer, by setting up selective mechanisms in consciousness which deny pain information entry into self-awareness, are successful in a proportion of individuals (Hilgard and Hilgard, 1975; Oakley and Pearce, 1984, unpublished observations). Some hypnotic subjects are able to achieve, upon suggestion, a level of anaesthesia and local analgesia sufficient to allow painful surgical procedures to be carried out without apparent discomfort or distress, and often with reduced bleeding and salivation. In these subjects physiological indices of pain may also be absent (Chertok, 1981). One hypnotized subject, Mrs D., underwent an operation to remove a ganglion in her left wrist and a foreign body in her right index finger. In a later interview, also under hypnosis, she was able to recall the people in the operating theatre, the numbness in her arms and the fact that she had asked for, and been given, a drink of water during the operation. During the surgical procedures she had thought mainly of a holiday, and had experienced the sun shining as she sailed in a pedal-craft. She had known that the operation was taking place but had felt nothing of it. A suggestion designed to call the hidden observer, however, produced a different story. The thermocautery was 'so hot. . . . It was burning . . . it was agony . . . as bad as the incision'.

The dissociation between the hypnotized subject and the hidden observer is even more similar to the multiple personality case where the subject is regressed either to an earlier stage in their own lives or to an apparent 'former life'. In both cases a subjectively real experience is created from episodic memory, often using material which is available to the waking subject only with great difficulty, if it is available at all. The hidden observer in these circumstances remains non-hypnotized and at the subject's real age. The age-regressed subject appears to relive the experiences as they occur and will talk of them in the first person, present tense, becoming emotionally involved in the events as they unfold, excitedly anticipating what the outcome might be, wondering, for instance, who will find whom in the hide-and-seek game in which they are engrossed. The hidden observer, at a pre-arranged signal, can simultaneously relate in more lucid terms, and in the third person, what is happening, what his younger self is wearing and why he is behaving in a particular way. This is often useful information, especially where the age-regressed or 'former life' subject is reluctant to speak on their own behalf. One of our own hypnotized subjects, for instance, had adopted a former life as Gerena, a goatherd. She was, as it turned out, a singularly taciturn goatherd and we called on the hidden observer for more details. Apart from information on her life and style of dress we discovered that other people were nearby, and Gerena was reluctant to speak out in answer to the questions which seemed to come from nowhere, lest she be discovered doing so and thereby risked being burned as a witch.

The information upon which hypnotically induced 'former life' experiences seems to depend is often unavailable to the subject in their waking state (the condition of cryptomnesia – literally 'hidden memory'). In some cases it has been possible to trace independently the source of such information to an historical novel, which the subject does not recall reading, but which contains all the same details, events, names, and so forth (see Wilson, 1982). In other cases the source has been discovered using hypnosis, with procedures akin to those of the hidden observer, in which consciousness systems can be accessed for information not normally available to self-awareness. In these cases the subjects appear to have retained almost verbatim the contents of a novel, a film or a similar source, and to have reworked the information as a former life, frequently identifying themselves with a minor character in the original and relating events in a different, but chronologically accurate, order. It is important for our model to note that the reworking of material takes place in conscious processing systems, and that the resultant narrative is fed into self-awareness as a continuous experiential event. This conspiracy by consciousness produces so immediate and sometimes so terrifying a sense of reality that many subjects and onlookers have accepted that what is being experienced in a hypnotically induced 'former life' regression is truly a re-enactment of a previous existence, and have taken it as proof of reincarnation or of some form of genetic or communal memory (see Iverson, 1976; Moss and Keeton, 1979).

Our own observations suggest that the interplay of hypnotized subject and hidden observer is no mere alternation of states but the selective entry of the products of two concurrent and parallel streams of processing into self-awareness. When an age-regressed subject is recounting an experience and the hidden observer is called, the hidden observer can relate from its own perspective what has gone before as well as how the experience is continuing. Once the hidden observer is dismissed and the age-regressed individual is returned to, it is evident that the childhood events which he was recounting have progressed whilst the hidden observer was speaking, and we pick up the same story at a later stage in its development. It would appear from our questioning of such subjects that the hypnotized individual is not aware of the hidden observer, though the hidden observer is fully cognizant of the hypnotized person. During one session, for instance, one of our subjects who was familiar with the hidden observer procedure had been regressed to the age of 5 years, and was being quizzed about 'B'. She appeared confused and offered the information 'Daddy calls me "flea".' Pressed a little further she blurted out 'It's me!' Posthypnotically this subject was able to explain that as a 5-year-old she did not know who 'B' was or what the question meant, and that she found the situation disturbing and puzzling. As the questioner persisted, however, the hidden observer had come to the fore to say 'It's me!', whereupon she had returned to her 5-year-old state. The one-way amnesia seen between the hypnotized subject and the hidden observer is also found, as we noted earlier, in dual personality states, as is the continuous existence in consciousness systems of both the primary and secondary personalities.

Hysteria

Though its greater prevalence in females is not generally disputed, the use of 'hysteria' as a single diagnostic category is contentious, especially where its application is intended to include the overdramatizing or over-reaction to situations which is implicit in the everyday use of the term (Almgren, Nordgren and Skantze, 1978; Chodoff, 1982; Reed, 1975; Stefanis, Markidis and Christodoulou, 1976). Reed has suggested that this type of behaviour is better described as 'histrionic', and should not be used as a criterion for classifying patients as hysterics, especially when they would otherwise be assigned to other diagnostic categories. We would like to accept his definition of hysteria as typified by the presence of either dissociative or conversion symptoms. In Reed's own survey this criterion revealed a small group of patients showing pure hysteria (13 per cent of a sample of 113 previously diagnosed 'hysterics'), a larger group presenting hysteria combined with affective symptoms, particularly depression and anxiety (33 per cent of the sample), and excluded a still larger group (54 per cent of the sample) whose 'hysterical' symptoms were either of the histrionic, attention-seeking type, or later proved to be due to undiagnosed, and often fatal, organic disorders. Dissociative conditions include the fugue and multiple personality states, which we have already considered above, as well as more limited amnesic blockades which isolate a single traumatic episode from recall. Conversion symptoms are changes in sensory capacity (such as blindness, deafness, tunnel vision, analgesia, pain) or in motor functions (paralyses, tics, tremors, convulsions, aphonia) for which no physical cause can be found, and which are therefore presumed to be of psychological origin. Also the symptoms do not correspond to any known anatomical functions, neurological pathways or segmental distributions.

In this section we would like to consider the conversion symptoms of hysteria, with particular reference to psychogenic blindness, though the account is intended to be relevant to all sensory and motor manifestations of the condition. We have already noted that hysterical dissociations in the form of fugues, multiple personalities and selective amnesias have parallels in hypnosis. In a similar way, the psychodynamic mechanisms underlying hysterical conversion symptoms appear to be the same as those employed in hypnosis to produce similar phenomena in normal individuals. Conversion symptoms have frequently been reported to remit under hypnosis, and the behaviour of subjects rendered deaf or blind by hypnotic suggestion is very similar to that of hysterically deaf or blind patients (Sackeim, Nordlie and Gur, 1979). It is a part of clinical folklore that it is the hysterically blind patient who bumps (gently) into every tree in the park, or selects the only occupied chair in a room, though it is noticeable that they do not seem to walk in front of cars. Similarly clear, if paradoxical, visually guided behaviours are also revealed by more formal testing. In one study, for example, a hysterical patient reporting total blindness was found to perform at a significantly below-chance level on a three-choice visual discrimination task. An apparently casual remark by a confederate of the experimenter, to the effect that the results were peculiar in that there were fewer correct responses than a blind man would make, was followed by an improvement in the patient's performance closer to chance levels (Zimmerman and Grosz, 1966). Similarly, hysterically blind patients can be classically conditioned using visual stimuli (Cohen, Hilgard and Wendt, 1933, cited by Sackeim, Nordlie and Gur, 1979).

Using two good hypnotic subjects and standard hypnotic induction procedures, Sackeim, Nordlie and Gur (1979) have reported that where suggestions of blindness were given under highly motivating conditions the subject scored well below chance on a happy/sad face discrimination task. Less motivating instructions were given to the second subject, who produced 100 per cent correct responses on the same discrimination task. Both subjects said they saw nothing of the visual targets or of the room in which they were tested. For much of the time, in fact, the second subject believed that she had her eyes closed. When confronted with her accurate performance she appeared astonished and, like the 'blindsight' patients, maintained that she had been guessing throughout, but added that sometimes 'it feels like a happy face'. The honesty of the subjects is indicated perhaps by the fact that during the test sessions both had raised their hands to signal that the blindness was lifting, whereupon testing was stopped and the suggestions of blindness were readministered. A non-hypnotized subject who was asked to simulate blindness in the same experiment produced chance levels of performance on all test sessions. The fact that both hysterically and hypnotically blind subjects claim not to be able to see, and yet produce performances which are significantly worse or better than they would if they were really blind, raises the question of malingering or attempts to deceive (or please) the experimenter. It seems unlikely that these individuals are deliberately trying to cover up the fact that they can really see. First, a simulating subject without prompting can make a far better job of appearing blind. Secondly, we have no reason from outside the testing situation to believe that either the patients or the hypnotic subjects are being dishonest when they report that they cannot see. During our own investigations of hypnotically induced blindness we have seen that some subjects become quite agitated, particularly the first time that blindness is produced, and after the session they report that this was because they were uncertain whether they would be able to see again once the suggestions were removed.

Physiological recording is no more reliable an index than behavioural measures, so far as gauging subjective experience is concerned. In patients with hysterical hemianaesthesia, evoked responses recorded over somatosensory cortex are sometimes, but not always, reduced on the affected side, and the same applies to hypnotically induced anaesthesia (see Lader, 1973). In hypnotically induced analgesia, which has been far more widely investigated, measures such as heart-rate and skin resistance frequently, though again not always, show changes in the expected direction, despite subjective reports that pain has been reduced or is absent (see Bowers, 1976; Wagstaff, 1981). A recent review of experiments in which visual evoked responses were monitored during either hypnotically induced or hysterical blindness revealed that, of eight studies, in two (both using hypnosis) a reduction or elimination of evoked responses was claimed, in four (two hypnosis and two hysteria) there was no change in the physiological measure during blindness, and in the final two (both hypnosis) the results were mixed (Snaith, 1983, unpublished dissertation). Our own observations on two subjects confirm that visual evoked responses to a reversing chequerboard stimulus are at most only slightly reduced (in one subject) during hypnotically induced blindness, even though our subjects reported complete subjective blindness (P. Eames, L. C. Eames and D. A. Oakley, 1982, unpublished observations).

Taken as a whole the physiological recording data indicate that physiological responses to sensory events persist in the majority of subjects, despite hypnotically or hysterically induced diminution or abolition of subjective awareness of those events. The evoked response studies make the further point that the sensory events are processed at a cortical level in such instances. In view of the exceptional cases, however, the possibility remains that a few occurrences of subjective sensory change are produced by inhibition of inputs prior to their cortical registration. This possibility is also supported by one case which used an unusual method for abolishing selected visual inputs at a subjective level. Schatzman (1980) has reported that one patient, 'Ruth', was able to hallucinate friends and members of her family, and eventually learned to control the behaviour of these hallucinations.

Under experimental conditions, and with EEG recording, Ruth produced an hallucination of her daughter sitting on her lap, in a position that would interrupt her view of an alternating chequer-board display. When the apparition blocked the display the typical evoked response recorded over her visual cortex was abolished, returning to normal levels once the apparition was dismissed. Subsequently several more hallucinators have been discovered to have the ability to abolish cortical evoked responses in this way (P. Fenwick, 1983, personal communication).

In terms of our model of awareness, we see hysterical conversion symptoms as involving a blockade of representations from re-representation within self-awareness. Information is processed quite normally within consciousness to the highest cognitive level, but selective mechanisms within consciousness itself prevent access to it by self-awareness mechanisms. In the case of hysterical blindness, for example, the consciousness systems do not pass perceptual representations to self-awareness and thus the individual remains subjectively blind. Behaviourally, however, cortical representational systems can allow perfectly accurate performance on visual tasks, though where there is a strong motivational component they appear to use the visual information to produce the paradoxical behaviour of making significantly more 'wrong' choices than would be expected by chance. This has been interpreted in psychodynamic terms as 'denial' (Sackeim, Nordlie and Gur, 1979). In cases of correct behavioural performance on visual tasks despite subjective blindness, consciousness may sometimes pass the outcome of its processing into self-awareness. When this happens the individual will become aware that, to use an earlier example, 'this is a happy face', despite being denied the perceptual information which led to that decision. The blindness in such cases is subjectively real and is the product of a deception perpetrated by consciousness upon self-awareness. The view that hysterics indulge in self-deception is in this sense true. It is a deception to which the individual is an unwitting party.

A similar account would apply to other hysterical conversion symptoms involving sensory changes, as well as to parallel phenomena produced by hypnotic suggestion. Hypnosis seems to serve as a means of influencing those mechanisms in consciousness which decide what will be re-represented into self-awareness. Motor symptoms of hysterical conversion states may be a product of denying self-awareness its usual priority over motor control systems. This may result in a local or more general muscular paralysis so far as voluntary activity is concerned, or in the inability to exert voluntary control over repetitive or even convulsive motor discharges generated within consciousness systems. The failure of re-representation of such acts in self-awareness will further prevent subjective awareness of the fact that they are consciously generated and are not the product of some more caudal neurological disorder. The so-called pseudoseizures produced by some hysterics, which have led historically to an association being drawn with epilepsy, are pseudo only in the sense of not having a physical cause (Trimble, 1983). In our terms they are quite real, and experienced by the subject as just as involuntary as those of epilepsy itself. Indeed it would seem that hysterical seizures may occur alongside physically based seizures in some epileptics, and not be distinguished by the individual concerned.

Conclusions

We have presented a view of human mental life which stresses that the representational processing which underlies perception and problem solving, as well as thinking about ourselves and our environments, constitutes consciousness, and that only a small sample of these representations are re-represented in self-awareness systems at any one time. It is only when representations have been re-represented in self-awareness that they become part of our subjective life. Within consciousness systems several lines of thought may proceed simultaneously, and two or more parallel self-representations and personal histories may be created. The subjective unity of self, of thought and of personal experience is an illusion created by the limited capacity of self-awareness systems and their need to process information sequentially. The illusion is enhanced, in our model, by the suppression of the self-awareness system in one hemisphere by its partner in the other hemisphere. Self-awareness systems, we suggest, normally exercise priority over our behavioural output, and it is this which creates effective, consistent actions, which focuses attention on immediate problems and which underlies their adaptive significance.

Conscious systems exercise a considerable control over the contents of self-awareness. If our subjective existence is delimited by the contents of our self-awareness systems, 'we' do not fully control the direction of our attention or of our thoughts. In some instances 'we' may be denied access to whole classes of sensory data, which nevertheless continue to be fully processed in consciousness systems and may influence our actions. Conversely 'we' may be fed information from memory by our consciousness systems in the guise of current experience, which we accept as subjective reality. 'We' may even be ousted at times, when self-awareness is filled with re-representations belonging to another individual housed in our representational systems, though when 'we' return our subjective experience seems unbroken. 'We', in other words, experience what our consciousness systems decide to re-represent in self-awareness. The vested interest which consciousness systems have in our survival normally ensures that the information which is passed on to self-awareness is compatible with a realistic and unified view of the world and of ourselves. It is this need which conceals from us the plurality of processing that exists within consciousness. Our unitary perspective of our own conscious processes is a consequence of the constraints imposed by our viewing them through the limited window of self-awareness.

Acknowledgement

The authors are grateful to Peter Fonagy for access to his reprint collection on hysteria.

References

Almgren, P-E., Nordgren, L. and Skantze, H. (1978) A retrospective study of operationally defined hysterics. *British Journal of Psychiatry 132*: 67–73.

Baker, R. R. (1981) *Human Navigation and the Sixth Sense.* London: Hodder & Stoughton.

Bliss, E. L. (1980) Multiple personalities: a report of 14 cases with implications for schizophrenia and hysteria. *Archives of General Psychiatry 37*: 1388–97.

Bowers, K. S. (1976) *Hypnosis for the Seriously Curious.* Monterey, Calif.: Brooks-Cole.

Cheek, D. B. and LeCron, L. M. (1968) *Clinical Hypnotherapy.* New York: Grune & Stratton.

Chertok, L. (1981) *Sense and Nonsense in Psychotherapy: The Challenge of Hypnosis.* Oxford: Pergamon Press.

Chodoff, P. (1982) Hysteria and women. *American Journal of Psychiatry 139*: 545–51.

Coons, P. M., Milstein, V. and Marley, C. (1982) EEG studies of two multiple personalities and a control. *Archives of General Psychiatry 39*: 823–5.

Davidoff, J. (1982) Information processing and hemispheric function. In
A. Burton (ed.) *The Pathology and Psychology of Cognition*, 24–47.
London: Methuen.

Dimond, S. J. (1972) *The Double Brain*. Edinburgh: Churchill Livingstone.

Dimond, S. J. (1979) Symmetry and asymmetry in the vertebrate brain. In
D. A. Oakley and H. C. Plotkin (eds) *Brain, Behaviour and Evolution*,
189–218. London: Methuen.

Dixon, N. F. (1981) *Preconscious Processing*. Chichester: Wiley.

Dixon, N. F. and Henley, S. H. A. (1980) Without awareness. In M. A. Jeeves
(ed.) *Psychology Survey 3*: 31–50. London: George Allen & Unwin.

Galin, D. (1974) Implications for psychiatry of left and right cerebral specialization: a neuropsychological context for unconscious processes. *Archives of
General Psychiatry 31*: 572–83.

Gazzaniga, M. S. (1967) The split brain in man. *Scientific American 217*: 24–9.

Gazzaniga, M. S. (1978) Is seeing believing: notes on clinical recovery. In
S. Finger (ed.) *Recovery from Brain Damage: Research and Theory*,
409–14. New York: Plenum Press.

Gibson, H. B. (1982) *Pain and its Conquest*. London: Peter Owen.

Goldstein, L. H. and Oakley, D. A. (1985) Expected and actual behavioural
capacity after diffuse reduction in cerebral cortex: a review and suggestions
for rehabilitative techniques in the mentally handicapped and head
injured. *British Journal of Clinical Psychology 24*: 13–24.

Griffin, D. R. (1976) *The Question of Animal Awareness: Evolutionary
Continuity of Mental Experience*. New York: Rockefeller University Press.

Herron, J. (1980) *Neuropsychology of Left-handedness*. New York: Academic
Press.

Hilgard, E. R. (1977) *Divided Consciousness: Multiple Controls in Human
Thought and Action*. New York: Wiley.

Hilgard, E. R. and Hilgard, J. R. (1975) *Hypnosis in the Relief of Pain*, Los
Altos, Calif.: William Kaufmann.

Hoppe, K. D. (1977) Split-brains and psychoanalysis. *Psychoanalytic
Quarterly 46*: 220–44.

Howe, M. J. A. (1980) *The Psychology of Human Learning*. New York:
Harper & Row.

Humphrey, N. K. (1980) Nature's psychologists. In B. D. Josephson and V. S.
Ramachandran (eds) *Consciousness and the Physical World*, 57–80.
Oxford: Pergamon Press.

Iverson, J. (1976) *More Lives than One?* London: Souvenir Press.

Jerison, H. J. (1973) *Evolution of the Brain and Intelligence*. New York:
Academic Press.

Jerison, H. J. (1976) Palaeoneurology and the evolution of mind. *Scientific
American 234*: 90–101.

Keverne, E. B. (1983) Pheromones. In J. Nicholson and B. Foss (eds) *Psychology Survey 4*: 247–65. Leicester: The British Psychological Society.

Lader, M. (1973) The psychophysiology of hysterics. *Journal of Psychosomatic Research 17*: 265–9.

LeDoux, J. E., Wilson, D. H. and Gazzaniga, M. S. (1979) Beyond commissurotomy: clues to consciousness. In M. S. Gazzaniga (ed.) *Handbook of Behavioral Neurobiology*, vol. 2, 543–54. New York: Plenum Press.

Ludwig, A. M., Brandsma, J. M., Wilbur, C. B., Bendfeldt, F. and Jameson, D. H. (1972) The objective study of a multiple personality: or, are four heads better than one? *Archives of General Psychiatry 26*: 298–310.

Moss, P. and Keeton, J. (1979) *Encounters with the Past*. Harmondsworth: Penguin.

Nottebohm, F. (1979) Origins and mechanisms in the establishment of cerebral dominance. In M. S. Gazzaniga (ed.) *Handbook of Behavioural Neurobiology*, vol. 2, 295–344. New York: Plenum Press.

Oakley, D. A. (1979) Cerebral cortex and adaptive behaviour. In D. A. Oakley and H. C. Plotkin (eds) *Brain, Behaviour and Evolution*, 154–88. London: Methuen.

Oakley, D. A. (1981) Brain mechanisms of mammalian memory. *British Medical Bulletin 37*: 175–80.

Oakley, D. A. (1983a) The varieties of memory: a phylogenetic approach. In A. Mayes (ed.) *Memory in Animals and Humans*, 20–82. Wokingham: Van Nostrand Reinhold.

Oakley, D. A. (1983b) Learning capacity outside neocortex in animals and man: implications for therapy after brain injury. In G. C. L. Davey (ed.) *Animal Models of Human Behaviour*, 247–66. Chichester: Wiley.

Reason, J. (1979) Actions not as planned: the price of automatization. In G. Underwood and R. Stevens (eds) *Aspects of Consciousness*, 67–89. London: Academic Press.

Reed, J. L. (1975) The diagnosis of 'hysteria'. *Psychological Medicine 5*: 13–17.

Russell, I. S. (1980) Encephalization and neural mechanisms of learning. In M. A. Jeeves (ed.) *Psychology Survey 3*: 92–114. London: George Allen & Unwin.

Sackeim, H. A., Nordlie, J. W. and Gur, R. C. (1979) A model of hysterical and hypnotic blindness: cognitition, motivation and awareness, *Journal of Abnormal Psychology 88*: 474–89.

Schatzman, M. (1980) *The Story of Ruth*. London: Duckworth.

Schreiber, F. R. (1973) *Sybil*. Harmondsworth: Penguin.

Sperry, R. W., Zaidel, E. and Zaidel, D. (1979) Self recognition and social awareness in the disconnected minor hemisphere. *Neuropsychologia 17*: 153–66.

Springer, S. P. and Deutsch, G. (1981) *Left Brain, Right Brain*. San Francisco: W. H. Freeman.

Stefanis, C., Markidis, M. and Christodoulou, G. (1976) Observations on the evolution of the hysterical symptomatology. *British Journal of Psychiatry 128*: 269–75.

Trimble, M. (1983) Pseudoproblems: pseudoseizures. *British Journal of Hospital Medicine 29*: 326–33.

Valentine, E. (1978) Perchings and flights: introspection. In A. Burton and J. Radford (eds) *Thinking in Perspective*, 1–22. London: Methuen.

Wagstaff, G. F. (1981) *Hypnosis, Compliance and Belief*. Brighton: Harvester Press.

Weiskrantz, L. (1977) Trying to bridge some neuropsychological gaps between monkey and man. *British Journal of Psychology 68*: 431–45.

Weiskrantz, L. (1980) Varieties of residual experience. *Quarterly Journal of Experimental Psychology 32*: 365–86.

Weiskrantz, L. and Warrington, E. K. (1979) Conditioning in amnesic patients. *Neuropsychologia 17*: 187–94.

Wilson, I. (1982) *Reincarnation?* Harmondsworth: Penguin.

Zaidel, E. (1976) Auditory vocabulary of the right hemisphere following brain bisection or hemidecortication. *Cortex 12*: 191–211.

Zihl, J. and Von Cramon, D. (1980) Registration of light stimuli in the cortically blind hemifield and its effect on localization. *Behavioral Brain Research 1*: 287–98.

Zimmerman, J. and Grosz, H. J. (1966) 'Visual' performance of a functionally blind person. *Behaviour Research and Therapy 4*: 119–34.

Name index

Figures in italics refer to bibliographical references

Able, L. P., *95*
Abramson, N., 77, *95*
Adams, R. D., 160, 162, *186, 188*
Akelaitis, A. J., 165, *186*
Akert, J., *191*
Alba, A., 136, *150*
Albert, M. L., 164, *186*
Allport, D. A., 153, 154, *186*
Almgren, P-E., 243, *248*
Andersen, P., 80, *95*
Angeli, F., *214*
Anscombe, G. E. M., *58*
Ardilla, A., *215*
Aristotle, 173
Armstrong, D. M., 197, *214*
Attneave, F., 1, *28*
Auerbach, E., 49, *56*

Bach-y-Rita, P., *189*
Baker, R. R., 103, *128*, 139, *149*, 223, *248*
Banker, B. Q., 168, *188*
Barlow, H. B., 62, *95*
Barnard, M., 49, *56*
Barnes, C. A., 88, *96*
Bartlett, F., 33, 46, *56*, 102, *128*

Bateson, G., 46, *56*
Bateson, P. P. G., *129, 150*
Bättig, K., 116, *129*
Beach, F. A., *57*
Beck, B. B., 108, 109, *128*
Becker, J. B., 76, *98*
Bender, M. B., 163, *186*
Bendfeldt, F., 234, *250*
Benson, D. F., 162, *191*
Benton, A. L., 171, *187*
Beritoff (Beritashvili), J. S., 102, *128*
Best, P., 80, *97*
Bever, T. G., 148, *151*
Biber, M. P., 162, *191*
Bisiach, E., 171, *186*
Bitterman, M. E., 24, 25, *28, 131*
Blakemore, C., 181, *186, 215*
Bliss, T. V. P., 80, *95*
Bliss, E. L., 238, *248*
Bloch, V., 154, *186*
Blough, D. S., 27, *28*
Bogen, J. E., 165, 166, *186, 194*, 199, *214*
Bolles, R. C., 99, *128*
Bond, M., 153, *190*
Botez, M. I., 178, *186*

Bourne, Rev. A., 232
Bowers, K. S., 245, *248*
Braitenberg, V., 79, *95*
Branch, M., 80, *97*
Brandsma, J. M., 234, *250*
Brattstrom, B. H., 137, *149*
Bridgman, P. W., 3, *28*
Brion, S., 160, *188*
Broadbent, D. E., 71, *95*, *192*
Brooks, N., 153, *190*
Brown, A. J., 232
Brucker, B. S., 136, *150*
Bruner, J. S., *128*
Bruyn, G. W., *188*, *190*
Buchtel, G., 186
Bucy, P. C., 110, *129*
Buerger, A. A., 136, *151*
Bullowa, M., *56*
Burton, A., *249*, *251*
Butler, R. A. B., 118, *128*
Butters, N., 160, 162, *186*, *195*
Buzsaki, G., 86, *95*

Cairns, H., 178, *187*
Campbell, C. B. G., 24, 25, *29*, *131*
Capaldi, E. D., 117, *128*
Caplan, L., 160, *186*
Caramazza, A., *196*
Carleton, L. R., 103, *130*
Carlson, N. R., xiv
Carpenter, M. B., xiv
Carr, T. H., 184, *187*
Carterette, E. C., 3, *28*, *30*
Cartwright, B. A., 139, *149*
Castro-Caldas, A., 173, *188*
Caveness, W. F., *194*
Cazzullo, C. L., 153, *187*
Ceram, C. W., 175, *187*
Chedru, F., 160, *187*
Cheek, D. B., 223, 224, *248*
Chertok, L., 240, *248*
Chodoff, P., 243, *248*
Christodoulou, G., 243, *250*
Chui, H. C., 170, *187*
Clarkson, J. K., 101, *128*
Cleland, G. C., 136, *150*

Clowes, M., 39, 40, 41, 42, *56*
Cobb, S., 57
Cohen, L. H., 244
Cohen, N. J., 163, *187*
Cohen, Y., 178, 179, 184, *193*
Colby, K. M., 50, *56*
Cole, M., *58*
Collett, T. S., 139, *149*
Collins, G. H., 162, *186*
Coltheart, M., 154, 174, *187*
Condon, W. S., 50, *56*
Conkey, R. C., 159, *187*
Conway, D. H., 81, 82, 88, *97*
Cools, A. R., 183, *187*
Coons, P. M., 237, *248*, *190*
Cowan, J. D., 42, *58*
Cowan, W. M., 83, 88, *97*, *98*
Cowey, A., 174, *187*
Cowie, R. J., 106, *128*
Craik, K. J. W., 9, 10, *28*, 33, 35, 38, *56*
Cresson, A., *58*
Crick, F., 179, *187*
Critchley, M., 169, *187*, *194*
Culver, C., 200, *216*
Cummins, B. H., 159, *187*
Curry, H., 159, *187*
Curtiss, S., 167, *187*, *188*

Damásio, A. R., 161, 163, 164, 170, 171, 173, 184, 186, *187*, *188*
Damásio, H., 161, 163, 164, 170, 173, *187*, *188*
Dandy, W. E., 165, *188*
Darley, F. L., *194*
Darwin, C., 15, 22, *28*
Davey, G. C. L., *30*, 120, *128*, *130*, 136, *150*, *195*, *250*
Davidoff, J., 186, 219, *249*
Davidson, R. J., 154, *188*
Davidson, T. L., 117, *128*
Deecke, L., 184, *190*
Delafresnaye, J. F., 71, *95*, *190*
Delay, J., 160, *188*
Delgado, J. M. R., 115, *128*
de Maupassant, G., 180
Dennett, D. C., 152, *188*

Denny-Brown, D., 168, 171, *188*
De Renzi, E., 163, 164, *188*
Descartes, R., 34, 72, 73, 162
Deutsch, G., 219, 229, *250*
Deutsch, J. A., 101, *128*
Diamond, I. T., 3, 8, *29, 30*, 75, *95*
Dickinson, A., 102, *128*
Dimond, S. J., 219, 227, 228, 229, 231, *249*
Disterhoft, J. F., 154, *188*
Divac, I., 183, *192, 193*
Dixon, N. F., 65, *95, 140, 149*, 220, 222, 226, *249*
Dorsett, S., 233
Dostoevsky, F. M., 180
Doty, R. W., *189*
Downs, R. M., 103, *128*

Eames, L. C., 136, 141, *150*, 245
Eames, P., 159, *195*, 245
Eccles, J. C., 11, *29*, 73, *95*, 185, *188*, 197, 200, 202, *214, 215*
Eddington, A., 185, *188*
Edelman, G. M., *30*
Egan, J., 118, 121, *128*
Eichler, V. B., 75, *96*
Einon, D. F., 119, *129*
Eisenberg, J. F., *29*
Eliot, G., 55, 56
Ellis, A. W., *193*
Ely, D. L., 116, *129*
Eriksen, C. W., 204, *214*
Evans, P., 185, *188*
Ewer, R. F., 116, 120, *129*

Fabrigoule, C., 105, *129*
Falk, G., 42, *56*
Feldman, M., 163, *186*
Fenwick, P., 246
Ferro, J. M., 173, *188*
Finger, S., *249*
Fisher, C. M., 160, *188*
Fisher, E. D., 165, *186*
Fivizzani, A. J., 74, *96*
Flannelly, K., 111, 119, *129*
Fodor, J. A., 197, *214*
Fonagy, P., 248

Foss, B., *249*
Fowler, H., *130*
Fox, S. E., 84, *95*
Frederiks, J. A. M., 153, 155, *188*
Friedman, M. P., 3, *28, 30*
Fromkin, V., 167, *188*
Funnell, E., 153, *186*

Gabor, D., 78, *95*
Gage, P., 178
Galef, B. G., 120, *129*
Galin, D., 227, 231, *249*
Gallup, G. G., 25, 26, *29*, 93, *95*, 144, 145, 146, 147, *149, 151*, 203, *214*
Gandolfi, G., 120, *130*
Garnett, M., 64, *96*
Gauthreaux, S. A., *95*
Gazzaniga, M. S., 163, 166, 167, 179, *188, 190, 194*, 198, 199, 200, 201, 202, 205, 206, 207, *214, 215, 216*, 228, 229, 230, 231, *249, 250*
Gelade, G., 179, *194*
Georgopoulos, A., 171, *192*
Geschwind, N., 157, 158, 159, 164, *188, 189, 191*, 198, *214*
Gibson, H. B., 240, *249*
Gibson, J. J., 66, *95*
Gibson, K. R., 26, *30*
Gispen, E. H., *96*
Glass, A. V., 163, *188*
Glickstein, M., 127, *129*
Goffman, E., 52, *56*, 134
Gogolak, G., 84, *97*
Goldberg, M. E., 171, 173, *189, 193, 195*
Goldstein, L., *189*
Goldstein, L. H., 221, *249*
Goodale, M. A., *195*
Goodwin, B., 56
Gould, S. J., 1, 25, 26, *29*
Grasselli, A., *56*
Gray, J. A., 84, *95*
Greenberg, N., *149, 150*
Griffin, D. R., 3, *29*, 133, 142, 143, 148, *149*, 219, *249*
Grosz, H. J., 244, *251*
Gur, R. C., 226, 243, 244, 246, *250*

Guzman, A., 42, *56*

Hardiman, M. J., 127, *129*
Harlow, H. F., *128*
Harlow, J. M., 178, *189*
Harnad, S., *189*
Harré, R., 52, *57*
Harris, L. P., 146, *150*
Head, H., 153, *189*
Hebb, D. O., *57*, 62, 68, *95*, 179, 180,
    181, 182, 185, *189*
Hécaen, H., 168, *189*
Heilman, K. M., 168, 169, 170, 171,
    172, *187*, *189*, *193*, *195*
Held, R., 4, *29*
Helmholtz, H. von, 38, *57*, *58*
Henley, S. H. A., 140, *149*, 220, 222,
    226, *249*
Henry, J. P., 116, *129*
Herman, L. M., 21, 27, *29*, 31
Herron, J., 228, *249*
Heywood, S., 173, *189*
Hicks, L. H., 91, *95*
Hilgard, E. R., 226, 232, 238, 240, 244,
    249
Hilgard, J. R., 240, *249*
Hillyard, S. A., 159, *189*
Hinde, R. A., *129*
Hink, R. F., 159, *189*
Hiorns, R. W., 10, *31*
Hippocrates, 152, 185
Hirst, W., 64, *97*, *215*
Hodos, W., 24, 25, *29*
Hoeler, F. K., 136, *151*
Holtzman, J. D., 179, *190*
Homer, 47
Honig, W. K., *130*
Honzik, C. H., 101, 115, *131*
Hook, S., 197, *214*
Hoppe, K. D., 229, 231, *249*
Horenstein, S., 171, *188*
Horney, K., 51, *57*
Hotton, N., *131*
Hovancik, J. R., 117, *128*
Howe, M. J. A., 225, *249*
Hubel, D., 75, *96*
Huffman, D., 40, *57*
Hull, C. L., 100, 101, 102, 116, 127, *129*

Hulse, S. H., *130*
Humphrey, N. K., 10, *29*, 54, *57*, 62,
    96, 119, 124, 125, *129*, 163, *192*, 223,
    249
Humphreys, A. P., 119, *129*
Huxley, J., 24, *29*
Huygens, C., 37, *57*
Hytier, J., *195*

Ince, L. P., 136, *150*
Ingle, D. J., *195*
Iversen, S. D., 170, *190*
Iverson, J., 242, *249*

Jackson, J. H., 157, 177, 180, *190*
Jacobs, J. L., 136, *150*
James, W., 4, *29*, 63, 67, 69, *96*, 152,
    157, 182, *190*, 232
Jameson, D. H., 234, *250*
Jasper, H., 155, 158, *192*
Jaynes, J., 44, 45, 46, 47, 48, 49, 54, *57*,
    189
Jeeves, M. A., *130*, *149*, *249*, *250*
Jennett, B., 153, *190*
Jerison, H. J., 2, 5, 11, 14, 15, 17, 19,
    26, *29*, 127, *129*, 133, 148, *150*, 219,
    249
John-Stenier, V., *58*
Johnson, M., 33, 43, 44, *57*
Johnson-Laird, P. N., 46, 56, *57*
Jolly, A., *128*
Jones, E. E., 93, *96*
Jones, E. G., 7, *29*
Josephson, B., *57*, *95*, *96*, *129*, *249*
Jouvet, M., 156, *190*

Kaas, J. H., 8, 12, *30*, 75, *96*
Kanouse, D. E., *96*
Karten, H. H., 139, *150*
Katz, J. M., 54, *57*
Keeton, J., 242, *250*
Kelley, H. H., *96*
Keverne, E. B., 223, *249*
Kleinman, D. G., *29*
Klopfer, P. H., *151*
Klüver, H., 9, *30*, 110, *129*
Koestler, A., 175, *190*
Köhler, W., 109, *129*

Kolb, B., 75, 76, *98*, 104, 105, *131*, 136, *150*, *151*
Kolers, P., 163, *190*
Kornhuber, H. H., 184, *190*
Kraschen, S., 167, *188*
Krauthamer, G., *189*
Krebs, J. R., 106, *128*, *130*
Kubie, J. L., 80, 82, 88, 91, *96*
Kubota, K., 184, *190*
Kubzansky, P. E., *191*

Lackner, J. R., 64, *96*
Lader, M., 245, *250*
Lakoff, G., 33, 43, 44, *57*
Lande, R., 19, *30*
Landfield, P. W., 78, 83, 86, *96*
Larsen, B., 184, *193*
Larsen, N. A., 184, *193*
Lashley, K. S., 34, 42, *57*, 107, 108, 117, 127, *129*, 155, 183, *190*
Latto, R., 168, 173, *190*
Lazarus, R. S., 204, *214*
Lechevallier, B., 160, *188*
LeCron, L. M., 223, 224, *248*
LeDoux, J. E., 166, 167, *188*, *190*, 200, 201, 203, 205, 206, 207, 212, *214*, *215*, *216*, 230, 231, *250*
Leiderman, P. H., *191*
Leith, E. N., 77, *96*
Lemperière, T., 160, *188*
Lennerstrand, G., *189*
Leung, L-W. S., 85, 86, *95*
Levi, L., *129*
Levinson, B., 224
Levy, J., 166, *190*
Lewin, R., *58*
Lewis, A., 162, *191*
Lewis, M., *149*
Lhermitte, F., 160, 169, 180, *187*, *191*
Linden, E., 14, 147, 148, *150*
Lindsley, D. B., 169, 181, *191*, *195*
Lishman, W. A., 168, *191*
Lloyd Morgan, C., 182
Lohman, A. H. M., *190*
London, P. S., 155, *191*
Lore, R., 111, 119, *129*
Lorenz, K., 36, *57*

Ludwig, A. M., 234, 237, *250*
Lunzer, E. A., 154, *191*
Luria, A. R., 178, *191*
Luzzatti, C., 171, *186*
Lynch, J. C., 157, 179, *191*, *192*
Lynch, S., 171, *195*

McCleary, R. A., 204, *214*
McEntee, W. J., 162, *191*
McFarland, D. J., *58*
MacFarlane, D. A., 100, *129*
McGrew, W. C., 109, *129*
MacKay, D., 200, 202, *215*
Mackintosh, N. J., 25, *30*, 91, *96*, 102, *129*
McKee, J., 165, *187*
MacLean, P. D., 5, 12, *30*, *149*, *150*
McNaughton, B. L., 88, *96*
Macphail, E. M., 22, 24, *30*, 139, *150*
Maddison, S., 171, *193*
Magoun, H. W., 155, *191*, *192*
Mancia, M., 153, *187*
Manikowski, S., 121, *131*
Mansfield, R. J. W., *195*
Marcel, A. J., 174, 175, *191*, 205
Markidis, M., 243, *250*
Marley, C., 237, *248*
Marr, D., 75, *96*
Marsden, C. D., 183, *191*
Marshall, J. C., 154, 167, 174, 186, *187*, *191*
Martin, J. R., 116, *129*
Martin, R. D., 14, 21, *30*
Mason, W. A., 25, *30*
Massion, J., *194*
Masterson, R. B., *131*, *189*
Masterton, R. B., 3, *29*, *30*
Maurel, D., 105, *129*
Mayes, A., *130*, *150*, 175, *191*, *250*
Mayman, C., 160, *187*
Maynard Smith, J., 24, *30*
Mead, G. H., 51, 52, 54, *57*
Medcalf, S., 49, 56, *57*
Meier, A. H., 74, *96*
Mellgren, R. L., *95*
Meltzer, B., *57*
Mendelson, J. H., *191*

Menzel, E. W., 106, 112, 113, 114, 117, 122, 126, *130*
Merzenich, M. M., 8, 12, *30*, 75, *96*
Mesulam, M-M., 159, 160, *191*, *195*
Metzgar, L. M., 117, *130*
Meyer, J. S., 171, *188*
Michel, F., 173, *192*
Michie, D., *57*
Mikami, A., 184, *190*
Milner, B., 160, 161, 162, 163, 178, *191*, *192*, *193*
Milstein, V., 237, *248*
Mishkin, M., 162, 168, *192*, *195*
Mitchell, J., 139
Mitchell, S. J., 87, *96*
Moare, I., 103, *130*
Moore, R. Y., 75, *96*
Morgan, C. T., *57*
Morgan, M. J., 134, *150*
Morris, R. G. M., 104, 105, *130*
Moruzzi, G., 155, *192*
Moss, P., 242, *250*
Mountcastle, V. B., 8, 10, 11, 12, *30*, 171, *192*, *195*
Mrosovsky, N., 75, *96*
Muller, R. U., 91, *96*
Myers, R. E., 199, *215*

Nadel, L., 76, 79, 84, 85, 86, 92, *97*, 103, 117, *130*, 136, *150*
Neisser, U., 64, *97*, 204, *215*
Newcombe, F., 154, 163, 164, 165, 174, *191*, *193*
Nicholas, D. J., 134, *150*
Nicholson, J., *249*
Nielsen, 169
Nilsson, L-G., *186*, *194*
Nisbett, R. E., *96*
Nissen, H. W., *57*
Nordgren, L., 243, *248*
Nordlie, J. W., 226, 243, 244, 246, *250*
Norman, D. A., 178, *192*
Northcutt, R. G., 139, *150*
Nottebohm, F., 227, *250*

Oakley, D. A., *31*, 32, 42, 56, *58*, 94, 102, 105, 107, 126, 127, *130*, 133, 134, 135, 136, 141, *150*, *151*, 219, 221, 240, 245, *249*, *250*
Oatley, K., 36, 42, 44, *58*, 134
Öberg, R. G. E., 183, *192*, *193*
O'Keefe, J., 76, 79, 80, 81, 82, 84, 85, 86, 87, 88, 91, 92, *96*, *97*, 103, 117, *130*, 136, 140, 149, *150*, 220
Oldfield, R. C., 178, *187*
Olds, J., 154, *188*
Olton, D. S., 80, 81, 88, *97*, 104, *130*
Ostrom, J. H., 17, *30*
Ostrovsky, F., *215*
Oxbury, J. M., 163, *192*
Oxbury, S. M., 163, *192*

Paillard, J., 173, 176, 179, 186, *192*, *194*
Palkavits, M., *187*
Pallaud, B., 121, *131*
Pandya, D. N., 160, *195*
Papert, S., 34, *58*
Parisi, V., 120, *130*
Parker, S. T., 26, *30*
Passingham, R. E., 26, *30*, 108, 109, 120, 122, 123, *130*, 148, *150*
Patterson, K. E., 154, 174, 175, *187*, *191*
Pavlov, I. P., 100
Pearce, S., 240
Penfield, W., 155, 158, 180, 182, *192*
Pennybacker, J. B., 178, *187*
Perani, D., 171, *186*
Perl, D. P., 162, *191*
Perret, D., 171, *193*
Perret, E., 178, *193*
Petsche, H., 83, 84, *97*
Pettito, L. A., 148, *151*
Piaget, J., 26, 27, 122, *130*, 146
Piercy, M. F., 154, 163, *193*
Plato, 34
Plotkin, H. C., 25, *30*, *31*, *58*, *130*, *150*, *249*, *250*
Pollio, H. R., 183, *193*
Pöppel, E., 172, *196*
Popper, K., 185, 197, *215*
Posner, J. B., 163, *188*
Posner, M. I., 4, *30*, 178, 179, 184, *193*, 204, *215*

Powell, T. P. S., 7, 10, *29*, *31*
Premack, D., 26, 27, *30*
Pribram, K. H., 57, *192*
Puchetti, R., 201, *215*
Puerto, A., 171, *193*
Putnam, H., 197, *215*

Radford, J., *251*
Rafal, R. D., 179, *193*
Ranck, J. B., 80, 82, 84, 87, 88, 91, *95*, *96*, *97*
Ramachandran, V. S., 57, *95*, *96*, *129*, *249*
Ratcliff, G., 163, 164, 165, 173, 186, *189*, *193*
Reason, J., 176, 184, *193*, 225, *250*
Reches, A., 164, *186*
Reck, A. J., *57*
Redshaw, M., 146, *150*
Reed, G. F., 181, *193*
Reed, J. L., 243, *250*
Reeves, A. G., 200, *216*
Reid, J. B., 110, *130*
Reis, D. J., *215*
Rensch, B., 1, 24, *30*
Requin, J., *191*
Richards, D. G., 27, *29*, *31*
Rigler, D., 167, *188*
Rigler, M., 167, *188*
Risse, G. L., 205, *215*
Roberts, L. G., 42, *58*
Roberts, L., 180, 182, *192*
Robinson, D. L., 171, 173, *188*, *193*
Robinson, T. E., 84
Rockel, A. J., 10, *31*
Roland, P. E., 184, *193*
Rolls, E. T., 171, *193*
Roper-Hall, A., 171, *193*
Rorty, R., 45, *58*, 197, *215*
Rose, G., 87, *97*
Rose, F. C., 160, 161, *193*
Rosenblith, W., *28*
Rosenblum, L. A., *149*
Rosene, D. L., 160, *195*
Rubens, A. B., 164, *193*
Ruesch, J., 159, *193*
Rusak, B., 74, 75, *97*

Russell, I. S., 14, *31*, 127, *130*, 136, *150*, 221, *250*
Russell, W. R., 156, *193*
Ryle, G., 163, 197, *215*

Saayman, G. S., 118, 121, *131*
Sackeim, H. A., 226, 243, 244, 246, *250*
Sakaguchi, J. E., *215*
Sanders, R. J., 148, *151*
Sarno, M. T., 163, *188*
Satinoff, E., *98*
Schatzman, M., 245, *250*
Schiller, C. H., *31*
Schiller, P. H., 118, *130*
Schmitt, F. O., *30*, *194*, *215*
Schneider, W., 177, *194*
Schreiber, F. R., 233, 236, *250*
Schreier, A. M., *128*
Schroeder, H., 39, 41, *58*
Schüz, A., 79, *95*
Scoville, S. A., 87, *97*
Scoville, W. B., 162, *193*
Scribner, S., *58*
Seifert, W., *95*, *96*, *97*
Shallice, T., 62, *97*, 154, 178, *192*, *194*
Sheer, D. E., *189*
Sherman, B. S., 136, *151*
Sherrington, C., 185, *194*
Sherry, D. F., 106, *128*
Shettleworth, S. J., 106, *130*
Shiffrin, R. M., 177, *194*
Sidtis, J. J., 179, *190*
Silverberg, R., 164, *186*
Simon, H. A., 6, 8, *31*
Simpson, G. G., 24, *31*
Skantze, H., 243, *248*
Skinhoj, R., 184, *193*
Skrede, K., 80, *95*
Slobodkin, L. B., 144, *151*
Smith, P. K., 119, *131*
Smylie, C. S., *214*
Snaith, K., 245
Snell, B., 49, *58*
Snoek, J., 153, *190*
Soczka, M., 121, *131*
Solomon, P., *191*
Solomon, R. C., 152, 153, *194*
Souberman, E., *58*

Southall, J. P. C., *57, 58*
Spelke, E., 64, *97*
Sperry, R. W., 4, *31*, 61, 62, *97*, 165, 166, *194, 196*, 197, 199, 203, *215*, 228, 229, 230, 231, *250*
Springer, S. P., *215*, 219, 222, *250*
Squire, L. R., 162, 163, *187, 194*
Stanton, G. B., 171, *193*
Stea, D., 103, *128*
Stefanis, C., 243, *250*
Stelmach, C. E., 173, *192*
Stephan, F. K., 75, *97*
Stephens, P. M., 116, *129*
Sternberg, R. J., *29*
Sternberg, S., 175, *194*
Stevens, R., *58*, 174, *187, 191, 193, 195, 250*
Steward, O., 87, *97*
Stollnitz, F., *128*
Strich, S. J., 156, *194*
Stumpf, C., 83, *97*
Suarez, S. D., 144, 146, *151*
Sussman, G. J., 45, *58*
Sutherland, R. J., 76, *98*, 104, 105, *131*, 136, *150, 151*
Swanson, L. W., 83, 88, *97, 98*
Sylva, K., *128*
Symonds, Sir C., 163, *194*
Symonds, C. P., 160, 161, *193*
Szentágothai, J., 10, *31, 187*

Taine, H., 43, *58*
Talland, G. A., 160, 162, 163, *194*
Tatam, J., 50, *58*
Tayler, C. K., 118, 121, *131*
Taylor, J., *190*
Teitelbaum, P., *98*
Terrace, H. S., 148, *151*
Teuber, H. L., 173, 184, *194*
Thompson, R. F., 127, *131*
Thorndike, E. L., 99, 127
Thorpe, S. J., 171, *193*
Tippett, J. T., *58*
Tolman, E. C., 100, 101, 103, 115, 116, 127, *131*
Tonoike, M., 184, *190*
Treisman, A. M., 71, *98*, 179, *194*
Trevarthen, C., *58*, 166, *190*

Trimble, M., 247, *251*
Trumbull, R., *191*

Underwood, G., *58*, 174, 175, *187, 191, 193, 195, 250*
Ungerleider, L. G., 168, *195*
Ungerstedt, U., 170, *195*
Upatnieks, J., 77, *96*

Valenstein, E., 168, 170, 172, *187, 189, 193*
Valentine, E., 225, *251*
Valéry, P., 183, *195*
Valins, S., *96*
van den Bercken, J. H. L., *190*
Vanderwolf, C. H., 84, 85, 86, *95, 98*
Van Hoesen, G. W., 88, *98*, 160, 161, 163, *187, 195*
Van Valen, L., 23, *31*
van Zweiten, P. A., 84, *97*
Velasco, M., 169, *195*
Victor, M., 162, *186*
Vignolo, L. A., 163, *195*
Vinken, P. J., *188, 190*
Vogel, P. J., 165, *186*, 199, *214*
Volpe, B. T., 179, *190*, 204, *214, 216*
von Cramon, D., 172, 173, *196*, 223, *251*
von Senden, M., 147, *151*
von Uexküll, J., 2, 3, *31*
Vygotsky, L. F., 53, 54, *58*

Wagstaff, G. F., 245, *251*
Walker, A. E., *194*
Walker, S., 99, *131*, 134, 137, 139, *151*
Wall, P., 94
Warren, J. M., 108, 109, *131, 191*
Warrington, E. K., 164, *195*, 222, *251*
Watson, F. M. C., 116, *129*
Watson, J. B., 100, *131*
Watson, R. T., 169, 171, 172, *189, 195*
Waugh, N. C., *194*
Weinberger, N. M., 169, *195*
Weiner, B., *96*
Weiskrantz, L., 172, *195*, 222, 223, *251*
Weizenbaum, J., 35, *58*
Wendt, G. R., 244
Wexler, D., *191*

Whishaw, I. Q., 75, 76, 84, *98*, 104, 105, *131*, 136, *150*, *151*
Whiten, A., 123
Whitteridge, D., 178, *187*
Whitty, C. W. M., *192*, *193*
Wiesel, T., 75, *96*
Wilbur, C. B., 234, *250*
Will, B., 121, *131*
Williams, M., 156, *195*
Wilson, D. H., 166, 167, 179, *188*, *190*, 200, 201, 206, 207, *214*, *215*, *216*, 230, 231, *250*
Wilson, E. O., 112, *131*
Wilson, I., 241, *251*
Winograd, S., 42, *58*
Wittgenstein, L., 43, 46, *58*
Wolfson, S., 84, *95*
Wolz, J. P., 27, *29*, *31*
Wood, R., Ll., 159, *195*
Woodruff, G., 26, 27, *30*
Worden, F. G., *194*, *215*
Wurtz, R. H., 173, *195*

Yarnell, P. R., 157, *195*
Yates, F. A., 34, *58*
Yeo, A. G., 136, *151*
Yeo, C. H., 127, *129*
Yin, T. C. T., 171, *195*
Yokum, M., 56
Young, A., *214*
Young, J. Z., 162, *195*

Zaidel, D., 166, *196*, *215*, 228, 229, 230, 231, *250*
Zaidel, E., 166, *196*, *215*, 228, 229, 230, 231, *250*, *251*
Zajonc, R. B., 205, *216*
Zangwill, O. L., 156, *192*, *193*, *195*
Zeki, S. M., 75, *98*
Zihl, J., 172, 173, *196*, 223, *251*
Zimmerman, J., 244, *251*
Zucker, I., 74, 75, *97*, *98*
Zurif, E., *196*

Subject index

absentmindedness, 175–6, 225
abstract memory, 219
abstract systems, 218
action: and attention, 175–9, 184; and consciousness, 69–71, 91–2, 175–7; and frontal lobe lesions, 178; not-as-planned, 176, 225; and self awareness, 140–1, 220, 224–5, 226
age regression, 240–2
agnosia, 163–8
allometry, brain/body, 13–22
Alzheimer's disease, 162
amnesia: global, 160–3; hypnotic, 238–9; post-anaesthesia, 224; post-traumatic, 156–7; retrograde, 156, 163
amnesics, conditioning in, 221–2
amygdala, xv, xvii
anaesthesia and self-awareness, 223–4
anagenetics, see evolution
analgesia, 240
anterior commissure, 205
Anton's syndrome, 169
apraxia, 176–8
arousal, 155–6
association learning, 135, 221–2
association systems, 218
attention, 69, 140–1, 177–9, 204, 209;

anatomy of, 183–4; disorders of, 158–60; and frontal cortex, 176, 178
attribution theory, 93
automatic processing, 177–8, 184, 209; see also action
awareness, 4, 217–20; comparative studies of, 132–49; definition of, 133; subdivisions of, 133

Balint's syndrome, 164
basal ganglia, xvi, 11–12, 139, 170
behavioural flexibility, 107
behaviourism, 99–100, 181–2
bicameral mind, 47–50
blindness: hypnotic, 244–5; hysterical, 243–4
blindsight, 172–3, 223
blindtouch, 173–4
body image, 182
brain size, 10–22
brainstem, xv, 74–5, 83, 88, 90

Cartesian theory of mind, 71–6
caudate nucleus, xvi, xvii, 115, 139, 170
cerebellum, xv, 12; and conditioning, 127
cerebral dominance, 227–8
cingulate gyrus, xv, xvii, 178

circadian rhythms, 35–7, 74
cladistics, *see* evolution
cognition, in animals, 99–128
cognitive evolution, 203
cognitive maps, 76–94, 100–6,
  116–17
colliculi, xv, 173
columns, 10–11
coma, 156–7
coma vigil, 155–6
communication, 12; across species,
  27–8, 147–8
confusional states, 159
consciousness, 4, 37, 43–56, 137–9,
  181–5, 218–20; biological theory of,
  89–94; and brain function, 60–1;
  comparative aspects of, 61–2, 137–9,
  202–3, 211; contents v. state, 153–4;
  definition of, 133; development of,
  50–1; and emotion, 212–13; evidence
  from classical mythology, 46–50; and
  the hippocampal cognitive map,
  89–94; language and, 50, 154; in
  machines, 61; neuropsychology of,
  152–85; plurality of, 217–48;
  properties of, 62–71; psychological
  model of, 60; and social role, 51–2; in
  split-brains, 165–9, 199–202; stability
  of, 65–7; states of, 155–8; theories of,
  59–62, 71–3; unity of, 65–7, 89–90,
  208–13, 226
conscious/non-conscious dynamics,
  206–7, 212–13, 221
controlled processing, 177–8, 184; *see
  also* action
conversion symptoms, 243–7
corpus callosum, xv, xvii, 139, 165, 219,
  227–9
corpus striatum, 139, 170, 183
cortex, xiv–xv, xvii, 217–18; auditory,
  xiv, 7; dorsal, 138; frontal, xiv, xvii,
  170–1, 176, 178, 184; motor, xiv,
  177; occipital, xiv, 204; parietal, xiv,
  168–71, 173, 177, 178, 179, 184, 204;
  pyriform, 138; somatosensory, xiv, 7;
  temporal, xiv, xvi, xvii; *see also*
  temporal lobe; visual, xiv, 7, 12, 223
cryptomnesia, 241

cultural evolution, and self-image, 55,
  144–5

diagonal band of Broca, 83–9
diencephalon, xv, 156
dissociation: between conscious and
  unconscious awareness, 165–74; in
  fugue and multiple personality,
  232–7; in hypnosis, 237–42
dorsal ventricular ridge, 138–9
dreaming, 125, 229
dual aspect theory, 71–2
dualism, 72–3
dyslexia, 174

emotion, 54, 125, 142, 205, 212–13,
  231
encephalization, 13–22; in archaic
  mammals, 19; in cetaceans, 20; in
  'higher vertebrates', 17; in hominids,
  21; in 'lower vertebrates', 16; and
  mental evolution, 23–4; in primates,
  20, 26; in prosimians, 20
endocasts, 15–17, 20, 22
epilepsy, 157, 181, 200; pseudoseizures
  in, 247
episodic memory, 141, 219; in hypnosis,
  239
entorhinal cortex, 79–80, 83, 86–9
entrainment, 37, 50–1
equipotentiality, 42, 183
evoked potentials, 159; and
  hallucinations, 246; and hypnotic
  blindness, 245
evolution: anagenetic, 1–2, 22–7;
  cladistic, 1–2, 24–7; cultural, 55; of
  encephalization, 15–22, 26–7; of
  human mind, 46–50; of mind, 1–28
experience, 4
exploration, 115–18
eye movement, control of, 178–9

filter theory, 71–2
foreground/background in
  consciousness, 66–7, 91, 182–3
former lives, 241–2
fornix, xv, xvi
fugue, 232

globus pallidus, xvi, xvii, 139, 170

hallucinations, 180–1; and episodic
memory, 239; in hypnosis, 239; and
temporal lobe stimulation, 180
hemispherectomy, 231
hidden observer, 238–42
hierarchies: in brain organization, 6–10;
and intelligence, 12–13;
physiological, 7–9
hindbrain, xv
hippocampus, xv, xvii, 138, 218;
anatomy of, 79; and attention, 183;
and cognitive mapping, 76–94, 117;
and consciousness, 77; and
holography, 77–89; and learning,
136; and memory, 160, 162; and
representational systems, 126, 135,
137, 218; and spatial mapping, 136
holograms, 77–89
hypnosis, 237–42; analgesia in, 240;
blindness induced by, 244–5;
hallucinations in, 239; and multiple
personality, 232, 234; and pain
control, 240
hypothalamus, xv, xvi, 75, 88, 183
hysteria, 242–7

imagery in animals, 99–128
imitation, 119–23
information processing: in brains, 8;
and brain size, 10–22
insight, 101, 109, 219, 225
insula, xvii
intellect, social function of, 55, 119
intelligence, 12–13, 109
internal capsule, xvii
introspection, 54–5, 62–4, 124–5,
219–20, 226; in animals, 124; from
the right hemisphere, 229–31
intruder tests, 111

Korsakoff psychosis, 160, 162–3

latch-box problems, 107–8, 117
language, 12, 27–8, 127; and cerebral
dominance, 227; and consciousness,
46, 50, 154, 198, 200–3; and the
hippocampal system, 92; and the
right hemisphere, 166–7, 200–2, 229;
and self-consciousness, 210; and
subjective reality, 210–11
latent learning, 116–17, 137
lateral ganglionic eminence, 138–9
learning, comparative studies, 24–5
limbic system, xv, 11, 160, 171, 184, 205

magnetic sense, 103
mammillary bodies, xv, xvi, 88–9,
183
mass action, 42
'me'/'me-ness', 51–2, 55, 66, 144, 217,
228, 232, 237
medial septal nucleus, 83–9
medulla, xv
memory: comparative studies, 162; and
consciousness, 66, 68–9, 91, 161; and
multiple personality, 237; and
representational systems, 141
mesencephalon, see midbrain
metaphors: deriving from technology,
34–5; in human thought, 43–5
metencephalon, see hindbrain
midbrain, xv, 156, 179; tectum of, xv;
tegmentum of, xv
mind: anagenesis of, 25–7; and brain
states, 198–9; comparative studies of,
25, 27–8, 99–128; continuity of
across species, 22–8; evolution of,
1–28, 213; and language, 4–6; as
metaphor, 46–56; neural basis of,
76–94, 199–200; unity of, 208–13
mirror recognition, 26, 93, 145–7
mismatch signals, 90–1
misplace cells, 82, 87
models: mental models, see
representations
modules: in limbic system, 11;
neocortical, 10–11, 74–6
multiple personality, 231–7
myelencephalon, see hindbrain

neglect: unilateral, 168–72; visual, 178,
204
non-conscious processing, 204–7, 212;
see also unconscious processes

neocortex, 74–6, 87–9, 159–60, 218; area of, 11; and behavioural flexibility, 108; and exploratory activity, 117; homologues of in reptiles and birds, 138; and learning, 127, 136, 221–2; modular organization of, 10–11; and representational systems, 135, 137, 218; and spatial mapping, 136
neocortical enlargement: and representational systems, 126; and social functioning, 53
neostriatum, 138, 170

object play, 118
observational learning, 119–23

pain control, 240
palaeostriatum, 170
parahippocampal cortex, xvii, 88
parental abuse, 125
Parkinson's disease, 179, 183
perception, 4; unconscious inference in, 37–43
perceptual defence, 225–6
perceptual worlds, 2–4, 6
pineal gland, 73
pituitary gland, xv
place cells, 80–9
place hypotheses, 88, 91
place learning, 103–5
play, 118–19
Poetzl effect, 222
pons, xv
preconscious processing, 149
priming, 175
pseudoseizures, 247
psychosomatic symptoms, 231
pulvinar, 173
putamen, xvi, xvii, 139, 170

Red Queen hypothesis, 23–4
reflective self-consciousness, 43–50
representational memory, 219
representational system, 218; and consciousness, 219
representational theory, 33–7; inadequacy of as a metaphor for mind, 45–6

representations: and conscious awareness, 37–8; of environmental events, 107–10; mental, 2, 60; of other animals, 110–14; of the physical world, 37–43, 100–10, 210–11; of reality, 2, 9, 12, 25, 211, 219; of the self, 92–3, 114–15, 143–8, 210–13; of the social world, 46–56, 111–14, 118–19, 210; of space, 103–6; spatial, 34
re-representations, 44–5, 140–1, 218, 220, 222–6, 246–7
reticular formation, xv, 155, 159, 181, 183
right hemisphere: and cognitive evolution, 203; and conscious awareness, 203; and emotion, 205, 231; and language, 200–2; and psychosomatic symptoms, 231; and self-consciousness, 201–2; and self-recognition, 230

schemata, 32–3, 42–3, 46, 49–50, 52–4
searchlight theory, 71
self-awareness, 66, 92, 139–48, 219–47; bidirectionality of, 144; definition of, 133; in machines, 141
self concept, 25, 210; see also self-image
self-consciousness, 92, 94, 201–2, 210–13
self-hypnosis and hysteria, 238
self-image, 51–2, 93, 114, 143–8; and cultural evolution, 55; development of, 144
self-observation, 123–6
self-recognition, 145–7
self-representation, 235–6
semantic memory, 219
sensory deprivation, 179–81
septum, 139, 183
similarities between normal and pathological data, 174–81
simple awareness, 134–7, 218
skills, 176
social models, 111, 124–6
social representations: in carnivores, 112; in chimpanzees, 112–14; in rats, 111–12

social theories, 52
sodium amytal, 206
spatial maps, 79, 105, 126, 137−8
spatial memory, 104−6
split-brains, 165−8, 199−202, 205−7,
    227−31; and consciousness, 200−2;
    and dreaming, 229; and mind,
    199−200; and self-consciousness,
    201−2; and willed action, 228
spinal cord, xv; and learning, 136
spokesman, 207, 209, 231
S-R learning, 100−1, 107, 116, 127
Stroop effect, 178
subcortex, 135, 218−19
subiculum, 79, 83, 87−9
subjective experience, in animals,
    142−3
subliminal perception, 222

teachers, animals as, 121, 123

temporal lobe, xvi, 12, 160, 162, 180,
    205
thalamus, xv−xvii, 11, 139, 158, 162,
    169, 183
theta: activity, 84−90; cells, 80, 84
thinking, 52−4, 219; as internal speech,
    53−4
tool use in animals, 108−10, 122−3
transient ischaemia, 160
travelling salesman problem, 106

umwelt, 1−4, 6, 211
unconscious processes, 65, 157, 175,
    184, 204−7, 209, 212, 224−5

ventricles: lateral, xvii, 138; third, xv
visual object agnosia, 164−5
visual suppression, 204

white matter, xvii
Wulst, 138